Lecturae Platonis   11

Diego Zucca | Roberto Medda [eds.]

The Soul/Body Problem in Plato and Aristotle

 ACADEMIA

The Deutsche Nationalbibliothek lists this publication in the
Deutsche Nationalbibliografie; detailed bibliographic data
are available on the Internet at http://dnb.d-nb.de

ISBN   978-3-89665-750-3 (Print)
         978-3-89665-751-0 (ePDF)

British Library Cataloguing-in-Publication Data
A catalogue record for this book is available from the British Library.

ISBN   978-3-89665-750-3 (Print)
         978-3-89665-751-0 (ePDF)

Library of Congress Cataloging-in-Publication Data
Zucca, Diego / Medda, Roberto
The Soul/Body Problem in Plato and Aristotle
Diego Zucca / Roberto Medda (eds.)
216 p.
Includes bibliographic references and index.

ISBN   978-3-89665-750-3 (Print)
         978-3-89665-751-0 (ePDF)

Visit our website
www.academia-verlag.de

Preface and Acknowledgements

This book brings together a selection of the papers presented at an international Conference held in Alghero (Sardinia, Italy) in September 2017 on the topic: *The Soul/Body Problem: Ancient Models and Contemporary Debates*. The conference was organized as part of a research project led by Diego Zucca (University of Sassari) on the ancient models of the mind and the ontology of the soul-body relation.

The papers in this book mainly focus on two of the most important models of the "mind" proposed in antiquity and revisited throughout the centuries up to the current debates in contemporary philosophy of mind: Plato and Aristotle. Many aspects of the "soul/body" issues that concerned Plato and Aristotle are addressed by various scholars, including cognitive psychology issues, epistemological dimensions such as the relation between perception, reason and thought, moral issues and those concerning action theory, ontological puzzles, as well as "theological" puzzles concerning how the human soul may both be rooted in the natural realm and yet be "divine" at the same time.

We would like to thank the Regione Sardegna, who financially supported the project of which this publication is the first outcome. We would also like to thank Professor Elisabetta Cattanei (University of Cagliari) who – as responsible for the project entitled *L'universalità e i suoi limiti: individui, nature, culture* – gave financial help for the organization of the conference.

A special thank you to Professor Maurizio Migliori, who as editor of the Academia Verlag's *Lecturae Platonis* Series, fully supported the project from the very outset, as well as taking part in the conference and contributing to this book with his paper.

We are especially grateful to Gabriele Meloni (University of Sassari), who played a pivotal role in organizing the conference together with us and in making everything come together so smoothly.

Thanks are due to the *University of Sassari* – in particular: the Department of Storia, scienze dell'uomo e della formazione – for its support, as well as the Department of Architecture for hosting the conference in its wonderful setting by the sea.

Finally, our most profound thanks go to the contributors of this book for their valuable work: with the generous contribution of such great scholars, this book may hopefully become a useful point of reference for future research in the field.

Diego Zucca, Roberto Medda

Introduction

What is the relation between soul and body? Does anything like "the soul" exist? Could it exist without the body? How can soul and body causally interact? What importance does their relation (be it one of harmony or one of opposition) have on our lives as agents with beliefs and desires and as subjects of knowledge? Such questions frame the soul/body problem in ancient philosophy and are quite differently addressed within what can be regarded as the two most influential models in the history of Western thought, those of Plato and Aristotle. This book draws together scholars of both philosophers, whose contributions explore these models from different interpretive perspectives and sensibilities, focusing on one or another dimension of the issue (metaphysical, psychological, moral and political, epistemological, eschatological). Of course, this is not the only book on these topics, and it does not aim to fill a gap in the literature. More modestly, the proposition is to enrich a discussion that already includes extensive contributions and numerous points of view.

Apart from a purely historical appreciation, what should a reader with philosophical interests today gain from considering in detail Plato's and Aristotle's views on the *mind/body* problem, rather than from consulting any of the huge number of contemporary works on the issue?

The mind/body problem has become an increasingly relevant issue in philosophy. The debate has flourished but despite the many refinements to the theoretical options, specific problems and arguments, in many respects it remains within the conceptual framework established by Descartes, who proposed to substitute the ancient notion of "soul" with the modern notion of "mind" and conceives of the latter as an ontological counterpart of matter/extension: a debate about how "the physical" and "the mental" can stay together in Nature. Although, mind as conscious subjectivity is simply an ingredient of the ancient soul as a factor responsible for life, and originally imbued with a moral, political and religious significance. Recovering classical models can be of theoretical interest, provided that we are prepared to put aside our underlying assumptions and be aware that our terms and notions do not automatically map to those of the ancient thinkers (although they may be the origins of our terms and notions, they have been fundamentally reconfigured throughout history). This obvious caveat holds for "soul" and "mind" as well as for "body", "matter", "nature", "cause" and the like, so we should be cautious in labelling this or that ancient position, for example, as "naturalism", "physicalism", "materialism", or as a theory about "mind-to-body causation". Neither is there a "incommensurability of contexts" such that the ancient soul/body problem has nothing to do with our mind/body problem. On the contrary, a historical view of the difference between these conceptual frameworks may be useful in both directions: first, to contextualize our underlying assumptions and concepts as the outcomes of a specific history; and second, to better understand and value the ancient views without naively superimposing our own theoretical requirements onto them.

So this is our position, in terms of the title and aim of this work. A cursory exploration of its contents is next provided, so that the reader can choose which paper to read first, and what to expect from the various contributions.

The soul/body problem primarily involves a question concerning *causality*. How is the soul causally related to the body, which is the material part of the whole individual?

Maddalena Bonelli addresses in her paper (*Matter is Not a True Cause*) the question of whether and to what extent *matter* has been conceived of as a genuine cause, to be distinguished from the notion of *condicio sine qua non*. She focuses on three fundamental models of ancient thought: Plato, Aristotle, and the Stoics. This first contribution acts as a preliminary entry into the main topic of the book: inquiring into the theoretical commitments of such philosophers to this or that view concerning the causal, or conditional, role of matter is a way to shed light on the metaphysical background on which the very soul/body problem emerges in the first place. To begin, the issue of the causal role of the body as the matter of a living being is of the greatest importance for both Plato and Aristotle. Both Plato's and Aristotle's αἰτίαι are "causes" and "becauses" at the same time, as causes figure as explanatory factors so they are reasonswhy. The Stoic model also closely associates cause and matter. As Bonelli shows, provided that Plato and Aristotle both reject the purely finalistic and the purely materialistic explanations, as each of them is structurally insufficient to account for natural beings and processes, both make an explicit distinction between "real" cause and *that-without-which* the cause would not act as a cause (i.e., *condicio sine qua non*). In particular, the body as a material constituent of the individual is characterized by Plato as the latter; more generally and even at a cosmic level, material causes are seen as auxiliary causes (συναίτια) of the "intelligent", purposeful causes. Although Aristotle – who shares with Plato the criticism of the exclusive appeal to material necessity in accounting for Nature – credits matter with being one of the four causes, Bonelli points out that in important passages he appears to consider material necessity more as a "that-with-out-which" than as a proper cause, unless the very distinction between cause and *condicio sine qua non* is overcome. From the Hellenistic age onwards, the cause/condition distinction is often replaced by the distinction between an *active* cause (which the Stoics take to be a body anyway), the only "true one", and the conditions *sine qua non*. Matter is among the latter, as it cannot be a true cause because of its passivity. The paper effectively explores the combination of such oscillations and changes from Plato to the Stoics through Aristotle, and in so doing introduces us, *in medias res*, to the ancient soul/body debate.

Maurizio Migliori opens his paper (*The Soul and Plato's Dialectical/Systemic Model*) by considering the limits of the "game" of writing in Plato, which is a quite serious but not standalone game as the philosopher must "help" it with his living, interlocutory speech. To some extent Plato echoes the Wittgensteinian motto that philosophy is an activity rather than a theory. Indeed, Migliori argues for a "multifocal" approach to Plato's philosophy: his inquiry should above all be seen as an attempt to affirm the multi-layered and originally plural dimension or reality, and the insurmountable limits of human knowledge in the face of such an irreducible plurality. This multifocal approach is here applied to Plato's different accounts of the soul and the soul/body relation, and allows the author to cope with the apparent contradictions in the Platonic *corpus* through a compatibilist commitment. For example, according to the dialogical contexts Plato either takes the human being to be made up of body and soul or he identifies the individual with his/her soul. At times he identifies the "true soul" with the rational part, but depending on the focus and perspective he either characterizes the human soul as simple, or made out of parts and if so then tripartite or bipartite. Plato stresses both the divinity and the bestiality of human beings; from the point of view of the soul itself the assimilation to God is the highest imperative if one is to be oneself, while from the point of view of the concrete "human" individuals, pleasure and thus the body play a pivotal role in happiness. This multifocal approach is a strategic hermeneutical tool concerning epistemology in addition to ethics and anthropology. Senses and reason are at

times regarded to be in total contrast, with senses portrayed as simply interference in the way of the absolute truth, but here Plato is not taking
the point of view of *human* knowledge, to which the absolute truth is indeed precluded and to which senses are necessary, even if far from sufficient. The repeated claims of human knowledge of the truth, of the
Forms/Essences and even of the Good itself are only apparently in contradiction with the many pessimistic allusions to the unreachability of the
truth (to fully reach the truth is a godly privilege). These are rather two
points of view of the same issue, and far from being the result of confu-
sion or discontinuous changes of mind on the part of Plato himself or the
lack of ultimate commitments due to the dialogue form, the continuous
transition from one to another is an essential part of the "serious game"
of philosophy.

Christopher Rowe (*Plato's Soul-Body Problem*) also favours a "holistic"
treatment of Plato's philosophy, rather than the piece-meal approach involving microscopic examinations of single passages, which has too often
prevailed. We should search for a bigger picture, in which the apparent
contradictions could be brought back to differences of perspective, of dramatic contexts, of choices of emphasis, etc. In his paper, Rowe focuses on
what is perhaps the most acute "soul/body problem" to be found in Plato:
that of accounting for how the human soul can be both a rational entity
and the activator of the body, and thus (even temporarily) located in the
body. The standard historical view is that Socrates took the "true" human
being to be pure reason while Plato saw reason as inevitably conflicting
with bodily rooted non-rational elements, but this is rejected by Rowe.
Rational and non-rational elements are for Plato not necessarily but only
potentially in conflict: such a conflict is *de facto* present in many people,
but by its nature reason can consider or not consider appetites and desires
in general, and eventually put under its control the "mortal kind" of soul
(with spirit and appetite). This in principle "optimistic" interpretation is
seriously challenged by some passages (e.g., in *Timaeus'* account of the tripartite soul), and particularly those where Plato depicts the embodiment
of the rational soul quite negatively, as involving a dangerous effect from
pleasures, pains, fear, boldness and the like, and of leading human beings
astray from the good and from the truth. Rowe argues that these effects
only occur when such non-rational affections are *not* under control of reason, a circumstance that is far from unavoidable. Other *prima facie* theoretical divergences – for example between *Phaedo* and *Republic* – are also
explained as differences in emphasis. In the (allegedly) Socratic view Plato

is "filling the gaps" rather than challenging the substance. The non-rational and non-contingently embodied parts of the soul may well serve the intellect and cooperate with it, even if the ideal of a life of pure thought remains more a regulative idea than a concretely instantiated reality. Thus, there is no contradiction in claiming that the self is the soul (the immortal rational part of it) but even this *qua* human and embodied soul requires the other parts, and tensions, reciprocal limitations, and sometimes lacerating conflicts, can surround this fact. Rowe to an extent deflects the controversial meaning of the eschatological myths and the related issue of reincarnation as allegories that directly concern our actual, earthly lives. In some cases people may look human but are actually beasts or even monsters, so the "story" concerning their future lives captures what they would find if they were to non-superficially ask themselves who they really are *now*. Plato's soul/body problem, then, is the paradoxically necessary cohabitation of two commitments: human souls are rational and god-like, but they are located or even trapped in bodies, so that their inhabitation makes the permanence of their very *humanity* only a possibility that is not guaranteed, a continuous challenge entirely dependent on our rational choices.

Aldo Brancacci (On the Relationship between Psuche *and the Senses in Plato's* Theaetetus*)* focuses on the epistemological *côté* of Plato's soul/body problem as it emerges in *Theaetetus*, focusing on the cognitive relation between the (rational) soul and the (embodied) senses. Though Brancacci first acknowledges the extreme complexity of such a multifaceted dialogue, which has understandably provoked a long-lasting debate concerning its status, aims and Plato's alleged theoretical commitments, he reads it as exhibiting positive solutions rather than being a merely "aporetic" dialogue. In particular, he closely examines the section (184c-187b) in which the soul/senses relation is articulated and the theory of common kinds (*koina*) is introduced. Here, genuine advancements are made by developing ideas present in dialogues such as *Phaedo* and *Republic*. As suggested in the *Phaedo*, experience of an F is necessary to think F, even if a confrontation between percept and idea shows the first to be defective (thus a pre-knowledge of the second is argued for, in terms of reminiscence). Brancacci also discusses the distinction found in the *Republic* (524d1-4) between perceivable objects that sensibility is able to grasp on its own, and "paracletic" objects, the perception of which calls for informational integration by reason and thought, insofar as the respective perceptual experiences involve apparent contradictions, oppositions and am-

bivalences: here, our senses appear to boost our intelligence, as they ex-
hibit, so to speak, "maieutic" powers in inviting reason to discursively
"mediate" these faltering contents, and to compare them and inquire into
them further. In the *Theaetetus* the cooperative interaction between senses
and reason is elaborated by refining the concepts of *psuchê* and *aisthesis*
further, in terms of their respective epistemological value and function.
In his reconstruction, Brancacci sheds light on the unifying cognitive
function of the soul, which the senses are instruments of as "organs"
through which we perceive, in a critical discussion of the relevant literature. The Platonic account of soul gets closer to the modern, contemporary concept of the "mind" in these passages than elsewhere, since soul is
meant in "operational" terms as a subject's unified set of cognitive functions. This is why the view presented in these passages is *also* a pioneering
piece of cognitive psychology. In considering the argument from the perspective of *koina* (common abstract and non-perceivable features the soul
grasps on its own) and Plato's further arguments on the superiority of rational knowledge and on thought as a discourse *in foro interno*, Brancacci
challenges the mainstream view, in which the senses are merely regarded
as passive receptors of environmental information. Senses are viewed as
active insofar as they "converge toward a single idea" (184d3-4), the "idea"
being the soul itself as a unitary subject of knowledge. In inverting Protagoras' discourse, in which the soul is simply a manifold bundle of ever-
changing perceptions, Plato assigns to senses an instrumental function.
However, contrary to the prevalent view in the literature, he credits them
with an *active* power towards reason: indeed, the oppositions, antitheses
and the "content-instability" that often characterize perceptual information are exactly what rational thought arises from.

Franco Trabattoni (On Soul-Body "Dualism" in Plato) challenges the received view, according to which Plato holds a clear-cut soul/body dualism
contrary to Aristotle's harmonic conception or hylomorphism. The contemporary sensibility naturally favours the Aristotelian model as metaphysically more plausible and more compatible with a unified view of
Nature, and as better fitting with our general experience. Plato's soul is in
this view a separate substance trapped in an ontologically heterogeneous
body, in contrast with Aristotle's model, which instead takes the soul to
be the act/form/essence of those specific *sunola* that are living beings.
This paper is thus an effective *trait d'union* between the first part of the
book, which mainly focuses on Plato, and the second, which concerns
Aristotle's model and its theoretical *Wirkungsgheschichte* in modern and

contemporary times (see *infra*). Trabattoni does not intend to deny any dualistic stand in Plato, but his main aim is rather to grasp the deeper meaning of the tension between the two broad, basic and irreducible dimensions, which find speculative expression at different levels, such as in the pairs of ideal/real, soul/body, theory/action, and philosophy/politics. These are not just abstract oppositions in which the superior term almost erases the other (as in Neoplatonic retellings); on the contrary, the first term illuminates the other by giving it a deeper significance and reconfiguring it throughout. The soul/body issue is then approached within a broader interpretive framework that involves ontology, psychology, epistemology and action-theory in addition to ethics and politics. The paper illustrates its general proposal by considering some crucial passages. First is the *Theaetetus'* digression on man's assimilation to God (176a8-c2). Trabattoni shows that despite the appearance of valuing an ascetic flight, the detachment from the world so hyperbolically described in the famous passage above in fact suggests a renewed and deeper way of being engaged with and *into* the world. This is how we should consider the only apparently paradoxical continuation of Socrates' speech, which concerns *virtue* and *justice* and thus accounts for an efficacious moral and political engagement in this world among embodied human beings living together. The same switch is to be found in the *Phaedo's* topic-transition from philosophy as an exercise of death to virtue, to confirm the identification of the true philosopher with the best politician, hinted at in the *Apology*, *Republic*, *Gorgias* and *Seventh Letter*. Trabattoni also argues that not only is Plato's "dualism" – in the moderate version described above – far from being detached from concrete human experience, but it is even *required* as an explicative model to account for experiential data, such as the dialectical tension (sometimes becoming opposition) between impulses, desires and physical needs on the one side, and values and spiritual goals on the other. In addition, the superiority of the latter dimension over the former is a well-established *topos* in the traditional conception (as a relevant part of "experience", in its broader meaning). In the last part of his paper, the author discusses and offers an original reading of a passage in Aristotle's *De anima* I 4, in the light of which Aristotle himself considers the Pythagorean doctrine of the soul as a harmony of the bodily parts (represented by Simmias in the *Phaedo*) to be the best explanation of why soul and body simultaneously pass away, and thus as a doctrine ultimately close to his own hylomorphism. Trabattoni then further argues that Plato's objections against Simmias' doctrine – *pace* Aristotle – would equally challenge and potentially defeat hylomorphism as well.

Giuseppe Feola begins the second part of this book – devoted to the Aristotelian model – with a paper (De An. *I 1, 403a25 and the* lógoi énuloi: *An Heraclitean Heritage in Aristotle's Psychology*) concerning the enigmatic and controversial characterization of psychical affections (*pathê*) as "*logoi enuloi*". Aristotle provides this in *De anima* I 1, 403a24-25, a *hapax* often translated as "enmattered forms" or "enmattered reasons". Examining this formula is a means of obtaining a better understanding of the hylomorphic framework. Feola first provides a lexicographical analysis of the term *enulos* and of other terms involved in the characterization (*pathos, logos*). By analogy with *enudros*, which can mean "(animal) that lives immersed in water" or "(place) that has water in it", *enulos* may refer either to something which is in matter or to something that has matter in it: the author favours the first hypothesis but also shows that it entails the second meaning. He then argues that the semantic parallelism of the two adjectives has philosophical relevance. Through this strange phraseology Aristotle suggests a conceptual kinship between his idea and the Heraclitean model: the Heraclitean tone of the passage emphasizes a specific aspect of the matter/form relation (thus of the hylomorphist view as applied to psychical affections), i.e., the form as a principle of permanence through change and as a regulative factor that imposes order and structure on the change. Indeed, the polarity between a *logos* (not just "discourse" but also the order, relation, ratio, and rule that binds everything together as a whole) on the one side, and an underlying flux that obeys this *logos* on the other, is the core of Heraclitus' view on Nature and the Cosmos. The image of liquid/water to represent the material substrate of change is quite common, not only in Aristotle and in Heraclitus – the river one cannot step in twice, for example – but also in Pre-Socratic thought, so the pair *enulos/enudros* resounded in the ears of people with a background of philosophical language as soon as they encountered the expression *logos enulos*. As the Heraclitean *logos* and the underlying flux are so intertwined that they cannot ever be separated, so are the form and matter of psychical affections. The second part of the paper considers the nature of such inseparability, broadening the focus to include the nature of the matter/form relation in living beings, and thus the soul/body relation in general. The example of a *logos enulos* provided by Aristotle in our text is that of anger, which he says should be defined as a movement M of the body/part/power B produced by A and for the sake of C. Anger is a *logos* as it is a structured relation between M, B, A and C, it is *enulos* as it has to be "immersed" in matter: the latter is relevant at the formal level in terms of "hypothetical necessity" (if *f* has to be, *m* must be in place). Feola inquires into the intertwining of matter and form and what point this arrives at, and how fine-grained the constraints matter puts onto the realization of a form may be, and how hypothetical necessity is determined in terms of matter. His conclusion is that constraints cannot be too fine-grained or determined, or they will prevent the in-principle possibility of a multiple realization of the same form/function by more than one material basis or constituent arrangement.

   Roberto Medda's paper (*Physiology and the Exemplar: Aristotle on Recognition and Moral Progress*) concerns a specific aspect of the soul/body relation in Aristotle, which is closely related to Aristotle's moral philosophy. Medda inquires about the psychological and physiological conditions for moral development and progress, thus critically assessing the contemporary applications of Aristotle by representatives of so-called virtue ethics. Medda's reconstruction is first aimed at showing that Aristotle's physiology, psychology and ethics are consistent and that his physiology and psychology have more explanatory power in terms of the understanding of ethics than is generally accepted in the literature. Aristotle's moral philosophy is often considered a form of exemplarism, insofar as the wise man (*phronimos*) is a benchmark that embodies and exhibits the features of a good life and a good agent. This view is used by virtue ethicists as an argument against the alternative models of deontologism and utilitarianism (often couched in consequentialist terms). However, as Medda argues, the Aristotelian view is not easily assimilated into contemporary exemplarism (e.g., Zagzebski, Merritt), as a single act does not have the normativity exemplarists require it to have, for the whole character of the wise man, as a second nature, matters for evaluating one or other of his actions. Aristotle also provides examples for each single virtue he introduces (included respective excesses and defects) but significantly does not provide any example of the architectonical practical virtue that wisdom consists of. This is no surprise, because Aristotle's view on wisdom is more focused on characters as dynamically immersed in particular contexts than on actions as such; in addition, some exemplarists view examples as having an effect at an intellectual level, i.e., to make us *think* about our moral adequacy according to our perceived discrepancy from an example normatively taken as paradigmatic. However, our *thought* about our moral selves is not the first worry in Aristotle's anti-intellectual ethics. The actions of the wise are context-driven and situated, as they "spring" from his character in a fast and immediate way, without effort, which is why they cannot have a prescriptive value beyond the way they are made by *this* wise man, *here* and *now* and in *this* context. In the second part of the paper, suggestions are made about the cognitive mechanisms (both psychological and physiological, according to the hylomorphic framework) through which a moral agent can practically exploit the example provided by the wise-in-action as a model. According to Medda, *phantasia* plays a pivotal role in internalizing particular cases that are not reducible to abstract rules, as it represents the power of using past information to cope with present contexts by foreseeing with "the eye of the soul". In addition to binding perception and practical reasoning it also binds the cognitive and the conative components underlying our behavior, and *phantasia* also allows for a detachment of a course of action from its contingent axiological value, so that the agent can virtually consider different possible courses of action and their respective consequences by mapping particular cases into analogous but different contexts. Such a psychological power can account for moral progress in youth, as it enables emulation (*zêlos*) in the first instance. However, emulation is only partially significant in moral progress as it can simply mean formal and exterior adherence, but it is a form of *imitation* (*mimesis*), a capacity that is connatural to human beings that also involves the work of *phantasia*. Thus *phantasia* may well be "pre-intellectually" responsible for the internalization of distinctive features of wise characters and their actions as paradigmatic. *Phantasia* is also a bodily movement in the hylomorphic model, brought about by perception and consisting of movements into the blood, involving paths from the heart to peripheral organs and to bodily parts responsible for locomotion. Medda offers interesting suggestions about how the physiological account of *phantasia*, consistently combined with its cognitive-psychological account, could concretely explain the capacity for moral progress.

   Diego Zucca (*What is Aristotle's Active Intellect?*) considers *De Anima* III 5, perhaps the most controversial lines in the Aristotelian *corpus*, where the so-called active intellect is introduced and characterized. It is commonly known that Aristotle's noetics is to say the least embarrassing, as it does not appear to fit the hylomorphic treatment of the soul/body relation. For example, *noûs* in III 4 is said to be separable from the body and not to be the actuality of any bodily part. The paper does *not* aim to accommodate this theory of *human* intellect within the hylomorphic framework, but aims to show that the active intellect (AI) introduced in III 5 does not introduce further problems for Aristotelian hylomorphism. A brief taxonomy of the classic interpretive options of what AI may be is first presented, and the pros and cons of each are then systematically considered by taking them at face value and checking whether and to what extent each is satisfied by Aristotle's pronouncements on active intellect in the chapter. Relevant versions of the *Divine Interpretation* (AI is God), the *Human Interpretation* (AI is a part or a function of the human soul), and the *Social Interpretation* (AI is a *habitus* belonging to the human kind as a whole) are considered and what they can and cannot explain is critically assessed. A proposal about the nature of AI is then advanced, referred to as *Content Interpretation*, in which AI is regarded as the unified system of principles or the very formal structure of the world. AI is not a part of the individual soul, but, as is the case in the divine and the social interpretation, it transcends individual intellects but it is not God, nor is it a habitus of the human kind, as it is humanity-independent. It is rather the (most excellent) *content* our intellects receive and "become" as soon as they grasp the principles, but the possession of this content by any individual intellect is a contingent and inessential property in terms of AI's objectivity and existence. In the paper it is argued that the Content Interpretation accounts for all Aristotle says about AI in III 5 better than other interpretive options put forward. This proposal is only indirectly related to Aristotle's soul/body problem, and it suggests that if there is a *noûs/* body problem in Aristotle that makes Aristotelian noetics inconsistent with the hylomorphic picture and with the definition of soul as the first act of a living body, we should *not* look for such a problem in III 5 but elsewhere. AI and III 5 do not threaten hylomorphism in any way, because they do not concern any part of our intellective soul, but rather its proper object.

Giulia Mingucci (*Aristotle and the "Cartesians' Error"*) offers a taxonomical interpretation of the range of positions in the contemporary debate over the *mind-body problem*. She argues that the influence of Cartesian dualism in this debate has been so overwhelming that even explicitly anti-Cartesian views start from the *a priori* assumption that Mind and Matter are two exclusive dimensions. Cartesian dualism also surreptitiously affects the interpretations of hylomorphism by Aristotelian scholars, even though Aristotle's hylomorphism could well be the very antidote to such an assumption. Indeed, Descartes' substitution of the modern "mind" as the centre of conscious subjectivity for the ancient "soul" as the principle of life has been retrospectively and illegitimately projected onto the soul/

body problem as treated by Aristotle. Mingucci offers a very useful taxonomy of the main theories concerning the mind-body relation, including *Strong Dualism* (as either token or type dualism), often associated with *Causal Interactionism* (or alternatively, in modern times, with *Parallelism*) and *Ontological Monism* (which can be *Physicalism, Immaterialism* or *Neutralism*). In the 20th Century debate we have *Strong* or *Weak* versions of physicalism, with the former holding both a type and token identity of physical and mental states, and the latter holding a token-identity but a type dualism, so allowing for mental descriptions/explanations that are irreducible to physical descriptions/explanations. The author duly focuses on the tension between the idea of an explanatory autonomy of the mental on the one side, and the principle of causal closure of the physical domain on the other: if any mental state M is token-identical with a physical state P and there are physically sufficient causes for *any* physical state to be brought about, where does the alleged explanatory autonomy come from? The puzzle chiefly concerns causation: either mental causation entails overdetermination (if physical causes are sufficient), or mental properties are purely epiphenomenal and causally inert, so they cannot be credited with an irreducible explanatory role. Referring back to Aristotelian hylomorphism, Mingucci shows how its many readings track the theoretical options referred to above. For example, Sorabji sees it as a form of Neutralism (a moderate "literalism" about the account of perception as involving reception of the form without the matter in the sense/organ), Slakey as a type of physicalist monism, Nussbaum/Putnam as a type of functionalism (best characterized as a weak physicalism involving token-identity, multiple realization and explanatory autonomy), Burnyeat as a form of dualist immaterialism ("spiritualism" about perception: reception of the form without the matter as a purely cognitive, non-physical reception), Caston as an type of Emergentism (weak physicalism with supervenience but also with causal efficacy, and thus with explanatory autonomy of the mental), and so on. All of these interpretive options, Mingucci points out, are imbued throughout with what she calls the "Cartesians' Error" (a label borrowed by the title of Damasio's famous bestseller). Even when they reject Cartesianism *apertis verbis*, original sin reveals a major conceptual distinction between the physical and mental components, which then can supposedly be identified and defined independently of each other.

William Jaworski is not an Aristotelian scholar but a contemporary philosopher who is representative of the ongoing revival of hylomorphism as a contemporary theory in metaphysics (particularly the metaphysics of life and mind). Although his approach is theoretical rather than historical, in his paper (*Contemporary Hylomorphisms and the Problems of Mind versus Body*) he also starts by introducing the different readings of Aristotelian hylomorphism: Functionalism (Putnam-Nussbaum, Wilkes, Hartman), Dual Attribute Theory reading (Barnes), Identity Theory (Slakey), Neo-parallelism (Ross), and so on. He agrees that contemporary philosophy has inherited its conceptual framework from Descartes, and thus when philosophers of mind ask how it is that the mind fits into the natural world they remain in this framework, no matter which of the many different answers they offer. Jaworski's version of hylomorphism is meant to "solve" the many mind/body problems that arise from this basic question: if everything – us included – is made of physical particles and entities (matter, energy and whatever else physical science quantifies) that have no mental properties (they are not conscious), how is it that *we* are mindful, and *we* are conscious? This contemporary perspective has some basic features in common with its Aristotelian "forerunner": first and foremost, it relies on the ontological and explanatory irreducibility of *form*; second, it conceives of form as an *unchanging structure* that "contains" and regulates changes in the individual in an orderly fashion, making it *one* and making it what it fundamentally *is* (as well as what *kind* it belongs to). Form, unity, permanence, behavioural regularity and kind membership are thus basic ingredients both of Aristotelian and contemporary hylomorphism.

Aristotle's form is introduced to account for change and becoming, but in living beings it is a special source of active causal power that individuates what a specific *sunolon* is, as an ordered unity of bio-cognitive capacities and activities. Contemporary hylomorphists such as Johnston and Fine along with Jaworski himself agree with Aristotle that hylomorphism best accounts for behavioural regularity in terms of a metaphysics of powers: form individuates a set of *structuring* powers, which makes a causal difference, and structured activities impose an order onto matter. Jaworski argues that this is why both the Aristotelian and the contemporary hylomorphist notions of form are not unscientific, and also why they best capture the notion of organization in modern biology, and are thus in fact required by the scientific framework. The structures exist in the real world – far from being description-dependent or, worse, mere *façons de parler* – they must be admitted as basic realities in the universe, which is not just a *continuum* of energy and matter but it is punctuated with centers of organized change and stability. According to Jaworski, being realistic about the forms or structures that do a causal job by being causally efficacious *on* the matter itself enables us to offer the best empirical description of the observed world. Jaworski suggests that from a Quinean position we should ontologically commit to the existence of entities that allow us to best explain observed reality, and we should consider forms or structures as *bona fide* basic entities genuinely belonging to the ontological arrangement of reality.

Each of the contributions briefly described above represents a new advancement in the respective field, and taken together they offer a better understanding of the Platonic and the Aristotelian view on the soul/body problem, and of their historical and dialectical connections. We hope this book can become a useful tool both for scholars and for non-academic readers who wish to gain new insights into this critical issue, as explored by the two main founders of Western thought.

Diego Zucca

Table of Contents

Preface and Acknowledgements   V

Introduction   VII

Matter Is Not a True Cause   3
Maddalena Bonelli

The Soul and Plato's Dialectical/Systemic Model   19
Maurizio Migliori

Plato's Soul-Body Problem   41
Christopher Rowe

On the Relationship between *Psuchê* and Senses in Plato's *Theaetetus*   55
Aldo Brancacci

On Soul-Body "Dualism" in Plato   75
Franco Trabattoni

*De An.*I 1, 403a25 and the *lógoi énuloi*: An Heraclitean Heritage in
Aristotle's Psychology   95
Giuseppe Feola

Physiology and the Exemplar: Aristotle on Recognition and Moral
Progress   115
Roberto Medda

What is Aristotle's Active Intellect?   133
Diego Zucca

Aristotle and the "Cartesians' Error"   159
Giulia Mingucci

Contemporary Hylomorphism and the Problems of Mind versus
Body   177
William Jaworski

Bio of the Editors   193

Index of Authors (with the exceptions of 'Socrates', 'Plato'
and 'Aristotle')   195

Matter Is Not a True Cause

Maddalena Bonelli

I have been working on and been concerned in the distinction between cause and *condicio sine qua non* in ancient philosophy for quite a few years now. Lately, in particular, I have been dealing with what, very early, in ancient philosophy, has been questioned the *status* of "cause" (αἰτία), being attributed, instead, the one of *condicio sine qua non*: that is to say the matter.[1]

In this contribution of mine I am going to talk about the concept of cause in Plato, Aristotle and the Stoics; then about matter as cause and/or *condicio sine qua non*; finally, I am going to try to work out whether or not it is possible to treat *condicio sine qua non* as cause.

I. 1 *"Because" as Cause: Plato*

As we know, it is in *Phaedo*, within the framework of the theory of the immortality of the soul, as opposed to the mortality of the body, that Plato addresses a general reflection on causality. Such reflection is introduced in Socrates' well-known autobiographical account, in which he explains that, in his youth, he had approached natural philosophy:

> ὑπερήφανος γάρ μοι ἐδόκει εἶναι, εἰδέναι τὰς αἰτίας ἑκάστου, διὰ τί γίγνεται ἕκαστον καὶ διὰ τί ἀπόλλυται καὶ διὰ τί ἔστι.
> I thought it splendid to know the *causes* of everything, *why* it comes to be, why it perishes and why it exists (*Phaed.* 96a8-10, tr. Cooper-Hutchinson, the underlining is mine).

---

1 See, in this regard, BONELLI (2009) and (2016).

What is important to underline in this passage is that the αἰτία of each single thing is equivalent to the διὰ τί, that is to say the "because" of things.[2]

In order to understand what Plato means when he speaks of the "because" of things, it is crucial to consider the examples he provides immediately after, all linked to answers to questions related to forms:

«why is x (or does become) F?».
(i) «why does x (man) grow up?» (96c7: διὰ τί ἄνθρωπος αὐξάνεται);
«*through* eating and drinking» (96c8: διὰ τὸ ἐσθίειν καὶ πίνειν);
(ii) «x is bigger than y *by* a head» (96e1: αὐτῇ τῇ κεφαλῇ);[3]
(iii) «ten is more than eight *because* two had been added» (96e2-3: διὰ τὸ δύο αὐτοῖς προσεῖναι);[4]
(iv) «two-cubit length is larger than a cubit *because* it surpasses it by half its length» (96e4: διὰ τὸ ἡμίσει αὐτοῦ ὑπερέχειν).[5]

These answers are considered as "materialistic" by Plato as they coincide with explanations calling for additions and subtractions of quantities and they evidently should provide *the cause* of the corresponding questions (see *Phaed.* 96e7: αἰτία).

Even when, considering such causes unreliable, Plato will appeal to "more certain" (*Phaed.* 100d),[6] or "more refined" (105c2)[7] causes, the role of αἰτία, at least in *Phaedo*, will be the one of providing the διὰ τί, in particular of explaining διὰ τί some things have, or happen to gain or lose, some specific properties.[8]

2 See also *Crat.* 413a3-4: δι᾽ὃ γὰρ γίγνεται, τοῦτ᾽ἔστι τὸ αἴτιον. On the Platonic cause as explanatory, which would not conflict with other Platonic ways to define cause, see HANKINSON (1998), p. 86-87.
3 Implied question: «why is x bigger than y? » In fact, the dative αὐτῇ τῇ κεφαλῇ is considered as αἰτία, i.e. as answer to the διὰ τί, and not as unit of measurement.
4 Implied question: «why is ten bigger than eight?».
5 Implied question: «why two-cubit length is larger than a cubit?».
6 Ideas, which are undoubtedly διὰ τί. Their causal efficacy is not a problem I will address here, as I do not deal with cause as an entity doing something. On the issue of the causal effectiveness or not of Ideas see, for example, NATALI (2013), p. 48-50 and note 27, providing a list of scholars, among whom many Italians, tilting against VLASTOS' thesis (1969), for the attribution of an efficient causation to Ideas.
7 Like, for example, fever which makes a body hot (or the soul, which makes it alive).
8 For this reason, Vlastos, in his famous 1969 article, preferred to speak not so much of Platonic "causes" but rather of "explanations" or "reasons". The article is

I.2 *"Because" as Cause: Aristotle*

At the beginning of the section on causes which is in the second book of *Physics*, Aristotle claims that:

> [...] ἐπισκεπτέον περὶ τῶν αἰτίων, ποῖά τε καὶ πόσα τὸν ἀριθμόν ἐστιν. ἐπεὶ γὰρ τοῦ εἰδέναι χάριν ἡ πραγματεία, εἰδέναι δὲ οὐ πρότερον οἰόμεθα ἕκαστον πρὶν ἂν λάβωμεν τὸ διὰ τί περὶ ἕκαστον (τοῦτο δ᾽ ἐστὶ τὸ λαβεῖν τὴν πρώτην αἰτίαν), δῆλον ὅτι καὶ ἡμῖν τοῦτο ποιητέον καὶ περὶ γενέσεως καὶ φθορᾶς καὶ πάσης τῆς φυσικῆς μεταβολῆς, ὅπως εἰδότες αὐτῶν τὰς ἀρχὰς ἀνάγειν εἰς αὐτὰς πειρώμεθα τῶν ζητουμένων ἕκαστον.
>
> [...] we must proceed to consider causes, their character and number. Knowledge is the object of our inquiry, and men do not think they know a thing till they have grasped the "why" of it (which is to grasp its primary cause). So clearly, we too must do this as regards both coming to be and passing away and every kind of natural change, in order that, knowing their principles,[9] we may try to refer to these principles each of our problems (*Phys.* II 3, 194b16-23, tr. rev. Barnes).

This well-known passage preludes to the doctrine of the four causes and it is extremely significant as, once established that it is not possible to know

---

rather criticized today for the positions, at times, by far, too drastic (see, for example, TRABATTONI, 2011, p. LXIII; LXXV-LXXVI; NATALI, 2013, p. 49-50); still, it is fundamental for any reflection on Platonic causality whatsoever.

9 Here we have a clear example of the equivalence between principle and cause. On such equivalence see, *Metaph.* Δ 1, 1013a16-17: ἰσαχῶς δὲ καὶ τὰ αἴτια λέγεται· πάντα γὰρ τὰ αἴτια ἀρχαί; *Metaph.* Γ 2, 1003b22-24: εἰ δὴ τὸ ὂν καὶ τὸ ἓν ταὐτὸν καὶ μία φύσις τῷ ἀκολουθεῖν ἀλλήλοις ὥσπερ ἀρχὴ καὶ αἴτιον [...].

10 For passages parallel to this definition of knowledge, see *Phys.* I 1, 184a12-14 (τότε γὰρ οἰόμεθα γιγνώσκειν ἕκαστον, ὅταν τὰ αἴτια γνωρίσωμεν τὰ πρῶτα καὶ τὰς ἀρχὰς τὰς πρώτας καὶ μέχρι τῶν στοιχείων); *An. Post.* I 2, 71b9-11 (Ἐπίστασθαι δὲ οἰόμεθ᾽ ἕκαστον ἁπλῶς, ἀλλὰ μὴ τὸν σοφιστικὸν τρόπον τὸν κατὰ συμβεβηκός, ὅταν τήν τ᾽ αἰτίαν οἰόμεθα γινώσκειν δι᾽ ἣν τὸ πρᾶγμά ἐστιν [...]); *Metaph.* Α 2, 983a25-26 (τότε γὰρ εἰδέναι φαμὲν ἕκαστον, ὅταν τὴν πρώτην αἰτίαν οἰόμεθα γνωρίζειν); *Metaph.* α 2, 994b29-30 (τότε γὰρ εἰδέναι οἰόμεθα ὅταν τὰ αἴτια γνωρίσωμεν). BARNES (1993), p. 90, points out this thesis arises from the well-known Platonic suggestion according to which true belief turns into knowledge if accompanied by causal reasoning (*Meno* 98a3: αἰτίας λογισμῷ).

without grasping the διὰ τί of each thing,[10] establishes an identity between the διὰ τί and the αἰτία πρώτη.[11]

In another passage, which maybe has not been taken sufficiently into
account, after restating the equivalence between αἰτία and διὰ τί
(1041a9-10), Aristotle explains how the διὰ τί should be regarded as. The
passage is at the end of *Metaphysics* Z, when the question about the nature of substance is discussed once again and, in particular about the substance as αἰτία. Here Aristotle claims:

> ζητεῖται δὲ τὸ διὰ τί ἀεὶ οὕτως, διὰ τί ἄλλο ἄλλῳ τινὶ ὑπάρχει. τὸ γὰρ
> ζητεῖν διὰ τί ὁ μουσικὸς ἄνθρωπος μουσικὸς ἄνθρωπός ἐστιν, ἤτοι ἐστὶ
> τὸ εἰρημένον ζητεῖν, διὰ τί ὁ ἄνθρωπος μουσικός ἐστιν, ἢ ἄλλο. τὸ μὲν
> οὖν διὰ τί αὐτό ἐστιν αὐτό, οὐδέν ἐστι ζητεῖν (δεῖ γὰρ τὸ ὅτι καὶ τὸ εἶναι
> ὑπάρχειν δῆλα ὄντα [...])· ζητήσειε δ᾽ ἄν τις διὰ τί ἄνθρωπός ἐστι ζῷον
> τοιονδί. τοῦτο μὲν τοίνυν δῆλον, ὅτι οὐ ζητεῖ διὰ τί ὅς ἐστιν ἄνθρωπος
> ἄνθρωπός ἐστιν· τὶ ἄρα κατά τινος ζητεῖ διὰ τί ὑπάρχει (ὅτι δ᾽ὑπάρχει,
> δεῖ δῆλον εἶναι· εἰ γὰρ μὴ οὕτως, οὐδὲν ζητεῖ), οἷον διὰ τί βροντᾷ; διὰ τί
> ψόφος γίγνεται ἐν τοῖς νέφεσιν;
> The 'why' is always sought in this form – why does one thing attach
> to another? For to inquire why the musical man is a musical man, is
> either to inquire – as we said – why the man is musical, or it is some-
> thing else. Now 'why a thing is itself' is doubtless a meaningless in-
> quiry; (for the fact or the existence of the thing must already be evi-
> dent [...]). But we can inquire διὰ τί a man is an animal of such and
> such a nature. Here, then, we are evidently not inquiring διὰ τί who is
> a man is a man; we are inquiring, then, διὰ τί something is predicable
> of something; (that is predicable must be clear; for if not, the inquiry
> is an inquiry into nothing). E.g. διὰ τί does it thunder? διὰ τί is sound
> produced in the clouds? (*Metaph.* Z 17, 1041a10-25, tr. rev. Barnes).

This is a complex passage, which though, in my view, highlights the fact
that to search for the διὰ τί means to investigate why *something attaches to
something else* (i.e. why this is that, or why F is predicable of x). This
would mean that every question and every respective answer (providing
the αἰτία) must always be in the form of "why x is F?". The examples in the

---

11 It is possible to interpret αἰτία πρώτη in two different ways. Either as the first
    cause, in turn not caused, of a series of causes (see, for example, *Metaph.* α 2,
    994b29-31); or as the proximate cause: see BERTI (2012), p. 160-168.

passage raise problems of interpretation,[12] but the thesis is clear: Aristotle too, like in the passage and the examples in the *Phaedo* we have seen, conceives the search for the διὰ τί, and therefore for the αἰτία, as investigation of why something *is* something, that is to say why x is F.

I.3 "Because" as Cause: Sextus Empiricus

In *Outlines of Pyrrhonism*[13] III 14 Sextus Empiricus, despite invoking the usual διαφωνία among Dogmatists about what "cause" is, provides a general definition of it, which sounds acceptable to everybody:

> δόξαι δ᾽ἂν αἴτιον εἶναι κοινότερον κατ᾽αὐτοὺς δι᾽ὃ ἐνεργοῦν γίνεται τὸ ἀποτέλεσμα.
>
> It would seem that a cause, according to their [= dogmatists] common view, is 'that because of which' (δι᾽ὃ), acting, the effect comes about (tr. Barnes).

This definition is echoed by Stobaeus' one (*Eclogae*, I xiii l^c):

> Χρύσιππος αἴτιον εἶναι λέγει δι᾽ὃ. Καὶ τὸ μὲν αἴτιον ὂν καὶ σῶμα [...] καὶ αἴτιον μὲν ὅτι, οὗ δὲ αἴτιον διά τι.
>
> Chrysippus says that a cause is that because of which (δι᾽ὃ) and that the cause is a body [...] and that the cause is 'because' (ὅτι), while that of which is cause is 'why?' (διά τι) (tr. Bobzien).

Sextus and Stobaeus speak of cause as δι᾽ὃ (Stobaeus also presents the closely related formulations ὅτι and διά τι, the interrogative form of which the αἴτιον is such). It is widely assumed that Sextus here retrieves the *standard* Stoic version, so much so that Stobaeus ascribes the definition of cause as δι᾽ὃ to Chrysippus.[14] However, there is nothing distinctively Stoic in such definition. First of all, διά is the ordinary Greek

---

12 On the complexity of the passage and the difficulty of the examples see BO-STOCK (1994), p. 237-238; FREDE/PATZIG (2001), p. 456.

13 From now onwards *PH*.

14 And also to Zeno: see *Eclogae* I xiii 1^c: Αἴτιον δ᾽ὁ Ζήνων φησὶν εἶναι δι᾽ὃ. On the corresponding Latin definition see Seneca, *ep.* 65.2: «there must be that from which (*unde*) something comes about, and that by which (*a quo*) it comes about: the latter is cause, the former matter».

preposition for expressing causality.[15] Moreover, as we have seen, Aristotle and, before him, Plato, speak of αἴτιον/αἰτία indeed in terms of διά τι (or, equivalently, of διότι[16]).

II.1 The Stoics and the Material Cause

On the other hand, in the passages, Sextus Empiricus and Stobaeus underline both the activity of cause and its corporeality. Whereas Sextus seems to present a general feature of cause (as δι'ὃ and ἐνεργοῦν) attributable to all Dogmatists, Stobaeus ascribes the definition he provides to Chrysippus (therefore to the Stoics).

Sextus Empiricus in *Against the Mathematicians*[17] IX 211, outlines the Stoic notion of cause:

> <οἱ> Στωικοὶ μὲν πᾶν αἴτιον σῶμά φασι σώματι ἀσωμάτου τινὸς αἴτιον γίνεσθαι, οἷον σῶμα μὲν τὸ σμιλίον, σώματι δὲ τῇ σαρκί, ἀσωμάτου δὲ τοῦ τέμνεσθαι κατηγορήματος.
>
> The Stoics say that every cause is a body which becomes a cause, to a body, of something incorporeal; as for instance the scalpel, which is a body, becomes a cause, to the flesh, which is a body, of the incorporeal predicate "being cut" (tr. Bobzien).

I will not dwell on the difficulties related to the comprehension of this text, like, for instance, the issue of the incorporeality of the predicate or the one of its coherence with other accounts of the Stoic cause.[18] What is relevant to underline here is that, for the Stoics, cause is closely associated with matter.[19]

---

15 See, for example, Apollonius Dyscolus, *De Conjunctionibus*, 242, 8-12. On this, cf. NATALI (2013), p. 46 n. 19.

16 BARNES (2014), p. 485.

17 From here onwards, as commonly abbreviated, *M*.

18 For these and other issues see the fundamental works by FREDE (1989), p. 495-496; BOBZIEN (1998), p. 18-27 and BARNES (2014), p. 487-491.

19 For the Stoics cause is closely related to matter, and that is basically for two reasons. First of all, because causality occurs exclusively between bodies, since they alone are capable to act and be acted upon (see, in this regard, Sextus Empiricus, *PH* III 38 and *M* IX 366; BOBZIEN, 1998, p.17; BARNES, 2014, p. 464). Secondly, because the fundamental principles of the universe are ultimately two: the active principle (which is corporeal), and the passive one, material. When Sextus Empiricus attacks causation, the causes and the principles in question are

As for the question of the activity of cause, neither Plato nor Aristotle are free from the characterization of the *aitia* in this sense.[20]

II. 2 Matter as Condicio sine qua non: *Plato*

In the already mentioned autobiographic section of the *Phaedo* Socrates expresses his disappointment at two kinds of explanations provided by natural philosophers: the materialistic ones (as seen above), and the seemingly finalistic ones. In particular, the disappointment of Plato (followed in this by Aristotle[21]) relates to Anaxagoras, who seemed to have identified the Intellect as responsible for the universe (which would therefore have been finalistically ordered, according to the criterion of the best), and then instead keeps identifying the αἰτία of things with material elements.

---

indeed the active and the passive ones (see, for example, Sextus Empiricus, *PH* III 1: παρὰ τοῖς πλείστοις συμπεφώνηται τῶν ἀρχῶν τὰς μὲν ὑλικὰς εἶναι, τὰς δὲ δραστικάς). Now, as the former ones look to the Stoics "more principles" than the material ones (Sextus Empiricus, *PH* III 1: ταύτας <ἀρχὰς> γὰρ καὶ κυριωτέρας τῶν ὑλικῶν φασιν εἶναι), Sextus' analysis will start from them. He describes and attacks a relative notion of causation (*M*, IX 207: τὸ αἴτιον τοίνυν, φασί, τῶν πρός τι ἐστίν. See also *PH* III 25), coinciding with a relationship between an *agent* (ποιοῦν) and a patients (πάσχον), both bodies, where the agent produces an effect on the patient. It should be noted that Sextus' criticism of the first principles, respectively active and material, starts with a description of the "most active" first principle, God (Sextus Empiricus, *PH* III 2), and of the completely inert principle, matter. So, the Sceptical attack is an attack at God as the most efficient cause of everything, and at matter as the passive cause of all. On the two Stoic principles, active and passive, of which one is God, the other the matter completely lacking in any quality, see Diogenes Laertius, VII 134. For an analysis of the Stoic causality considered in light of Sextus' criticism see BARNES (2014), in particular p. 463-511.

20 For Plato, see *Phil.* 26e6-8 (Οὐκοῦν ἡ τοῦ ποιοῦντος φύσις οὐδὲν πλὴν ὀνόματι τῆς αἰτίας διαφέρει, τὸ δὲ ποιοῦν καὶ τὸ αἴτιον ὀρθῶς ἂν εἴη λεγόμενον ἕν), *Soph.* 265b8-10 (Ποιητικήν, εἴπερ μεμνήμεθα τὰ κατ᾽ ἀρχὰς λεχθέντα, πᾶσαν ἔφαμεν εἶναι δύναμιν ἥτις ἂν αἰτία γίγνηται τοῖς μὴ πρότερον οὖσιν ὕστερον γίγνεσθαι); *Hipp. Ma.* 296e8-9 (Τὸ ποιοῦν δέ γ᾽ ἐστὶν οὐκ ἄλλο τι ἢ τὸ αἴτιον). For Aristotle see the whole extremely controversial issue of the "efficient cause", defined by him as «the primary source of change» (*Phys.* II 3, 194b30-32).

21 See *Metaph.* A 3, 984b15-22; A 4, 985a18-21.

Here is what Plato states commenting on this behaviour:

καί μοι ἔδοξεν ὁμοιότατον πεπονθέναι ὥσπερ ἂν εἴ τις λέγων ὅτι
Σωκράτης πάντα ὅσα πράττει νῷ πράττει, κἄπειτα ἐπιχειρήσας λέγειν
τὰς αἰτίας ἑκάστων ὧν πράττω, λέγοι πρῶτον μὲν ὅτι διὰ ταῦτα νῦν
ἐνθάδε κάθημαι, ὅτι σύγκειταί μου τὸ σῶμα ἐξ ὀστῶν καὶ νεύρων, καὶ
τὰ μὲν ὀστᾶ ἐστιν στερεὰ καὶ διαφυὰς ἔχει χωρὶς ἀπ'ἀλλήλων, τὰ δὲ
νεῦρα οἷα ἐπιτείνεσθαι καὶ ἀνίεσθαι [...] ἀμελήσας τὰς ὡς ἀληθῶς
αἰτίας λέγειν, ὅτι, ἐπειδὴ Ἀθηναίοις ἔδοξε βέλτιον εἶναι ἐμοῦ
καταψηφίσασθαι, διὰ ταῦτα δὴ καὶ ἐμοὶ βέλτιον αὖ δέδοκται ἐνθάδε
καθῆσθαι, καὶ δικαιότερον παραμένοντα ὑπέχειν τὴν δίκην ἣν ἂν
κελεύσωσιν·

That seemed to me much like saying that Socrates' actions are all due
to his mind, and then in trying to tell the causes of everything I do, to
say that the reason that I am sitting here is because my body consists
of bones and sinews, because the bones are hard and are separated by
joints, that the sinews are such as to contract and relax [...] but he
would neglect to mention the true causes, that, after the Athenians
decided it was better to condemn me, for this reason it seemed best
to me to sit here [e] and more right to remain and to endure whatever penalty they ordered (*Phaed.* 98c2-e5, tr. Cooper/Hutchinson).

Actually, Plato goes on arguing that to call the material components
"causes" would be too absurd:

εἰ δέ τις λέγοι ὅτι ἄνευ τοῦ τὰ τοιαῦτα ἔχειν καὶ ὀστᾶ καὶ νεῦρα καὶ ὅσα
ἄλλα ἔχω οὐκ ἂν οἷός τ'ἦ ποιεῖν τὰ δόξαντά μοι, ἀληθῆ ἂν λέγοι· ὡς
μέντοι διὰ ταῦτα ποιῶ ἃ ποιῶ, καὶ ταῦτα νῷ πράττων, ἀλλ'οὐ τῇ τοῦ
βελτίστου αἱρέσει, πολλὴ ἂν καὶ μακρὰ ῥᾳθυμία εἴη τοῦ λόγου. τὸ γὰρ
μὴ διελέσθαι οἷόν τ'εἶναι ὅτι ἄλλο μέν τί ἐστι *τὸ αἴτιον* τῷ ὄντι, ἄλλο δὲ
ἐκεῖνο *ἄνευ οὗ* τὸ αἴτιον οὐκ ἄν ποτ'εἴη αἴτιον·

If someone said that without bones and sinews and all such things, I
should not be able to do what I decided, he would be right, but surely to say that they are the cause of what I do, and not that I have chosen the best course, even though I act with my mind, is to speak very
lazily and carelessly. Imagine not being able to distinguish the real
cause from *that without which* the cause would not be able to act as a

cause[22] (*Phaed.* 99a5-b4, tr. Cooper/Hutchinson, the underlining is mine).

Hence, Plato presents a clear distinction between real cause (that, in this case, is the final cause, the one for which Socrates is held in prison, instead of being safe in Megara or in Boeotia) and the *condicio sine qua non*, bones, tendons, muscles, enabling Socrates to act as he has decided to act. Here we might though consider Plato's stance as particularly "strict" since this is an example of human action, though the general criticism is towards the failure to use the Intellect in Anaxagoras' universe. Instead, in *Timaeus*, Plato, committed to explain the origins and the development of our cosmos, opts for a distinction between "intelligent" causes (true causes operating according to a rational and purposeful design) and auxiliary causes (συναίτια), the material ones, enabling to explain the mechanical phenomena of nature, governed by necessity.[23]

Interesting is then the following passage taken from *Timaeus*:

διὸ δὴ χρὴ δύ᾽ αἰτίας εἴδη διορίζεσθαι, τὸ μὲν ἀναγκαῖον, τὸ δὲ θεῖον, καὶ τὸ μὲν θεῖον ἐν ἅπασιν ζητεῖν κτήσεως ἕνεκα εὐδαίμονος βίου, καθ᾽ ὅσον ἡμῶν ἡ φύσις ἐνδέχεται, τὸ δὲ ἀναγκαῖον ἐκείνων χάριν, λογιζόμενον ὡς *ἄνευ τούτων* οὐ δυνατὰ αὐτὰ ἐκεῖνα ἐφ᾽ οἷς σπουδάζομεν μόνα κατανοεῖν οὐδ᾽ αὖ λαβεῖν οὐδ᾽ ἄλλως πως μετασχεῖν.

That is why we must distinguish two forms of cause, the necessary and the divine. First, the divine, for which we must search in all things if we are to gain a life of happiness to the extent that our nature allows, and second, the necessary, for which we must search for the sake of the divine. Our reason is that without the necessary, those other objects, about which we are serious, cannot on their own be discerned, and hence cannot be comprehended or partaken of in any other way (*Tim.* 68e6-69a5, tr. Cooper/Hutchinson).

For Plato, the knowledge of necessary causes represents a vital step towards the one of intelligent causes. What is important to point out is that

---

22 According to FREDE (1989), in Plato there is a distinction between αἴτιον (active entity) and αἰτία (explanation). In Aristotle there is not such distinction, whereas there is, for example, in Chrysippus, at least according to Stobaeus who ascribes indeed to him the distinction between αἴτιον as causal entity and αἰτία as explanation of the αἴτιον (*Eclogae* I xiii 1[c]: Αἰτίαν δ᾽ εἶναι λόγον αἰτίου, ἢ λόγον τὸν περὶ τοῦ αἰτίου ὡς αἰτίου).

23 *Tim.* 46c7-e6. See also 68e-69a. On this, cf. FRONTEROTTA (2003), *Introduzione*, in particular paragraphs 4 and 6; p. 249-251, n. 179; p. 344-355, n. 310.

"what without which" (ἄνευ τούτων), which seems to identify matter as
condicio sine qua non (of the knowledge of divine causes but also of the
constitution of the world[24]) and as auxiliary cause. The question that then
arises and that we will be addressing in the conclusions is whether it is
possible to establish an identification of auxiliary causes with *condicio sine
qua non*.

II.3 *Matter as Cause or* Condicio sine qua non? *Aristotle*

Aristotle's theory of the four causes (and therefore of matter as cause) is
well-known, thus I am not going to dwell on it. Instead, it is interesting
to present a passage where, in my view, Aristotle swings between his own
position (matter as cause) and Plato's, who sees matter as *condicio sine qua
non*.

In fact, when, in the second book of *Physics*, Aristotle tackles the causal
role of matter, he shares Plato's criticisms towards those who consider the
materialistic causes as the only causes of natural events.[25] Indeed, though
Plato does not deny the presence of material necessity in natural processes, he criticises those who believe that the material components are the
only causes, whereas, as we have seen, they are instead just necessary conditions or at most auxiliary causes.

Aristotle, however, while maintaining, as we know, that matter is cause
along with the others,[26] in *Phys.* II 8 he seems to be instead very much in
agreement with Plato, defending finalism against those who (presumably
natural philosophers) assume that natural processes are entirely determined by nature and by the properties of natural elements. The question
is then brought up again in extremely interesting terms to us, in *Phys.* II
9.

To explain what happens in natural processes, Aristotle, as is often the
case, takes the building of a wall, namely an artefact, as an example. According to some, he points out, the building of a wall can be explained
simply relying on its material elements «just as if one were to suppose
that the wall of a house necessarily comes to be because what is heavy is

24 See *Tim.* 46c7-e6.
25 See *Tim.* 46c7-e6.
26 See *Phys.* II 3.

naturally carried downwards and what is light to the top».[27] That is to say the wall comes to be as a result of the nature of its elements, with stones and foundations at the lowest place, soil on top and timber further up, because of its lightness.[28]

But this is not what it is:

ἀλλ' ὅμως *οὐκ ἄνευ* μὲν τούτων γέγονεν, οὐ μέντοι *διὰ ταῦτα* πλὴν ὡς δι' ὕλην, ἀλλ' ἕνεκα τοῦ κρύπτειν ἄττα καὶ σῴζειν. ὁμοίως δὲ καὶ ἐν τοῖς ἄλλοις πᾶσιν, ἐν ὅσοις τὸ ἕνεκά του ἔστιν, *οὐκ ἄνευ* μὲν τῶν ἀναγκαίαν ἐχόντων τὴν φύσιν, οὐ μέντοι γε *διὰ ταῦτα* ἀλλ' ἢ ὡς ὕλην, ἀλλ' ἕνεκά του, οἷον διὰ τί ὁ πρίων τοιοσδί; ὅπως τοδὶ καὶ ἕνεκα τουδί. τοῦτο μέντοι τὸ οὗ ἕνεκα ἀδύνατον γενέσθαι, ἂν μὴ σιδηροῦς ᾖ· ἀνάγκη ἄρα σιδηροῦν εἶναι, εἰ πρίων ἔσται καὶ τὸ ἔργον αὐτοῦ.

Whereas, though the wall does not come to be *without* these,[29] it is not *because of* these, if not *because of* matter; it comes to be for the sake of sheltering and guarding certain things. Similarly, in all other things which involve *that for the sake of which:*[30] the product cannot come to be *without* things which have a necessary nature,[31] but it is not *because of* these, if not as matter: it comes to be for an end. For instance, why is a saw such as it is? To effect so-and-so and *for the sake of* so-and-so. This end, however, cannot be realized unless the saw is made of iron. It is, therefore, necessary for it to be of iron, if we are to have a saw and perform the operation of sawing (*Phys.* II 9, 200a5-13, tr. rev. Barnes slightly modified, the underlining is mine).

This passage has been the subject of much debate, for several reasons, first of all the issue of the sense and attribution of necessity ἐξ ὑποθέσεως.[32] We find it interesting because it highlights some sort of sway – if not

27 Aristotle, *Phys.* II 9, 199b35-200a3: νῦν μὲν γὰρ οἴονται τὸ ἐξ ἀνάγκης εἶναι ἐν τῇ γενέσει ὥσπερ ἂν εἴ τις τὸν τοῖχον ἐξ ἀνάγκης γεγενῆσθαι νομίζοι, ὅτι τὰ μὲν βαρέα κάτω πέφυκε φέρεσθαι τὰ δὲ κοῦφα ἐπιπολῆς.
28 *Phys.* II 9, 200a3-5: διὸ οἱ λίθοι μὲν κάτω καὶ τὰ θεμέλια, ἡ δὲ γῆ ἄνω διὰ κουφότητα, ἐπιπολῆς δὲ μάλιστα τὰ ξύλα· κουφότατα γάρ.
29 The material elements.
30 Among which natural processes.
31 As ROSS (1960), p. 531 points out, they are materials which *must* have a certain nature to be matter of certain things.
32 For such issues refer to the remarkable book by QUARANTOTTO (2005), and especially to p. 178-212, for a detailed analysis of the most recent views on the subject.

identification – between matter as cause and matter as *condicio sine qua non*.

It is extremely interesting to see in Simplicius' comment to this passage the adoption of a solution consisting in identifying the (weak) causality of matter precisely because of its being *condicio sine qua non*:[33]

> ἕνεκα γὰρ τοῦ τέλους γίνεται τὰ γινόμενα, οὐκ ἄνευ μέντοι τῆς ὕλης, πλὴν οὐχ ὡς διὰ τὴν κυριωτάτην αἰτίαν τὴν ὕλην, ἀλλὰ διὰ τὴν ἧς οὐκ ἄνευ.

> For what happens does so for the sake of the end, although not without the matter; however it happens not because the matter is the overriding cause, but because it could not happen without it (Simplicius, *in Phys.* 387, 26-28, tr. Fleet slightly modified).[34]

Simplicius, while stressing repeatedly the hypothetical necessity of matter, subordinate to the end and form,[35] tries to keep the causal role of matter, indeed identifying it with its being *condicio sine qua non*.

In so doing, Simplicius claims that in this way Aristotle reveals himself as utterly Platonic (388, 11-12: καὶ ἐν τούτῳ δὲ τῷ κεφαλαίῳ Πλατωνικῶς ὁ Ἀριστοτέλης ἀναστρεφόμενος φαίνεται).[36] As proof, he quotes both the passage of *Timaeus*, in which two kinds of causes are distinguished,[37] and the passage of *Phaedo* where Plato distinguishes between *condicio sine qua non* and true cause,[38] claiming that, in fact, here too, two kinds of causes

---

33 Simplicius, *in Phys.* 386, 3-389, 15, *ad Phys.* 199b34-200a15.

34 See also Simplicius *in Phys.* 386, 30-34: δι'οὖ δείκνυσιν ὅτι *οὐκ ἄνευ* μὲν τῆς ὕλης γίνεται τὰ γινόμενα, οὐ μέντοι *διὰ τὴν ὕλην* ὡς διά τινα κυρίως αἰτίαν, ἀλλ'ὡς δι' ὕλην μόνον καὶ δι'ὑλικὴν αἰτίαν. τὰ γὰρ ἐξ ὑποθέσεως ὡς ὕστερα τῶν προϋποτιθεμένων καὶ ἧττον αἴτιά ἐστι, τὸ δὲ κυρίως αἴτιον τὸ τέλος ἐστὶ καὶ τὸ οὖ ἕνεκα («He uses it to show that things are not produced on the one hand *without* their matter, but that on the other hand things are not what they are *because of their matter* as some sort of overriding cause, but only as their matter and their material cause. For whatever depends on the prior conditions is posterior to them and *less of a cause*, while the true cause is the end and the purpose» (tr. Fleet slightly modified, the underlining is mine). Simplicius also claims that matter is among causes καθ'αὑτά, but κυριωτέρα are ἡ μορφὴ καὶ ὁ λόγος καὶ τὸ τί ἦν εἶναι (387, 12-14).

35 See, for example, Simplicius, *in Phys,* 386, 3-30.

36 On the veridical use of φαίνεσθαι plus participle see BARNES (2011), p. 175, n. 1.

37 *Tim.* 68e6-69a5, see *supra*, p. 17-18.

38 *Phaed.* 99a5-b4, see *supra*, p. 16-17.

are distinguishable.[39] In this way, the Platonic *condicio sine qua non* is some sort of cause too, even though in a weak sense.[40]

Conclusions

All the philosophers we have been considering accept some sort of equivalence or identity between "cause" and "because".

As regards the role of matter, from Plato to the Stoics, through Aristotle, a more or less accepted and aware distinction arises between matter as cause and matter as *condicio sine qua non*. This distinction is overlapped and then replaced by another distinction, that is found in a number of "Dogmatics" from the Hellenistic age onwards, between *active cause* and conditions *sine qua non*:[41] the material ones at first, to which will be added also those considered by Aristotle as primarily causal, like form and end. In fact, not only matter, but also the other Aristotelian causal factors, namely form and end, eventually, will become, for the Stoics, mere necessary conditions for the only true cause, the active one.[42]

Against this position and in line with Simplicius' exegesis,[43] will instead take a stand Clement of Alexandria, who, unlike the "Dogmatics" mentioned above, will prefer to adopt a solution more similar to Simplicius' one, or even a stronger one. Indeed, even though he acknowledges that matter is a *condicio sine qua non*, or perhaps precisely because, he will argue that it is a cause:

39 Simplicius, *in Phys.* 388, 21-22: τὰ αὐτὰ δὲ περὶ τούτων τῶν διττῶν αἰτίων καὶ ἐν Φαίδωνι διώρισται σαφῶς [...].
40 See *supra*, p. 20-21.
41 This is a rather common distinction: see, for example, Cicero, *top.* xvi, 61 (*hoc igitur sine quo non fit, ab eo in quo certe fit diligenter est separandum*); *de fato*, xvi, 36 (*nec id sine quo quippiam non fit, causa est, sed id, quod cum accessit, id, cuius est causa, efficit necessario*); Seneca, *ep.* lxv 2 (*esse ergo debet unde fiat aliquid, deinde a quo fiat: hoc causa est, illud materia*). See also Galen, *caus. Procat.* vii 84 (*haec <= materia> igitur secundum accidens sunt omnia et rationem habent eorum sine quibus non, abscidentia quidem, si non affuerint, et generationem prohibentia eius, ipsa autem nichil in essendo presentia cooperantia*); Clement of Alexandria, *Stromata* VIII, ix, 25, 1 (Αἴτιον δὲ κυρίως λέγεται τὸ παρεκτικόν τινος ἐνεργητικῶς).
42 See, for example, Seneca, *ep.* lxv 4-6, in particular 4: *Stoici placet unam causam esse, id quod facit*. On such reduction see FREDE (1987), p. 492-494; BOBZIEN (1998), p. 20.
43 See *supra*, p. 20 and note 34. Simplicius was probably influenced by Alexander of Aphrodisias: see BONELLI (2009) and (2016), p. 182-183.

τῶν ὧν *οὐκ ἄνευ* λόγον ὁ χαλκὸς ἐπέχει πρὸς τὸ γενέσθαι τὸν ἀνδριάντα καὶ ὁμοίως ἐστὶν *αἴτιον*. πᾶν γὰρ οὗ χωρὶς οὐκ ἐνδεχόμενον γενέσθαι τὸ ἀποτέλεσμα, κατὰ ἀνάγκην ἐστὶν αἴτιον, αἴτιον δὲ οὐχ ἁπλῶς. οὐ γάρ ἐστι συνεκτικὸν τὸ οὗ μὴ ἄνευ, συνεργὸν δέ.

The bronze has the status of *sine qua non* with regard to the coming to be of a statue and it is a *cause* accordingly: everything without which an effect cannot come about is necessarily a cause, but it is not a cause without qualification. For the *sine qua non* is not synectic but auxiliary[44] (*Stromata*, VIII ix 28, 3,1-4,1, tr. Havrda slightly modified).

That is to say, matter, being passive, cannot be cause, as ineffective. Nonetheless, it still is auxiliary cause as, with its "patient" quality, enables the true cause to act. Therefore, in this case too, the solution adopted seems to be Platonic and, to some extent, Aristotelian.

Instead, as regards the characterization of cause as "because", we will see that, in the end, Clement will connect the true cause (the active one) to a species of the "because" genus:

καὶ εἰ μέν τί ἐστιν αἴτιον καὶ ποιητικόν, τοῦτο πάντως ἐστὶ καὶ δι'ὅ, εἰ δέ τί ἐστι δι'ὅ, οὐ πάντως τοῦτο καὶ αἴτιον.

if something is cause and it is active, then, necessarily, it is also δι'ὅ. But if something is δι'ὅ, it is not necessarily also a cause (Clement of Alexandria, *Stromata* VIII, ix, 27, 3, 1-3, tr. Havrda modified).

References

ANNAS, J.; BARNES, J. (2000). Sextus Empiricus. *Outlines of Scepticism*. Cambridge. Cambridge University Press.

BARNES, J. (1984). Aristotle. *Physics*. In: Barnes, J. (ed.). *The Complete Works of Aristotle. The Revised Oxford Translation* I and II. Princeton. Princeton University Press.

_____ (1993[2]). Aristotle. *Posterior Analytics*. Oxford. Oxford University Press.

_____ (2011). Aristotle and the Methods of Ethics, in Bonelli, M. (ed.). *Jonathan Barnes: Method and Metaphysics*. Oxford. Oxford University Press, p. 174-194.

---

44 In the Stoic theory Clement has in mind, συνεκτικόν is the main cause and συνεργόν the auxiliary one.

_____ (2014). Pyrrhonism, Belief, and Causation. In: Bonelli, M. (ed.). *Jonathan Barnes: Proof, Knowledge, and Scepticism*. Oxford. Oxford University Press, p. 417-511.

BERTI, E. (2012). *Profilo di Aristotele*. Roma. Studium.

BOBZIEN, S. (1998). *Determinism and Freedom in Stoic Philosophy*. Oxford. Oxford University Press.

BONELLI, M. (2009). Alexandre d'Aphrodise et la cause matérielle. *Journal of Ancient Philosophy*, 3, p. 1-17.

_____ (2016). La materia nell'antichità: causa o *condicio sine qua non?*. In: Viano, C. (ed.), *Materia e causa materiale in Aristotele e oltre*. Roma, Edizioni di Storia e Letteratura, p. 171-186.

BOSTOCK, D. (1994). *Aristotle, Metaphysics Z and H*. Oxford. Oxford University Press.

COOPER, J.; HUTCHINSON, D.S. (1997). Plato. *Phaedo*. In: Cooper, J.; Hutchinson, D.S. (eds.), Plato. *Complete Works*. Indianapolis. Hackett Pub. Co. Inc.

FLEET, B. (1997). Simplicius. *On Aristotle Physics 2*. London, Bristol Classical Press.

FREDE, M. (1989). Les origines de la notion de cause. *Revue de Métaphysique et de Morale*, 4, p. 483-511.

_____; PATZIG, G. (1988). *Metaphysik Z*. München. C.H. Beck Verlag (It. tr.: *Il libro Zeta della Metafisica di Aristotele*, ed. by N. Scotti Muth. Vita & Pensiero. Milano, 2001).

FRONTEROTTA, F. (2003). Platone. *Timeo*. Milano. Rizzoli.

HANKINSON, R.J. (1998). *Cause and Explanation in Ancient Greek Thought*. Oxford. Oxford University Press.

HAVRDA, M. (2017). *The So-Called Eight Stromateus by Clement of Alexandria*. Leiden. Brill.

NATALI, C. (2013). *Aitia* in Plato and Aristotle. From Everyday Language to Technical Vocabulary. In: Viano, C.; Natali, C.; Zingano, M. (eds.). *Aitia I. Les quatre causes d'Aristote: origines et interprétations*. Leuven. Peeters Publishers, p. 39-73.

QUARANTOTTO, D. (2005). *Causa finale, sostanza, essenza in Aristotele*. Napoli. Bibliopolis.

ROSS, D. (1960). Aristotle. *Physics*. Oxford. Oxford University Press.

TRABATTONI, F. (2011). Platone. *Fedone*. Torino. Einaudi.

VLASTOS, G. (1969). Reasons and Causes in the *Phaedo*. *Philosophical Review*, 78, p. 291-325.

The Soul and Plato's Dialectical/Systemic Model[1]

Maurizio Migliori

I. Preliminary Remarks

I believe it is always useful, if not necessary, to clarify the methodological premises of a work. My first premise is the clear-cut distinction between theoretical readings and historical readings. This is a complex topic, which I have discussed elsewhere. As I cannot delve into it here, I will refer to my previous contributions.[2] Here I will only note that I operate exclusively as a historian. I try to bring out Plato's own voice, as far as this is possible, and therefore to express his thought in the clearest possible way, without being too influenced by what I personally think – or what we generally think, 2500 years after the philosopher in question.

In brief, I might clarify the matter as follows: I *do not believe* in the existence of the soul and believe that this *great invention* of Greek thought – which in its Christian version shaped two millennia of Western thought – offers more (for the most part unsolvable) aporias than it does solutions, as is shown by the very history of such an idea. In my intentions, this should in no way influence our interpretation of Plato, who instead believed in the actual existence of an immortal soul and in the theoretical usefulness of the concept.

---

1 Many of the points I will briefly make – and which may seem "odd" to the reader, or at any rate not in line with the traditional view of Platonic philosophy – are only justified within the framework of this reconstruction. I must therefore refer here to my extensive monograph: MIGLIORI (2013). I have recently published a more succinct and linear exposition of this new interpretation: MIGLIORI (2017b).

2 See MIGLIORI (2013), p. 1220-1250.

My second premise concerns Platonic writing,[3] a theme which the philosopher himself discusses in the *Phaedrus*:

> writing speeches is not a disgrace in itself [...]. But the disgrace, I fancy, consists in speaking or writing not well, but disgracefully and badly (258d1-5).

According to Plato, communication is always difficult. Precisely for this reason, he makes it the object of an extensive discussion, within which he also provides some suggestions for constructing a good speech: 1) we must know the truth about what we are speaking/writing about; 2) we must not shun the "formal" element: each speech must be written as a unitary composition, with a suitable arrangement of the various parts – as though it were a living being – by drawing upon the contributions provided by the masters of rhetoric (264c); 3) we must know the nature of the soul we are discussing. Socrates then addresses the issue of "writing":

> What is left is for us to speak of the appropriateness and inappropriateness of writing, *in what conditions it is good to do so and in which it is not appropriate* (274b6-7).

This is followed by an exposition of the myth of the god Theuth, which I will gloss over, since it is well-known and has been widely discussed. Its purpose is to highlight the limits of writing. As regards its effects, writing does not strengthen memory but rather weakens it: for if we rely on writing we no longer exercise memory as we ought to. Moreover, the written word does not convey true knowledge, which is the outcome of research, but only the semblance of it. Hence, because of all the information they have, readers will believe that they are learned, when in fact they know nothing at all, and it will be difficult to discuss things with them.

Besides, we have the intrinsic flaws of every written text: it cannot answer questions and repeats the same things over and over; it is incapable of defending itself and requires the help of its author (275e; 276c); it cannot be controlled and can fall into anyone's hands; it does not know when to speak and when to keep silent. In brief, the written text is a weak tool that is open to countless misunderstandings and

> only a simpleton will believe that a text can convey any clear and stable knowledge (τι σαφὲς καὶ βέβαιον, 275c6).

---

3 For an in-depth discussion of the issue, see MIGLIORI (2013), p. 25-190.

This might seem like an absolute condemnation, but it is not, as written speech is only the legitimate, if weaker, brother of oral speech, which is written into the interlocutor's soul through the suitable knowledge. This saves written speech, which – despite its weaknesses – can be used, within certain limits and with all due precautions.

Plato refers to this activity as a "game": he who has knowledge of the just, the beautiful and the good will be wise and

> he will not seriously write them in black water, sowing them through a reed with discourses which cannot defend themselves by argument and cannot adequately teach the truth [...]. But he, it seems, will sow them in the gardens of writing and he will write, when he writes, as a game (παιδιάς) (*Phaedr.* 276c7-d2).

No doubt, these are far from futile games: they are actually most beautiful (276e), and – most notably – useful. Plato not only shows that he does not scorn them, but *even claims that they are so important and serious that one can devote one's whole life to them* (276d). It seems most unlikely that in writing this sentence Plato did not have the dialogues he had already "published" before the *Phaedrus* in mind. The game of writing is even presented as the defining feature of the philosopher. If someone, even a prominent orator like Lysias, writes down laws or public or private speeches, believing that these written works have great stability and clarity (μεγάλην τινὰ ἐν αὐτῷ βεβαιότητα ἡγούμενος καὶ σαφήνειαν, 277d8-9), this will bring him much shame, even if the multitude praises him. However, the situation is the opposite for the person

> who believes that in a written discourse on any subject there is bound to be *the playing of a game* (παιδιάν) and that no work in verse or prose that deserves to be treated with much seriousness (σπουδῆς) has ever been written (277e5-8).[4]

---

4 This tension between writing and seriousness is further confirmed by the *Seventh Letter*: «Every serious man must not write serious things, lest he expose them to the aversion and lack of understanding of men. In brief, it must be acknowledged that whenever one sees a man who has written some works – be they the laws of a legislator or any other kind of text – these are not the most serious things for him, if he is serious, because such things abide in the fairest region he possesses. If, however, he has written these things, taking them to be serious things, 'then certainly' not the gods but mortal men 'have deprived him of his wits'» [the reference here is to Homer, *Iliad* VIII, 360; XII, 234] (344c1-d2).

If someone

> has composed these works *knowing the truth* and being able to *support them* when he is challenged with regard to the things he has written, and *if by his own oral speech he is capable of showing the weakness of texts that he has written*, such a man ought to be referred to by a name drawn not from such writings, but from that to which he has devoted himself [...]. I think, Phaedrus, that the epithet wise is excessive and befits only a god; but "lover of wisdom" (*philo-sophon*), or something of the sort, would be more fitting and moderate for such a man (278c4-d6).

Therefore, he who writes deserves the name of "philosopher" if he not only knows the truth, but possesses 1) further knowledge to come to the aid of his writing and 2) the capacity to show its weakness *in speech*. The contrast between the two forms of writing becomes particularly explicit in the almost mocking passage that follows:

> On the other hand, he who has nothing more valuable than the things he has composed or written, turning his words up and down at his leisure, both joining them together and cutting them out, will you not properly consider him poet or writer of speeches or lawmaker? (278d8-e2).

The difference lies herein: the philosopher uses writing with an awareness of what he is doing and without harbouring any illusions. He writes so that the reader might ponder the issues raised, as far as possible. In order to do so, however, it is necessary to help the reader discover existing problems and aporias, to make him uneasy, upset him and push him "to go on". One must not reveal, but allude to or suggest things: these are "games". Plato is inspired to take this path by the theoretical and practical example of Socrates: he seeks to promote Socratic maieutics through a weak tool such as writing. The dialogues must not so much convey information as lead the reader to think, since philosophy is not learned but practised. As Wittgenstein right notes, «philosophy is not a theory but an activity» (*Tractatus* 4.112).

Given all this, it is possible to show that Plato's approach to philosophical issues is always a multifocal one, not because he doubts the possibility of attaining the truth (a limited, human truth), but rather on account of 1) his belief in the simultaneously single and manifold nature of reality, which requires different approaches; 2) his certainty as regards the limits of human knowledge, which is never perfect and must therefore approach the truth of the *ousia* by all available avenues; 3) the appropriateness and/or the need – inferred from the sophists' teaching – to grasp the relations constituting reality with a dialectic that must take account of the different perspectives implied by such relations.[5]

It is possible to demonstrate that Plato engaged in this kind of written philosophising through extensive analyses of the philosophical content of the dialogues – something I cannot provide here.

Fortunately, Plato himself reveals this interpretative key in the *Laws*, just after the Athenian Stranger has expressed an extremely disparaging judgement about human beings, by describing them as *puppets, who share in truth to a small extent* (*Leg.* 804b2-4). This claim requires some justification, which is provided forthwith:

> Do not marvel, Megillus, but understand me: for when I spoke thus, I had my mind set on the Divinity, and was under its influence. But, if you wish, we can grant that the human race is not worthless, but worthy of some attention (*Leg.* 804b7-c1).

It is possible to pass one judgement *from the point of view of the Divinity* and another *from the human point of view*, clearly with different outcomes. Likewise, it is possible to pass judgement from the point of view of man or from the point of view of his soul, from the point of view of absolute Truth or that of human truth, and so on.

II. Some Introductory Examples of the Multifocal Approach

This element, the *multifocal approach*, lies at the basis of many misunderstandings related to Plato's thought. When read "ingenuously", Plato's text constantly presents (apparently) unacceptable or contradictory elements. These "discrepancies" are almost invariably interpreted as reflecting changes of opinion on the philosopher's part. This interpretation finds no confirmation in ancient philosophy: while frequently criticising his master, Aristotle *never* accuses him of having constantly changed his views. This conventional interpretation conflicts with one additional element, as will emerge precisely from my analysis of the topic of the soul.

---

5 See MIGLIORI (2016), (2017a).

Let me anticipate one point. Here I do not at all wish to argue that according to Plato all points of view carry the same weight; on the contrary, the reader is often forced to adopt a particular point of view. The real issue is that for each choice there must be a reason, which it is necessary to identify and understand. For example if we are speaking of man, the fact that he is made up of body and soul is something that Plato repeats countless times – it would be rash to argue that this is not the case. However, we also find a great many statements concerning a particular man or a particular situation, in which the point of view adopted is that of the individual's soul.

Consider, for instance, Socrates' suggestion with regard to punishment, which is often deemed excessive or paradoxical. In *Gorg.* 474c-475d Socrates argues that the person who does not expiate his guilt by undergoing the right punishment finds himself in the worst possible situation. Undoubtedly, punishment is nothing pleasant; however, it is useful because it frees the soul from an illness. This reasoning is further reinforced by drawing a parallel with medicine: just as a sick person is happy after suffering because of the action of a good physician, so he who has committed an injustice can be happy, provided he purifies himself through the expiation of his guilt (476b-479e). While Socrates is speaking of a human being, made up of soul and body, the point of view adopted is that of the soul, which obviously then *reverberates* through the whole person. To further confirm this, punishment is presented as having the same function both on earth and in the afterlife: despite the pain, it must be embraced because it helps heal those souls that can be cured (525a-b).

Later, in *Resp.* 591a-b, these claims are justified in the light of the tripartition of the soul. It is not advantageous to commit an injustice without getting caught or punished for it, because in the case of those who are punished the bestial element is restrained and the docile one freed: the soul is restored to the best possible condition.

While all this might seem excessive or at any rate inadequate to justify the notion of a multifocal approach, consider Plato's suggestion with regard to the best way to lead a human life. From the point of view of the soul,

> by living in harmony with what is divine and orderly, the philosopher will become orderly and divine in the measure permitted to man (*Resp.* 500c9-d2).

Given all the evils in the world, *one must flee from Earth as soon as possible in order to reach Heaven* and "assimilate oneself to God", within the limits of human possibilities (*Theaet.* 176a-b). Plato's reasoning is more explicitly laid out in the *Laws*: it is right to *follow the best things in the best way*. There is no human possession that is more suited than the soul for choosing what is excellent (*ariston*) and spending the rest of one's life with it (728c-d).

> Therefore, the wise man is to become a friend and follower of the Divinity, which is the supreme measure of all things. It is necessary to make oneself as similar to it as possible (*Leg.* 716c-d).

This holds true from the point of view of the soul, not least because any reference to the afterlife can only apply to it.

In confirmation of this, Plato repeatedly argues that human life cannot be happy without a share – even a considerable share – of pleasures.[6] What emerges is a very "concrete" view of life:

> we assert this to be the thing worthy of the greatest consideration in our eyes: *everyone should live his life in peace for as long as he can and in the best possible way.* What, then, is the right way? We should live out our lives *playing at certain pastimes, sacrificing, singing and dancing,* so as to be able to win Heaven's favour and to repel our foes and vanquish them in fight (*Leg.* 803d6-e4).

Evidently, the point of view adopted in this case is the "human" one, which is say that of the concrete human being made up of body and soul. And I could go on with many other examples, for which I must refer to MIGLIORI (2013).

III. The Soul-Body Relation on the Gnoseological Level[7]

Plato's multifocal approach becomes even more evident if we address the question of the soul starting from the epistemological problem, as the *Phaedo* does. Socrates explains in what sense philosophy is an exercise in

---

6 On the issue of Plato's view of pleasures, which should not be mistaken for a condemnation of hedonism, see MIGLIORI (2013), p. 949-988.

7 For an overall treatment of the question of the soul, I will refer to MIGLIORI (2013), p. 725-858; (2017), p. 175-206.

dying. The philosopher, who concerns himself with the soul and not bodily pleasures (64d-e):

> unlike other men, seeks to free the soul from its communion with the body as far as possible (*Phaed.* 65a1-2).

This also holds true on the level of knowledge: the senses have no truth-bearing power, but rather prove misleading and distracting; therefore, the soul can only attain truth if its reasoning is not disturbed by the senses (65b-c). This is difficult and problematic, which is why the philosopher's soul *utterly despises the body* (65c11-d1).

Once this radical contrast between soul and body has been achieved, the theme undergoes a change 1) in its references: Plato speaks of Ideas by mentioning the just, the beautiful and the good, i.e. by referring to the essence (*ousia*, 65d13) of all things, that which makes them what they are; and 2) in tone. This text presents an eruption of superlative and absolute forms, in redundant and extremely emphatic passages: *absolute* truth (τὸ ἀληθέστατον, 65e2) is not attained through the body; rather, those who strive to think *to the utmost* (μάλιστα, 65e2) *will get very close* (ἐγγύτατα, 65e4) to knowing it. Plato speaks of absolute truth, which in a way is rather paradoxical: for he *always* claims that only the Divinity possesses wisdom (*sophia*); therefore, the dialogues show in countless different ways that man *never* attains the absolute. So if Plato speaks of absolute truth here, he cannot have limited human knowledge in mind and the truth man can attain. In this respect, the rejection of the body seems like a coherent and logical step: the perspective adopted is exclusively that of the soul. As further evidence, we only need to consider how the text goes on to state that the *purest way* (καθαρώτατα, 65e6) of proceeding is for the soul to act *to the utmost* (μάλιστα, 65e7) through thought alone, without any interference from the senses. In other words, the soul must separate itself *to the utmost* (μάλιστα, 66a4) from the senses that prevent it from acquiring truth and knowledge; in such a way,

> employing thought, self-contained and pure (αὐτῇ καθ'αὑτὴν εἰλικρινεῖ τῇ διανοίᾳ), let it seek each thing, self-contained and pure (αὐτὸ καθ'αὑτὸ εἰλικρινὲς) (66a1-3).

Therefore, if we wish to know something in a pure way (καθαρῶς, 66d8), we must cast off the body and gaze *at things themselves with the soul itself* (αὐτῇ τῇ ψυχῇ θεατέον αὐτὰ τὰ πράγματα) (66e1-2). All this emphasis on "purity" shows that Plato is not speaking of human knowledge: as long as the soul is bound to the body, it is impossible to adequately (ἱκανῶς, 66b6) attain this absolute truth.

The game the text is suggesting is "rigged", so to speak: Plato knows – and has repeatedly argued – that it is *impossible* for a human being to see the Ideas in themselves, in all of their perfection. This is only possible for the soul in the afterlife, i.e. after the death of the body. As we will be pure (καθαροὶ, 67a7) there, we will come to personally know what is definite (πᾶν τὸ εἰλικρινές), which is to say the truth, because it is not lawful for the impure to grasp what is pure (μὴ καθαρῷ γὰρ καθαροῦ, 67a8-b2).

IV. Man's Attainment of the Truth

Perfect knowledge, therefore, is only possible among pure elements: the soul vis-à-vis the Ideas. Why should this entail the impossibility for man to truly attain knowledge? Plato repeatedly and variously argues that man does attain truth, if only in a limited and "human" form, confirming that from a multifocal perspective truth itself is manifold. However, to avoid possible misunderstandings, on this occasion too he states – *for the second time* – that *over the course of our lives* we can come «very close to knowledge» (ἐγγυτάτω ἐσόμεθα τοῦ εἰδέναι, 67a3), if we have little intercourse with the body and keep ourselves pure (καθαρεύωμεν, 67a5).

Two considerations are in order. First of all, the *Phaedo's* argument does not at all imply that it is impossible to know the Ideas, but only that it is impossible to know them in their absolute perfection. Within the limits of human nature, it is indeed possible to know them. In the *Republic*, Socrates asks:

> Will you not call he who can account for the essence of each thing a dialectician? (534b).

This even applies to the highest Idea, that of the Good:

> This reality, then, that gives their truth to the objects of knowledge and the power of knowing to the knower, you must say is the Idea of Good; as it is the cause of knowledge and truth, *you must deem it knowable (Resp. 508e1-4).*

Dialectical knowledge may be considered akin to the faculty of sight, by which one seeks to look at living beings first, then at the stars, and finally at the sun itself. Likewise, with the dialectical procedure, by leaving all

sense-perceptions aside, a person starts to approach the essence of each
thing through reasoning alone and does not stop until he has grasped *the
very essence of the Good* with his intelligence; in such a way, this person
will reach the very limits of intelligibility, just as the first person will
reach the limits of visibility (532a2-b2).[8]

From a broader perspective, Plato's dual move is quite clear. On the
one hand, he repeatedly emphasises the limits of human knowledge. Already in the *Apology* Plato attributes to the Delphic Apollo a praise of
Socrates, who is aware that

> human wisdom is of little or no value (23a6-7); in truth, <his own>
> wisdom is of no value (23b3-4).

This is repeated again and again in the dialogues, down to the *Laws*, in
which Plato suggests that human beings should

> mould their lives according to that nature whereby we are almost
> complete puppets, *who share in small parts of the truth* (804b2-4).

More generally, it is widely known that according to Plato God alone is
sophos (*Phaedr.* 278d). On the other hand, in the *Phaedrus* Plato repeatedly
states that the first condition to create a good speech is *the knowledge of
the truth*. In the *Laws* we read that

> of all goods the *truth* stands first for gods and men alike: let every
> man partake of it from his earliest days, if he wishes to be blissful and
> happy, so that he may live in the *truth* as long as possible (730c1-4).

In the same text, therefore, Plato argues both that man has little or no
contact with the truth, and that living in the truth is possible, very useful,
indeed almost necessary.

V. *The True Human Being*

This constant, almost "systematic", transition through different points of
view as a means to evaluate the "human" condition finds theoretical justification in the answer to the question of what the *true* human being is.
The adjective *true* is a theoretical element that Plato repeatedly resorts to

---

8 On the knowledge of the Good and its nature as Measure according to the *Philebus*, see MIGLIORI (2013), p. 558-644; REALE (2003), p. 315-344; 435-453.

in order to distinguish between "one X", which is X, from "the true X", which expresses the true nature of X.[9] Thus in the *First Alcibiades* Plato asks what the true being of man is, what his *true self is*, i.e. what man is in his innermost nature (128d-e). Man's true self is not the body, nor the combination of soul and body, but rather the soul, which uses the body just as craftsmen use their tools (129c8; 129d4). So, *in the proper sense*, which is to say in the deepest and truest sense, man is only his soul (130c). However, Plato goes even further, as in this dialogue too he does not overlook the structural duality of the human being:

> So is its proper to take the view that when you and I are conversing with each other, making use of words, one soul is addressing another? [...] when Socrates is conversing with Alcibiades, using speech, he is not addressing the latter's face, as it seems, but Alcibiades – that is, his soul (130d8-e6).

When Socrates uses *words* and looks Alcibiades in the *face*, the true relation is not the external, visible one, but the deeper intercourse between two souls that communicate with one another *through* the body, which therefore *cannot be left out*. The duality is immediately reaffirmed in an ever more explicit way:

> So he who urges us to know ourselves[10] bids us to know the soul [...]. Therefore, anyone who knows something belonging to the body knows something about himself, but not himself (130e8-131a3).

To speak of the human being and to know the body, on the one hand, and to speak of the true human being, on the other, are two very different things. Yet, the same applies to the soul itself. In order to grasp the usefulness of the Delphic injunction, a comparison is drawn with sight. If the inscription told the eye to "look at itself", the latter could see itself in another eye, provided it gazed at its *best* part, namely the pupil, which would then act as a mirror:

---

9 Thus Plato distinguishes the true cause from secondary causes (*Phaed.* 98e), identifies the truest nature of the soul (*Resp.* 611b) and the true craftsman who, as such, cannot make mistakes, since if he did, he would lose the knowledge that qualifies him, thereby ceasing to be a craftsman (*Resp.* 340e).

10 The reference here is to the famous inscription from the temple of Apollo at Delphi, which Socrates/Plato often quotes: «know thyself», γνῶθι σαυτόν.

If the soul too is to know itself, it must surely look at a soul, and especially at that space (*topon*) of it in which the virtue of the soul, wisdom (*sophia*), occurs (133b7-10).

Plato, therefore, takes the various parts of the soul for granted and presents the rational one as the true soul, the part expressing its "virtue", which is to say the part in which the most perfect nature of the soul is realised. Within this context, however, it is worth noting two interesting points:

1. Throughout his lengthy exposition, Plato avoids using the word "part", even when it seems necessary to do so; rather, he speaks of *a space*, in relation to both the eye and the soul. This effort to avoid a word even when the alternative adopted sounds ridiculous (as in the case of the "space" of the soul) can only be explained by an eagerness to make the reader reflect on the matter and lead him to raise the problem of the "partition" of the soul – something I will be discussing in the next section.
2. In the same exposition Plato stresses that in the soul there is nothing more divine than that part (although this word is carefully avoided) in which knowledge and thought are located (133c2):

    > This resembles God, and whoever looks at it knows all that is divine, both God and thought, and will thereby know even himself in the best way (μάλιστα) (133c4-6).

The conclusion is that, by examining both the Divinity and the soul's virtue,

> we will be able to see and know ourselves in the best way (μάλιστα) (133c15).

When it comes to knowing an individual, the knowledge provided by the soul might not be complete, but it is still the best possible knowledge.

VI. *The Soul's Complexity*

As we have seen, already in the *First Alcibiades* the soul is presented as consisting of different parts, one of which is better than the others. Due to space constraints, I will not analytically demonstrate that the attempt to present the parts of the soul as mere functions is unconvincing.[11] I will only list some basic evidence in support of an interpretation of different Platonic passages as implying a division of the soul into various parts:

1. In the *Timaeus* the generated gods *add something to the immortal soul* which the Divinity has fashioned; they receive the immortal principle, fashion a mortal body, and *craft another sort of soul within it, the mortal one* (69c);
2. Only if the soul has parts the various souls can have different origins and (mortal or immortal) destinies, as Plato repeatedly claims;
3. If the souls described in the texts are not ontologically different parts, but only functions associated with the body, they ought to vanish with death; but – as we will soon see, particularly in relation to the Myth of Er – in Hades the souls actually preserve their human features;
4. If the soul is only one and does not comprise different parts, the whole argument about justice formulated in the *Republic* becomes rather incomprehensible, and the comparison with a city comprising different parts with a high degree of autonomy no longer works;
5. If there are no parts, the *Timaeus'* description of their place within the human body becomes rather incomprehensible, or even ridiculous, given the need to separate the rational part from the other two through the neck;
6. Only the interplay of different parts makes sense of why, *on the functional level*, the volitive part works together with the rational part against the appetitive one, whereas *on the ontological level* the bond is always between the human, mortal and irrational parts, and the rational, divine and immortal one; this remains separate and plays a leading role, which makes little sense if there are no parts;
7. If there are no parts, the image of the chariot in the *Phaedrus* may even be regarded as misleading.

The fact of the matter is that Plato speaks of the soul in unitary, binary, and ternary terms. These different formulations cannot be regarded as conflicting treatments for two reasons. First of all, a piece of textual evidence is provided precisely by a crucial dialogue, the *Phaedrus*. Initially the term *psuchê* occurs without ever suggesting the existence of different parts; then, in 245c2-3, Plato *introduces* his demonstration *by mentioning the divine soul and the human one*, a binary distinction which is *never taken*

---

11 See MIGLIORI (2013), p. 776-781; (2017b), p. 182-183.

up in the rest of the dialogue. Even the demonstration of the immortality of the soul (245c-246a) makes no reference to this duality: the treatment provided is a unitary one. Therefore, it is up to the reader to decide whether both souls are immortal, or only one. Plato then presents his most classic ternary image, that of the winged chariot, without any reference to the issue of immortality, but only to the life of the soul prior to the birth of the living being into which it becomes embodied.

We find three different presentations within a few pages of the same dialogue. If what we were dealing with were three conflicting models – unitary, binary and trinary – then we ought to conclude that Plato got into a real muddle *precisely in the dialogue in which he provides the rules to correctly impart a teaching.*

Secondly, even a superficial reading of Plato's models shows that it is impossible to regard them as being mutually opposed. The winged chariot, consisting of three elements, is *a single whole*, which has *one* defining feature and *one* specific nature (depending on the divine figure it has followed in its "initial" flight). In brief, leaving the mythical framework aside, each individual soul has its own unique and unitary features.[12] At the same time, the chariot is binary: what we have is a contrast between a human being, the charioteer, and two animals, the horses; the same also occurs in *Resp.* 588c7-8, where we find a creature with many animal heads, a complex and protean entity (in *Tim.* 80e this part is described as a wild animal in chains), with a lion component and a human-like one. At the same time, the chariot is ternary, since each element has its own dynamics, capacity, etc.; hope always lies in the collaboration between the charioteer and the white horse, between the rational soul and the volitive soul.

It is important to stress once again – and to always bear in mind – that the soul is a whole consisting of parts, according to the model which Plato emphasises in his dialectical works, and which I cannot examine in detail here.[13] However, it is intuitively clear that it is possible to view it from different perspectives, as a whole, as the specific parts of that whole, and as the dynamics between the various parts. Indeed, this is precisely Plato's assessment. To sum up, we might say that 1) when Plato is discussing the

---

12 As is always the case with wholes, these features are closely connected to the parts constituting the whole itself.

13 On this articulation of Plato's dialectical argument, see MIGLIORI (2013), p. 413-428.

nature of the human being or is demonstrating the immortality of the soul, he is not interested in distinguishing its different parts; 2) instead, when he discussing the structure of the soul from an ontological perspective, he presents it according to a binary scheme, by drawing a distinction between the divine and immortal part of the soul and the human and mortal one; finally, when he focuses on the operative function of the soul, the model becomes a ternary one.

Nevertheless, even this last reconstruction cannot be accepted as the "definitive" one. Plato has a far more complex view of the soul, something which the dialogues only hint at. In the *Republic* the appetitive soul is presented as «a single *idea* (ἰδέαν) of a composite and multi-headed beast» (588c7-8). This seems obvious, given the variety of human desires, which frequently conflict with one another: a point that apparently Plato is not interested in exploring in depth. However, even in relation to the mythical figure of the *Phaedrus* various other factors come into play, such as the wings, which have given rise to a complex hermeneutic debate, seeing that it is difficult to define their place. As for the complex problems raised by the crafting of the soul in the *Timaeus* via a twofold operation – first the highly complex operation performed by the Demiurge, then the "additional" one carried out by the generated gods – they fall beyond the scope of the present article.

One last question confirms the fact that it is impossible to confine Plato within the simple schemes adopted in many handbooks. The claim that, on the one hand, the appetitive soul's function is to desire does not rule out the possibility that other parts too might be subject to a kind of drive that could be referred to as "desire". In the *Republic* Plato explicitly states that there are three classes of pleasures, each pertaining to one of the three parts of the soul; likewise, there are three classes of desires and principles (580d8). Each soul is assigned a specific *philia*: the appetitive part loves wealth, the volitive part honour, and the rational part knowledge (580d-581b). Therefore, we have a generic form of desire, which pertains to the appetitive part, and more specific forms of desire, pertaining to the other parts. Are we to conclude that these are independent activities that are carried out separately? I have (yet?) to find a suitable answer in Plato's writing; however, I have identified certain elements that suggest more complex interrelations. With regard to the desires of the lower parts of the soul, Socrates states:

those who, following knowledge and reason, and pursuing their pleasures in conjunction with them, take only those pleasures which reason approves, will enjoy the truest pleasures [...] and also those that
are proper to them (τὰς ἑαυτῶν οἰκείας), if for everything that which
is "best" may be said to be "most its own" (οἰκειότατον) [...]. So if the
entire soul follows the philosophical part without any dissension, the
result for each part, in addition to everything else, is that it accomplishes its own task (τὰ ἑαυτοῦ πράττειν) and is just, and likewise that
each enjoys its own proper pleasures, the best pleasures and, *so far as
such a thing is possible*, the truest [...]. But when one of the other parts
gets the mastery the result for it is that it does not find its own proper
pleasure and constrains the others to pursue an alien pleasure and not
the true one (*Resp.* 586d5-587a5).

Plato states here that 1) the desires of the various parts may be influenced
by the indications provided by the rational part; 2) if they follow these indications, the parts attain the pleasures that are most proper to them and
hence the truest; 3) if we have the predominance of one part, this prevents the other parts from finding their own pleasure. Therefore, the
three parts of the soul influence one another not just on the gnoseological level, but on other levels too, such as that of desires, something which
– unlike knowledge – Plato never discusses in detail in his writings.

On the other hand, precisely because we are dealing with parts of the
soul, we cannot expect them to all have the same function: rationality is
bound to have its specific principles and desires, to which particular pleasures correspond, given that it is so different from the other two parts as
to be immortal; and the same applies to the other two parts, which are
always portrayed using images the highlight their diversity.

VII. The Immortality of the Soul

The topic which has elicited most debate has certainly been that of immortality. Plato explicitly states that the soul is immortal on several occasions and demonstrates it by means of four proofs, which revolve around
the same issue in a protreptic crescendo. The close connection between
the various arguments emerges from the fact that the soul, as the cause of
life and movement, is intrinsically linked to these two elements. This notion is expressed 1) on the onto-predicative level in the *Phaedo*: the Idea of

life represents an essential predication, which rules out any link with the Idea of death; 2) *e contrario* in the *Republic*, given the evident non-existence of any proper evil capable of making the soul die; 3) in the *Phaedrus* through the necessary capacity of a principle to move itself, which implies an immortal life; 4) in the *Laws* by elucidating the nature of the Prime Mover, which is anterior to all things and to time – a "movement capable of moving itself". *The theoretical horizon is always the same*: the *Phaedo* and the *Republic* offer the same reasoning from a positive and a negative perspective, whereas the *Phaedrus* and the *Laws* clarify the foundations of all this, namely the soul's capacity for self-movement. According to this reading, the sequence of proofs is both well-ordered and justifiable.

However, immortality does not apply to the soul as a whole, but only to its divine part. After demonstrating the soul's immortality, Socrates claims that we must not assume that, in its *truest nature* (*Resp.* 611b1), the soul possess a great variety of forms and discordances; he adds that

> it is not easy for a thing, which is composed of many elements not put together into a most beautiful composition, to be immortal (*aidion*) as now appeared to us to be the case with the soul (*Resp.* 611b5-7).

However, the tripartite soul will not necessarily disappear with the death of the body. This seems unlikely for various reasons:

1. Plato repeatedly stresses the fact that it is an ontologically superior entity compared to the body; therefore, it would be strange if they were to disappear together, despite this profound difference;
2. If the soul died with the body, this would invalidate the strong point of the *Republic*, which claims that it is absurd for a thing to perish owing not to any defect of its own, but to another thing's defect (609d); this *other* defect can only exert some influence if somehow it is made *proper* to the thing itself; in any case, if no proper defect can destroy an object, this result cannot be attained by "another" defect. The death of the body is not a sufficient reason for the death of the soul. This is the cornerstone of the "simple" argument advanced in the *Republic*:

> when an external evil occurs in a thing, but the evil proper to such a thing does not emerge within it, we must not suffer it to be said that the soul or anything else perishes in this way (610b6-c2).

3. Two pieces of textual evidence:
   3.1. In his objection, Cebes accepts the recollection argument: the
        soul is pre-existent to its union with the body, but this does not
        prove that it continues to exist after the latter's death. It is con-
        ceivable that the soul outlives the body and dies in the end,
        whereas the hypothesis that the soul is immortal remains to be
        demonstrated (86e-88b). The underlying theme that is alluded to
        here ought to lead one to reflect on the difference between "sur-
        viving the death of the body" by virtue of a superior nature and
        "being immortal".
   3.2. In the Myth of Er we find that tripartite souls survive: they pre-
        serve the memories, weaknesses and all other traits of human per-
        sonality. As we have seen (and as seems obvious), these souls are
        mortal. Still, they live long and become embodied ten times (ac-
        cording to the myth). At the end of a long year (the equivalent of
        10000 years, as the *Phaedrus* states) only the divine and immortal
        part of the soul remains.

However, an even more radical consequence follows from Plato's argument: the soul survives, whereas the subject does not. As the Myth of Err
recalls, after 100 years on Earth and 900 in Hades, the soul chooses a new
destiny for itself, which is to say a new life and the new subjects in which
it will be incarnated; it then visits the River Lethe, drinks from it, and for-
gets all its previous experiences. The concrete subject that existed is nulli-
fied, the soul reverts to its "virgin" state, and can reincarnate in the subject it has chosen – be it a man, woman, or animal. While this is only a
myth, if the soul of a Plato scholar is to reincarnate itself as a lion, this is
the only path it can take: it will annihilate the subject, while the soul itself will live on.

This also explains why in other dialogues, such as the *Symposium* and
Laws, Plato speaks of immortality by referring to descendants: offspring
represent the only immortality available to the human subject, made up
of body and soul.

VIII. The Multifocal Approach

What we have, then, are multiple levels: man can live 100 years, his soul –
as the soul of that specific subject – will disappear after 1000 years, and the

soul – *as a tripartite entity* – will endure 10000 years; then the mortal parts of the soul will meet their destiny and the cycle will start anew, with a new intervention on the part of the gods, who will once again add some mortal parts to the immortal soul, so as to ensure a new cycle of existence.[14] This is consistent with what I have sought to illustrate with reference to Plato's texts, and in particular to Plato's view of the "human being", which in a way coincides with his rational soul, while from another perspective the soul is tripartite, and from yet another coincides with both soul and body. This is what I would refer to as the multifocal approach.[15]

This element, the multifocal approach, allows us to face one last problem. Scholars have been arguing about Plato for decades, without agreeing on practically any issue – he is the only philosopher to cause so much variance. While the scope for disagreement in philosophy is frequently vast, it is usually well-defined and circumscribed; yet in Plato's case, it seems as though anything and everything can be argued. Leaving all excesses aside, this disagreement is due to structural reasons: many views are as *true* – which is to say as textually well-founded – as their opposites. The debate is endless because scholars tend to unilaterally focus on this or that topic put forward by Plato – an outstanding pupil of the greatest and most coherent of all sophists, the Athenian Socrates. The only way to deal with such a complex reality – in our case, with such a difficult topic as the soul – is to adopt a differentiated approach to problems and bring various points of view into play; in this case we can hope to identify the truth, as far as this is possible for a limited creature such as man:

---

14 What lies at the basis of all this is a cosmological model, which is illustrated for instance by the myth of the *Statesman*: the world endures by virtue of a cyclical process based on divine intervention. The Divinity establishes the greatest possible order; it then leaves the cosmos to its own resources; by virtue of its nature, the universe gradually loses its divine order and reverts to its former state of disorder; when it is about to dissolve, the Divinity newly intervenes. We thus have two cycles which eternally repeat themselves: the Divinity ensures the only possible form of eternity for this higher yet material reality, which by its own nature is disorderly. For a more in-depth analysis, see MIGLIORI (1996), p. 80-102; 216-222; 314-331.

15 I first started developing this interpretation in CATTANEI/FERMANI/ MIGLIORI (2016), a volume featuring various contributions: FERMANI (2016c), EUSTACCHI (2016), FERMANI (2016a), MIGLIORI (2016), PALPACELLI (2016a), FERMANI (2016b), PALPACELLI (2016b), CATTANEI (2016).

I think, Socrates, as perhaps you do yourself, that it is either impossible or very difficult to acquire clear knowledge about such matters in this life. And yet he is a weakling who does not test in every way what is said about them and persevere until he is worn out by studying them on every side. For with regard to such matters we must do one of two things: either we must learn how things stand from others or discover this on our own, or if that is impossible, we must take whatever human reasoning is best and hardest to disprove and, embarking upon it as upon a raft, sail upon it through life in the midst of dangers, unless we can sail upon some stronger vessel, some divine argument (*Phaed.* 85c1-d4).

If nothing better is available, we must make do with those arguments which are the hardest to disprove. The only possibility that is ruled out is giving up because the argument is difficult and too removed from our experience: we must take a risk. Socrates himself, in the *Phaedo*, confirms this attitude the moment in which he "also" raises the problem of destiny and of the soul's abodes after death:

to affirm with certainty that things are as I have exposed them would not be suitable for an intelligent man; but to say that the things that concern our souls and their abodes are these or something like these, since the soul is shown to be immortal, this seems to me to be fit and worth taking the risk of believing – for the risk-taking is beautiful (*Phaed.* 114d2-6).

References

CATTANEI, E. (2016). In conclusion. In: CATTANEI/FERMANI/MIGLIORI (2016), p. 221-222.

_____; FERMANI, A.; MIGLIORI, M. (eds.) (2016). *By the Sophists to Aristotle through Plato*. Sankt Augustin. Academia Verlag.

EUSTACCHI, F. (2016). At the Source of the Multifocal Approach: Relations in the Sophistic Context. In: CATTANEI/FERMANI/MIGLIORI (2016), p. 33-66.

FERMANI, A. (2016a). Man is Unhappy in Many Ways. Some Examples of the Multifocal Approach inside the Platonic Reflection. In: CATTANEI/ FERMANI/MIGLIORI (2016), p. 67-84.

_____ (2016b). Some Examples of the Multifocal Approach in Aristotle's Ethics. In: CATTANEI/FERMANI/MIGLIORI (2016), p. 153-186.

_____ (2016c). The Multifocal Approach as an Assumption of the Complexity of Reality: A Few Introductory Insights. In: CATTANEI/FERMANI/MIGLIORI (2016), p. 7-32.

MIGLIORI, M. (1996). *Arte politica e metretica assiologica*, commentario storico-filosofico al *Politico* di Platone. Milano. Vita e Pensiero.

_____ (2013). *Il disordine ordinato. La filosofia dialettica di Platone*, 2 vv., I. *Dialettica, metafisica e cosmologia; II. Dall'anima alla prassi etica e politica*. Brescia. Morcelliana.

_____ (2016). Plato: a Nascent Theory of Complexity. In: CATTANEI/ FERMANI/MIGLIORI (2016), p. 85-118.

_____ (2017a). A Hermeneutic Paradigm for the History of Ancient Philosophy: The Multifocal Approach, «Giornale di Metafisica», NS 39, p. 187-207.

_____ (2017b). *Platone*. Brescia. Els La Scuola.

PALPACELLI, L. (2016a). The Multifocal Approach in *Metaphysics* V. In: CATTANEI/FERMANI/MIGLIORI (2016), p. 119-152.

_____ (2016b). Time and the Stars: Two Examples of Multifocal Approach in Aristotle's Works on Physics. In: CATTANEI/FERMANI/MIGLIORI (2016), p. 187-220.

REALE, G. (2003). *Per una nuova interpretazione di Platone. Rilettura della metafisica dei grandi dialoghi alla luce delle "Dottrine non scritte"*. Milano. Vita e Pensiero (orig. ed. 1984).

WITTGENSTEIN, L. (1922). *Tractatus logico-philosophicus*. London. Kegan Paul, Trench, Trubner, and Co.

Plato's Soul-Body Problem[1]

Christopher Rowe

I.

For those who like myself have no time for any notion of "soul" at all, and for whom the existence of bodies is for the most part uncomplicated, anyone who *does* have time for "souls" will necessarily have a soul-body problem (are they lodged somehow in the body? If so, where in the body? Corporeal or incorporeal? If incorporeal, how do they relate to and inter-

---

1 The text of this paper is very close to that of the original as delivered in Alghero in September 2017. Its originality, if such it has, lies chiefly in the fact that it attempts to make a single whole out of the many different things Plato says or hints at about the relationship of soul and body across the complete range of his dialogues. Such projects of synthesis are relatively out of fashion in contemporary scholarship, for two reasons in particular: (1) that if Plato is thought to hold firmly to any substantial views at all, he is also thought by many, especially in the English-speaking world, to have changed those views radically over the course of his life; and (2) that modern philosophical practice (again, especially in the English-speaking world) generally favours microscopic examination of particular ideas, theses or arguments over the construction of a world-view, and tends to shape its treatment of Plato accordingly, preferring to engage minutely with individual passages or contexts independently of any larger picture – if indeed it overtly recognises that there is such a larger picture worth taking notice of in the first place. My own approach is to begin with the assumption that Plato's thinking is all of one piece, and that it is our business as interpreters to try as far as we can to fit together what may appear to be widely varying positions on the same subjects in a way that reduces at least the apparently most significant differences to differences of perspective, themselves corresponding to differences in the *dramatis personae* and the dramatic circumstances of particular dialogues. This is not to say that I dismiss altogether the possibility of changes of mind on Plato's part, only that we should not start from there – given that, despite the *Seventh Letter*, and despite any evidence we may think we have from Aristotle, we know far too little about Plato's intellectual biography to be able to use it as a basis for the interpretation of his written works.

act with the corporeal? And, plainly, so on and so on).[2] As for Plato, *his* version of the problem – or problems – may sometimes appear about as extreme as it can get, insofar as he can write about human souls and bodies in such a way as to suggest that it is *bodies* whose presence is problematic; for he can propose, for example, that it is our chief and perhaps only serious business in life to assimilate ourselves to gods, who by his account need not have bodies at all. On such a view, we appear to be reducible not just to our souls but to the thinking, rational aspect of our souls, our bodies being no more than unfortunate encumbrances to be sloughed off at the first opportunity (however rare and remote).

II.

And yet: to characterise Plato's views like this would be wholly one-sided. As Sarah Broadie[3] has argued, the human soul for Plato is always *both* a rational entity *and* the activator of the body, what brings life to it. He does not confuse the two functions, but rather combines them. The serious problem, in Plato, is about how his view of the human soul as a fundamentally rational entity, akin to his exclusively rational gods (who, if they have a body at all, seem to have the same sort of relationship to it as horsemen to their horses), is to be combined with the inevitable fact that, being a *human* soul, it must typically, if not in fact permanently,[4] be located in a body – which inconveniently provides what is at best an uncertain environment for the favoured activity of such a rational entity (i.e., pure reasoning). This will be the focus of the present paper.

III.

There is a story about Plato that is told regularly in the modern period (and one that I used to peddle myself) that his dialogues contain two

---

2   "Soul" can of course be understood as "(principle of) life": see the beautifully produced KORNMEIER (2016), accompanying an exhibition of the same name; both are subtitled "Ancient ideas of life and body", thus conveying the plain fact that ancient explanations of life are always tied to a notion of soul (albeit sometimes in a way that actually does away with souls as such altogether).

3   BROADIE (2001), p. 295ff.

4   That is, except for intermissions between lives.

quite distinct views of human nature: one, that we are rational through and through, the other a version of the notion of original sin, namely that the rational capacity of each and every one of us, *qua* human, is under permanent threat from irretrievably non-rational elements in us. These two views are evidently irreconcilable, and according to the commonest version of the story in question are to be seen as the products of different minds: the first of Socrates', the second of Plato's. Such a solution fits well enough with the general tendency to separate off some (earlier) dialogues as "Socratic", leaving the others as representing a time when Plato became more of his own man and developed distinctive ideas of his own. But it (now) seems to me that this is a mistake: there is, I (now) claim, no clear evidence that Plato was ever committed to the second view, i.e., that human rationality is permanently threatened by an animal within us – even if we have an element in us that *is* animal, or at least "like a savage creature" (see §VII below). Despite appearances to the contrary, I believe that he never means to propose that *all* human souls are compounds of rational and a non-rational element or elements that permanently threaten to corrupt or even overcome reason; although he may propose that all human souls, *qua* human, are necessarily divided into rational and non-rational elements or parts, I do not believe him to be proposing that these elements or parts are necessarily or naturally in conflict with each other. The basis for this claim of mine is that the idea of a soul divided into naturally opposing elements or parts, as applied to the soul at least in its most extreme form, derives essentially from the *possibility* of internal conflict, or its presence in some souls, and – so I take Plato to say – there is nothing inevitable about such conflict, which occurs just through a failure of reason (the key text here is *Soph.* 228b2-4: «'Well now', he says, 'in a soul, *when people are in poor condition*, don't we observe beliefs disagreeing with desires, anger with pleasures, reason with pains, indeed all of these with each other?'»[5]). It is the business of reason to decide our priorities; let it choose the wrong priorities (for food and wine, say, or

---

5 The translation is from my translation of the *Theaetetus* and *Sophist* (ROWE, 2015); in a footnote, I comment «Such internal "disagreement" in the soul is treated, in Book IV of the *Republic*, as the basis of an argument for dividing the soul into three forms or parts; if that argument were starting from what Socrates says here in the *Sophist*, would the division only apply in the case of souls "in poor condition"?» The implied answer is (of course) *no*. I am far from wanting to deny that Plato acknowledges the existence of non-rational aspects of the soul (see §V below on the "mortal kind" of soul in the *Timaeus*); what I do deny is that

sex, over rational discourse), and the way is open to what can then be represented as a dispute between reason, on the one hand (supposing that the agent remains aware that his or her choices are wrong, or at any rate not obviously right), and a quasi-independent appetite on the other.

IV.

The intellectualist Socrates, the one to whom is usually attributed the notion of human nature as through and through rational, was said even in antiquity to have "done away with" the irrational part of the soul, and [so] with emotion and character.[6] The Stoics may well have thought that they were modelling themselves on him when they treated desires and emotions as cognitive states.[7] But both these interpretations – saying that Socrates "did away with" the emotions, and saying that he made them into cognitive states, in common with the Stoics – probably go beyond the evidence, at least so far as concerns the Socrates of Plato's dialogues. The theory of action on display in the so-called "Socratic" dialogues ties reason inseparably to desire, i.e., to a universal desire for the (real) good. About other desires, or the emotions apart from anger, the Socrates of these dialogues has little or nothing to say – this much is true, but it need signify no more than that the focus of these dialogues is such as not to call for a spelling out by their Socrates and his author of a position on "bodily" desires and emotions. We can fill the vacuum with Stoic doctrine, if we wish, but it seems more plausible to fill it instead in the way I propose Plato fills it, by treating such phenomena as what the *Phaedo*

---

he regards these as naturally and necessarily out of harmony with the rational. The picture of the soul that we are given in the *Republic* as the locus of warring parts that have to be schooled into agreement is developed through an analogy with a city that is luxurious (*truphôsa*, II, 372e3) and (so) already fevered (*phlegmainousa*, e8), and needs to be cured of that fever; a soul modelled on a city that was in better condition – not fevered, but healthy (372e7) – would look quite different: comprising different aspects, but unified, not conflicted. See, most recently, ROWE (2017).

6 [Arist.] *Mag. Mor.* I 1, 1182a15-17.
7 «The Stoics revert to Socrates' extreme intellectualism. They deny an irrational part of the soul. The soul is a mind or reason. Its contents are impressions or thoughts, to which the mind gives assent or prefers to give assent. In giving assent to an impression, we espouse a belief. Desires are just beliefs of a certain kind, the product of our assent to a so-called impulsive impression» (FREDE, 2000, p. 12).

calls the "distractions" provided by the body, and giving the soul the capacity to decide how, and to what extent, to respond to these. «The body», Socrates says there in the *Phaedo*, «provides us with a million distractions because of the need to supply it with food [...]. It fills us full of lusts, desires, fears, fantasies of all kinds [...]».[8] But we – our souls – are so constituted by nature as to be capable of deciding to treat all this exactly *as* a set of "distractions". Things may look attractive and desirable, but if they are not in fact good for us, then we will not desire them, and they can and should be set aside. If I am hungry, if I actually need to eat in order to stay alive and complete my projects, and if staying alive and completing my projects really is the best thing for me, then I really do want to eat, but otherwise not (even if my stomach feels empty, and even if it is). And if I really do need to defend myself, that being what is best for me, then I will really want to do that too, with whatever degree of emotional response is required and appropriate (i.e., as approved by reason in the circumstances).

V.

According to this perspective of the *Phaedo*, we can even choose whether or not to find things pleasant. «Does it appear to you [asks Socrates of Simmias] to be a philosopher's business to have worked hard at the so-called pleasures like, say, those of food and drink [...] or the so-called pleasures of sex [...] [or] acquiring distinctive cloaks or shoes [...] do you think that he attaches value to these, or does he rather refuse to do so, except in so far as he absolutely can't avoid having something to do with them?» He actually «fails to find [any] such things pleasant» (64d-65a). From this angle, the body is not just a nuisance; it is a prison, even, insofar as the soul finds itself perpetually trapped, hemmed in on all sides by demands that tend to cut it off from what it is its destiny to do, as something whose nature it is to reason and which left to itself yearns only to reason. However there are other perspectives available – other perspectives that Plato and his Socrates consider, alongside that of the *Phaedo*: most importantly, perhaps, that of humans living together in society. This is the perspective especially of the *Timaeus*, whose account of the creation of the world and its various contents is framed by a story about a success-

8 *Phaed.* 66b7-c3.

ful warrior society. In this context, Plato's Timaeus recognises a mortal kind (*genos*) of soul, comprising spirit and appetite (69c-72b), each with its own separate location, away from reason, but so arranged as to be under the control of reason. These, spirit and appetite, resemble the two lower parts of the soul as described in the *Republic* (though in the *Timaeus* the language of "parts" is less visible), but in comparison with the *Republic* they are introduced in a distinctly more positive way. They are constructed by the created gods as these gods «imitate [the Demiurge], taking over the/an immortal principle of soul» (*hoi de mimoumenoi, paralabontes archên psuchês athanaton*),[9] in other words to help bring the Demiurge's plans to fruition. Once a rational soul finds itself encased in a human body, its responsibilities necessarily expand in order to include all those functions required for human living, especially perception (69d4), a capacity for responding to external or internal threats, and «appetites for food and drink and whatever else [the aspect of the soul that has desires] has a need for because of the nature of the body» (70d7-8). The relation of these functions to reason, and the overall unity of the soul, is underlined by the connection between the marrow constituting the brain, containing the circular motions of reason, and the marrow containing the mortal soul, which is distributed throughout the rest of the body: «the marrow that was to contain the remaining, mortal [element] of the soul he [through the agency of the created gods] divided up into shapes that were both round and straight [...] and from these as it were from anchors he threw out bonds to bind the whole soul, thus fashioning now the whole of this body of ours around it [*sc.* the marrow]» (73d2-7).[10]

VI.

Thus if these functions are not actually extensions of the activity of reason itself, they are at any rate introduced as consistent with, even necessary to, that activity. There is at least one worry about Timaeus' account here, namely that we are not told what ingredients the created gods use to make the "mortal kind of soul". But it may be enough that they are said to divide up the non-cerebral marrow into both round and straight shapes,

9 *Tim.* 69c5-6.
10 This is in all essentials Thomas Johansen's interpretation, in JOHANSEN (2004), ch. 7.

and that they imitate (the example of?) the Demiurge, the point being to suggest a combination in the mortal soul of the straight-line movements typical of physical experience with the circular movement that is the mark of (constitutes?) reason.

VII.

A more serious difficulty with this interpretation is that the terms in which these new functions of soul are introduced appear, at least at first sight, distinctly less positive than the account in the previous section (§VI above) suggests. Thus (e.g.) «And within the body they built another kind of soul as well, the mortal kind, which contains within it those fearful (*deina*) and necessary (*anankaia*) experiences: of pleasure, first of all, most powerful lure to what is bad; then of pains, that cause us run away from what is good; besides these, boldness and fear, foolish counsellors both, anger, hard to assuage, and expectation that easily leads astray. These they fused with unreasoning sense perception and lust/passion ready to attempt anything (*epicheirêtêi pantos erôti*), and so constructed the mortal type of soul as was necessary (*anankaiôs*)».[11] It is not unexpected that human life, as resulting from the embodiment of the soul, should be said to require the experience of pleasures and pains, boldness, fear, and so on; what is surprising – that is, given the general line of approach adopted in the present paper – is that these things should be introduced, at least at first, in so apparently negative a way.

But there is an explanation for this. In each case, the negative descriptions ("fearful and necessary",[12] "most powerful lure", etc.) simply tell us what the effects of the various *pathêmata would* be if they were not located separately from and controlled by reason. As the created gods actually set them up, however, that control by reason will be provided for, and Timaeus spells out at some length the mechanisms by which it will be exercised. So, for example, with appetite, the "*erôs* ready to attempt any-

---

11 *Tim.* 69c7-d6; Donald Zeyl's translation (from COOPER/HUTCHINSON, 1997), heavily modified.

12 «And necessary»: "necessary" here, perhaps, refers especially to the force of the experiences in question, not so much their inevitability (at least in some contexts?).

thing": this may be "like a savage creature" in us,[13] but it is prevented, under the original disposition, and under any situation that properly mimics that original disposition,[14] from actually running wild.[15]

VIII.

The differences here from the *Republic* and the *Phaedo*, then, are on this account chiefly a matter of context and perspective, or of emphasis,[16] rather than of substance; the differences from the so-called "Socratic" dialogues will, more speculatively, be a matter of Plato's filling in the gaps, i.e., on the subject of the soul's relation to the body, and on the passions and emotions. The ideal of the life of pure thought is a constant in the dialogues,[17] and by itself, as in the *Phaedo*, can suggest a treatment of the body as at best a necessary concomitant, at worst a distraction. But such an ideal can happily sit beside another picture, according to which (I quote Thomas Johansen), «the lower parts [...] have assumed rational functions in the body [...]. The lower parts [...] are not just set apart from the intellect (though that happens too); they also work together with the intellect in bringing about the ends that the intellect prescribes. I talk [...] of *devolved* rationality to emphasize the positive point that the lower parts of the soul co-operate with the intellect in maintaining rational order in the entire living being».[18] Indeed in my view the two pictures

13 Appetite has to be tied down «like a savage animal, but one that has to be kept fed along with the others if ever a human race is to exist» (70e3-5).
14 Cf. 86b-90d.
15 See ROWE (2016).
16 Cf. JOHANSEN (2004), p. 153: «I would suggest that *Timaeus'* account of the tripartite soul is, generally speaking, different in *emphasis* from that of the *Republic* (footnote: «[...] I do not claim to have identified any disagreements or inconsistencies in doctrine between [the two dialogues]»). In the *Republic* the three parts of the soul are clearly distinguished in terms of the different objects that they desire: the intellect has a proper desire for truth, the spirited part for esteem, and the appetitive for bodily gratification (footnote: «[...] Note, however, that *Resp.* IV 436aff. seems, initially at least, to distinguish the parts of the soul by function (knowledge, anger, etc.) rather than by desires for specific objects»). I myself add that further distinguishing feature of the *Republic* treatment that it starts from the assumption of internal conflict (the institutions of Callipolis are intended, from the beginning, to cure an already "fevered" city): see §III above.
17 See specially SEDLEY (1999).
18 JOHANSEN (2004), p. 154-155 (my italics).

of the relation between soul and body – that of the *Phaedo* (e.g.) and that of the *Timaeus* – *must* sit side by side, insofar as the ideal of the life of pure thought is no more than an ideal, i.e., something unattainable: unattainable because human souls must inevitably remain human, however close to the sun, and the stars, they may fly.[19]

IX.

The body is in this way integrated into the Platonic idea of the human being. The self is the soul. True, "the soul" here is the immortal rational soul rather than the whole soul, i.e., the soul as including its mortal elements: knowing ourselves is knowing this truth about ourselves. Nevertheless, the immortal element of the human soul, *qua* human, still requires the mortal ones. Compare Socrates' question to himself in the *Phaedrus*, «whether I am actually a beast more complex and more typhonic than Typhon, or both a tamer and a simpler creature, sharing some divine and un-Typhonic portion by nature».[20] The terms of the question are explained later in the dialogue, if they needed explaining: Socrates is asking himself whether he is to be identified with many-headed beast of appetite, the black horse of the *Phaedrus* myth, or rather with the charioteer of reason. His answer, equally unsurprisingly, is the second: he is the charioteer, not the black horse. Realising his rational nature, in the mythical scheme of this dialogue, would free him from the body altogether, but even in the story he will acquire his liberty only for a time. To say, as Socrates does in the *Phaedrus*, that a human soul is forever destined to be in a body is to say that it is not and cannot be itself divine – it only *shares*

---

19 «But could [a] transition from a mortal to an immortal nature be accommodated to Plato's notion of either essential or conferred immortality? That is a question on which we are left to ponder», says SEDLEY (2009), p. 161. The transition in question is what would be involved in what Sedley calls "earned" immortality – earned, that is, by devotion to virtue and philosophy; "conferred" immortality is the sort, according to Timaeus, that belongs to the rational element of the human soul as well as the world, its soul, and the cosmic gods, while "essential" immortality is what Sedley calls the sort of immortality that the *Phaedo* argues for in the case of the soul. I incline towards thinking that the introduction of "conferred" immortality is merely a consequence of (what I regard as) the fiction of the creation of the universe by a divine Craftsman, and that Plato never intended "earned" immortality to be more than an aspiration.

20 *Phaedr.* 230a3-6.

«some divine [...] portion by nature», not possessing knowledge, only the capacity to progress in the direction of knowledge. It therefore belongs, not with the stars, but on the earth. Once it is there, the Timaeus of the eponymous dialogue considers the possibility that it could do just with a head, but of course it cannot; a human being consisting simply of circular movements fitted neatly into a globular shell would just roll around and get lodged in ditches. No, it needs the full paraphernalia, with trunk, arms, legs and so on; it can dream of joining the gods, and that is what it should aim to do to the best of its ability, being in its most important part divine, but the best it can do is to mimic the serenity, and the unity, of divine rationality.

X.

On the other hand, the more we associate with the mortal parts, and the less control our reasoning part comes to have, the less human (i.e., further still from the divine) our souls become. This idea usually appears in the context of talk, typically cast as story-telling, about what will happen to our souls after death, whether in the *Phaedo*, the *Republic*, or elsewhere. Thus the souls of organised, well behaved people will pass into the bodies of bees and ants,[21] of aggressive types into those of wolves and hawks,[22] and so on. But there is a serious question about when exactly the transformation takes place. After all, if the soul of one of those «who have practiced ravening gluttony or excessive fondness for wine»[23] – a banker, say – is already fit for the body of a donkey, why is it not already a donkey soul while the banker is still alive? Plato's eschatological scheme would give him a special reason for wanting to say this.[24] On this scheme, the person does not survive, only his or her soul, and this soul when lodged in a new body will apparently have no memory of any experiences it had when in a previous body. That is, there is no room for personal survival, only for the survival of individual packages, as it were, of soul-stuff (this is consistent with the Socratic-Platonic notion of self-knowledge[25]).[26] Yet at the

21 *Phaed.* 82b.
22 *Phaed.* 82a.
23 *Phaed.* 81e.
24 For the following argument, see ROWE (2005).
25 See §IX above.
26 See SEDLEY (1999), esp. p. 316-319.

same time the stories about reincarnation are plainly intended to be persuasive: to warn us what the dangers are if we do not look after our immortal souls as we should. If after death our banker won't know that he was once a "successful" banker when he becomes a donkey, and indeed he won't *be* a banker, or the particular banker he was, there will be nothing frightening about being told that his bit of soul-stuff will pass into a donkey (we can easily imagine him saying "so what? What is it to me?" And he would be right; to worry about what the donkey he will become might think *if* he could remember what he was would be mere sentimental nonsense). Plato's stories about our future lives are, I propose,[27] thinly disguised allegories about our lives in the present. The greedy banker is already a donkey,[28] even though he doesn't know it – and that ought to terrify him thoroughly, if only he knew it, or had even asked the question

27 And as many others have proposed: see e.g. ANNAS (1981), p. 351-352.
28 Compare the following passage, cited in ROWE (2005), from Flann O'Brien's novel, *The Third Policeman*:
«'The Atomic Theory' I sallied 'is a thing that is not very clear to me at all.'
'Michael Gilhaney' said the Sergeant 'is an example of a man that is nearly banjaxed from the principle of the Atomic Theory. Would it astonish you to hear that he is nearly half a bicycle?' [...]
'Are you certain about the humanity of the bicycle?' I inquired of him. 'Is the Atomic Theory as dangerous as you say?'
'It is between two and three times as dangerous as it might be' he replied gloomily. 'Early in the morning I think it is four times, and what is more, if you lived here for a few days and gave full play to your observation and inspection, you would know how certain the sureness of certainty is.' [...] 'The gross and net result of it is that people who spend most of their natural lives riding iron bicycles over the rocky road-steads of this parish get their personalities mixed up with the personalities of their bicycle as a result of the interchanging of the atoms of each of them and you would be surprised at the number of people in these parts who are nearly half people and half bicycles' [...]. The Sergeant's face clouded and he spat thoughtfully three yards ahead of him on the road. 'I will tell you a secret' he said very confidentially in a low voice. 'My great-grandfather was eighty-three when he died. For a year before his death he was a horse!'
'A horse?'
'A horse in everything but extraneous externalities. He would spend the day grazing in a field or eating hay in a stall' ...
'I suppose your great-grandfather got himself into this condition by too much horse-riding?'
'That was the size of it. His old horse Dan was in the contrary way and gave so much trouble, coming into the house at night and interfering with young girls during the day and committing indictable offences, that they had to shoot him [...] but if you ask me it was my great-grandfather they shot and it is the horse

"Who/what am I?" in the way that Socrates asks it about himself in the *Phaedrus*; after all, he is probably used to looking down on other people, let alone donkeys. The moral: (for the observer) the creature before you may look human, but beware – it could be a quite different animal, even a monster; (for the agent) what is at risk, in our life-choices, is our very humanity.

XI.

So here is Plato's resolution of what I call his "soul-body problem". Human souls are essentially, i.e. in their essential nature, rational, even god-like (with the emphasis on the *-like*). On the other hand, because they are not – and can never[29] become – gods, they are necessarily located in, indeed locked into, bodies.[30] And that makes their humanity a fragile matter: in such a (bodily) context it is not guaranteed that they *remain* human, even if they continue to inhabit human bodies. But that is entirely up to them/us; whether they/we stay human or not, even in the lives we are living now, is determined by their/our (rational) choices and by nothing else. We have something in common with other animals, and necessarily so, but *qua* human we have the power not to become (like) them,

---

that is buried up in Cloncoonla churchyard'». (O'BRIEN, 1993, p. 85-86, 89, 88, 93-94). The idea is that the parish, i.e. the universe, needs a policeman just to prevent things unravelling: thus the Sergeant keeps stealing bicycles and locking them up in the jail, just to try to slow the process of transformation down. The difference is that O'Brien is writing satire; Plato is deadly serious – the greedy banker, soul-wise, *is* a donkey, or at least so like a donkey as to be hard to distinguish from one.

29 Except in their dreams, and the stories they tell themselves.
30 Locked in, that is, until their bodies die, at which point, for Plato (I propose), they cease to be the individuals that they once were, i.e., when they were in their last body; the only difference between them will be generic, in the sense that given their condition at the point of (the body's) death some will be better adapted to some kind of non-human animal in its next life, while others will have enough about them that is still human to pass back into another human body. Having no memory of their previous lives (*Resp.* 621a-b), any vestige of individuality is stripped away.

whether in our present existences or, less importantly,[31] in any future existence "our" souls may enjoy or suffer through.[32]

31 Less importantly, that is, for us, just insofar as the memories of individuals will
    have been wiped, but perhaps just as importantly from the perspective of a uni-
    verse that is not only rationally constructed but is actually a reasoning entity –
    for which any diminution of rationality might well be a matter of concern (on
    the other hand, if the universe is eternal, its rationality must be equally durable.
    Balance must somehow be maintained; there can be no room for entropy. Phi-
    losophy, it seems, will be a crucial part of what keeps the world turning).
32 My warm thanks to the audience at, and the individual contributors to, the orig-
    inal conference in Alghero for their criticisms and suggestions; also to Diego
    Zucca, Roberto Medda and Gabriele Meloni for organising a meeting that was
    as pleasing to the body (aesthetically, for its surroundings and gastronomically)
    as it would have been to the rational soul, were there to be such a thing (see §I
    above).

54 Christopher Rowe

References

ANNAS, J. (1981). *An Introduction to Plato's Republic.* Oxford. Clarendon Press.

BROADIE, S. (2001). Soul and Body in Plato and Descartes. *Proceedings of the Aristotelian Society*, 102, p. 295-308.

COOPER, J.M.; HUTCHINSON, D.S. (eds.) (1997). Plato. *Complete Works.* Indianapolis, Cambridge. Hackett.

FREDE, M. (2000). The Philosopher. In: Brunschwig, J.; Lloyd, G.E.R. (eds.). *Greek Thought. A Guide to Classical Knowledge.* Cambridge (Mass.), London. Harvard University Press, p. 3-19.

JOHANSEN, TH. (2004). *Plato's Natural Philosophy: A Study of the* Timaeus-Critias. Cambridge. Cambridge University Press.

KORNMEIER, U. (ed.) (2016). *The Soul is an Octopus.* Berlin. Berliner Medizinhistorisches Museum der Charité and Excellence Cluster Topoi of Freie Universität Berlin and Humboldt-Universität.

O'BRIEN, F. (1993). *The Third Policeman.* Hammersmith, London. HarperCollinsPublishers (Flamingo).

ROWE, CH. (2005). Hommes et monstres: Platon et Socrate parlent de la nature humaine. In: Dillon, J; Dixsaut, M. (eds.). *Agonistes. Essays in Honour of Denis O'Brien.* Aldershot (UK), Burlington (US). Ashgate, p. 139-156.

_____ (2015). Plato. Theaetetus *and* Sophist. Cambridge. Cambridge University Press.

_____ (2016). On the Good, Beauty and the Beast in Plato's *Symposium.* In: Tulli, M.; Erler M. (eds.). *Plato in Symposium. Selected Papers from the Tenth Symposium Platonicum.* Sankt Augustin. Academia Verlag, p. 391-403.

_____ (2017). "The City of Pigs": A Key Passage in Plato's *Republic. Philosophie Antique. Problèmes, Renaissances, Usages*, 17, p. 55-71.

SEDLEY, D. (1999). The Ideal of Godlikeness. In: Fine G. (ed.). *Plato 2: Ethics, Politics, Religion, and the Soul.* Oxford. Oxford University Press, p. 309-328.

_____ (2009). Three Kinds of Platonic Immortality. In: Frede, D.; Reis, B. (eds.). *Body and Soul in Ancient Philosophy.* Berlin, New York. de Gruyter.

On the Relationship between *Psuchê* and Senses in Plato's *Theaetetus*

Aldo Brancacci

The *Theaetetus* is such a rich and complex dialogue that even outlining its completive physiognomy with a single definition turns out as a challenging task. Nevertheless, the fact that its hardship is largely due to its various and divergent interpretations leads me to declare from the beginning how I conceive this difficult dialogue. In my opinion, *Theaetetus* is, first of all, a contentious dialogue, in which the argument begins on the sophistic "ground" and ends on the Socratic one: Plato's polemical targets are beyond Protagoras' philosophy – which has the privileged role of "polemic idol" – and involve other philosophies, even though they are not explicitly mentioned.[1] Differently from most of contemporary scholars, I feel very close to previous ones in believing that it is crucial – and not irrelevant – to consider the polemic context (and in general the whole historic-philosophical dimension) of Plato's works. In fact, a Historian of Philosophy can absolutely not ignore the pattern of references – like pugnacious aims or interlocutors or antagonists – of a philosophical text and of a philosopher. From my point of view, this strong belligerent and contentious trait of *Theaetetus* is one of the reasons by which it is commonly defined as aporetic. Exposition and theoretical development of the rival thesis are, on one side, so wide to make it impossible for a dialogue – even for a dialogue of considerable dimensions like this one – to realize a further inquiry in order to give a complete exposition of Plato's concept of ἐπιστήμη (taking for granted by the sake of argument that Plato wished to do so in this work). On the other side, that dialogue is so concentrated, controversial, unsettled and complex, to necessarily require an additional introspection by both the philosopher reader – whose task is to get as close as possible to a correct comprehension of a given issue

---

1 I have already argued on it in BRANCACCI (1992). Because of the depletion of that volume, I also report the French version of my paper: BRANCACCI (2001), where I repeat my opinion in a wider way.

with his very own, autonomous commitment – and, probably, by Plato himself as well.

Inside a such problematic and puzzling frame, we have definitely not to ignore the important sections of the dialogue where Plato reaches positive solutions. In fact, the presence of these solutions leads us to reconsider the aporetic nature of the *Theaetetus*, and to admit – in contrast to many scholars' opinion – that it does not exhaust the texture of the dialogue. One of these sections is in the passage 184c-187b: it establishes a comeback to the question of what ἐπιστήμη is, after the conclusion of the attempt of confutation of Protagoras and the κομψότεροι. It is structured in two moments, which are both distinguished and strictly connected. Initially the issue of the relationship between *psuchê* and senses sparks out with very innovative theoretical acquisitions, afterwards it paves the road to the exposition of the theory of the κοινά. I will consider only the first moment of this wide passage, even though I will also keep in mind its end, that is the point where Socrates states that the result of the previous analysis led the research concerning what ἐπιστήμη is to the maximum degree of advancement. It is not trivial to remind that the one theme present in *Theaetetus* – and in all of Plato's work – is a pursuit (ζήτησις) addressed to discover and find out (εὑρίσκειν): whether this element is forgotten, the whole sense of Plato's dialogue and philosophy is lost for good. We shall first of all read this conclusion:

> Then, Theaetetus, perception and knowledge could never be the same.
> Evidently not, Socrates; and indeed now at last it has been made perfectly clear that knowledge is something different from perception.
> But surely we did not begin our conversation in order to find out what knowledge is not, but what it is. However, we have progressed so far, at least, as not to seek for knowledge in perception at all, but in some function of the soul, whatever name is given to it when it alone and by itself is engaged directly with realities.[2]

---

2 Plat. *Theaet.* 186e9-187a6: – Οὐκ ἄρ' ἂν εἴη ποτέ, ὦ Θεαίτητε, αἴσθησίς τε καὶ ἐπιστήμη ταὐτόν. – Οὐ φαίνεται, ὦ Σώκρατες. καὶ μάλιστά γε νῦν δὴ καταφανέστατον γέγονεν ἄλλο ὂν αἰσθήσεως ἐπιστήμη. – Ἀλλ' οὔ τι μὲν δὴ τούτου γε ἕνεκα ἠρχόμεθα διαλεγόμενοι, ἵνα εὕρωμεν τί ποτ' οὐκ ἔστ' ἐπιστήμη, ἀλλὰ τί ἔστιν. ὅμως δὲ τοσοῦτόν γε προβεβήκαμεν, ὥστε μὴ ζητεῖν αὐτὴν ἐν αἰσθήσει τὸ παράπαν ἀλλ' ἐν ἐκείνῳ τῷ ὀνόματι, ὅτι ποτ' ἔχει ἡ ψυχή, ὅταν αὐτὴ καθ' αὑτὴν πραγματεύηται περὶ τὰ ὄντα (the translations are taken from FOWLER, 1961).

The present contentions, in virtue of their conclusiveness concerning the first part of *Theaetetus*, are mainly directed against the definition of ἐπιστήμη as perception, initially suggested by Theaetetus and afterwards represented by Protagoras' and "the subtler philosophers'" doctrine through a series of progressive comparisons. Indeed, by them it is plainly meant that knowledge[3] is not perception, nor is it traceable back to perception. Anyway, we do not have to presume additional meanings from Plato's words: by these contentions he means that knowledge does not coincide with perception, nor even it is traceable back to perception. Vice versa, the focal point of that section consists in the development of a theoretical perspective based on a principle of cooperation between soul and senses, which Plato devises and increases with a high degree of complexity.

This theme is not new and unrelated to the rest of Plato's production. In *Phaedo* 74a-76a, namely in the context of an exposition and a justification of the theory of reminiscence, Plato stresses the fact that we can grasp the equal itself by thought (ἐννοεῖσθαι) only if we previously perceive with our senses objects which appears as equals to us. The term used by Plato in reference to it is ἐκ, which is present in many expressions,[4] whilst once there is a recurrence of ἀπό.[5] Both these prepositions point out the sensorial sphere as the ground to grasp (ἐννοεῖσθαι) the idea. First of all, the occasion to ἐννοεῖσθαι the idea is provided by the confrontation between an effective perception of an object – or of different objects – and its idea, which indicates the thing itself. That confrontation exposes how the sensible object is defective (τι ἐλλείπει, 74a6) of something in comparison to the idea, which differs from any other corresponding sensible instance, and to which we affix the formula αὐτὸ ὃ ἔστι (75d2). And whether it might be questioned where from (πόθεν, 74b4) would we acquire the very cognition of it, we know that it arises from the woods, or the stones, or any other kind of objects that can be perceived as alike one another, or that may seem alike to an individual and different to another one (79b4-9). The other element taking part in this cognitive process is the *in-itself*, the idea:

---

3 The word *epistêmê* could be also translated with "science". But in this paper I follow the common usage in the anglosaxon scholarship.

4 Plat. *Phaed.* 74b4 (ἐξ ὧν); 74b6 (ἐκ τούτων); 74c7 (ἐκ τούτων); 75a6-7 (ἐκ τοῦ ἰδεῖν ἢ ἅψασθαι ἢ ἔκ τινος ἄλλης τῶν αἰσθήσεων).

5 Plat. *Phaed.* 74c13-d1 (ἀπὸ ταύτης τῆς ὄψεως).

'Now then,' said he, 'do the equal pieces of wood and the equal things of which we were speaking just now affect us in this way: Do they seem to us to be equal as abstract equality is equal, or do they somehow fall short of being like abstract equality?' 'They fall very far short of it,' said he. 'Do we agree, then, that when anyone on seeing a thing thinks, 'This thing that I see aims at being like some other thing that exists, but falls short and is unable to be like that thing, but is inferior to it' he who thinks thus must of necessity have previous knowledge (προειδότα) of the thing which he says the other resembles but falls short of (ἐνδεεστέρως ἔχειν)?'.[6]

This conclusion brings clearly out the importance of this other element, to which runs parallel the προειδέναι. In the two fundamental descriptions of the προειδέναι itself it is possible to make out the first appearance in Greek philosophy of something partially similar to what – a few centuries later, and in a whole different theoretical context – will be called the *a priori*.[7] But even when the evidence of this second element of knowledge arises, Plato takes good care of reaffirming the crucial role of perceptions: «Indeed, we agree on such thing as well, that in no other way we could have possibly came up with this thought, nor would it have been possible to achieve it by any other means, if not by seeing or touching or using any other one of sensible perceptions».[8] In *Republic*, which is chronologically closer to *Theaetetus*, that role of perception is furthermore specified by the merging of a new concept. In fact, the theoretical context of *Phaedo* is held by two couples of concepts, plus a fifth one: the αἰσθάνεσθαι and the ἐννοεῖσθαι, connected by the transition from one to the other; the concomitant affirmation of the προειδέναι, on the side of the idea, and of the ἐλλείπειν, on the side of sensible object; to whom compels the ὀρέγεσθαι. In *Republic*, the new concept that breaks into the

---

6 Plat. *Phaed.* 74d9-e4.
7 Plat. *Phaed.* 74e9-75a3: « – Well then, is this just what happened to us with regard to the equal things and equality in the abstract? – It certainly is. – Then we must have had knowledge of equality before the time when we first saw equal things and thought, 'All these things are aiming (ὀρέγεται) to be like equality but fall short'». The second passage is found shortly after: « – Then before (πρὸ) we began to see or hear or use the other senses we must somewhere have gained a knowledge of abstract or absolute equality, if we were to compare with it the equals which we perceive by the senses, and see that all such things; yearn to be like abstract equality but fall short of it» (Plat. *Phaed.* 75b4-8).
8 Plat. *Phaed.* 75a5-8.

theoretical ground of senses is the παρακαλεῖν, which is a new development of the ἐκ and the ἀπό that in *Phaedo* would only trace back the up-
rising awareness of the in-itself (αὐτὸ τὸ ἴσον) to its source in the field of
sensitivity. In addition, and on a completely different level, it is a development of the ὀρέγεσθαι of *Phaedo* too. And παρακλητικόν is the function of
some perceptions which designs the activity of a stimulation to the act of
thinking, and which bestows a major degree of activity to the sensible
perception. So, Plato makes a distinction between two classes of sensible
objects: the ones which does not lead intelligence to a further research,
because they are adequately evaluated by sensation itself; the other which
do it, because from the heuristic point of view the single perception is
not capable of adding up to them anything useful. The second ones are
the so called paraclectic perceptions, which consist of an incentive for the
inquiry, because the single perception features at the same time one specific trait and its opposite. They are παρακλητικὰ τῆς διανοίας.[9] The first
ones, instead, cannot hence address a further research right because they
do not produce at the same time a contradictory depiction. All things in
which there is opposition (or proportion) are according to Plato sugges-
tive of reflection. The mere impression of sense evokes no power of
thought or of mind. The paraclectic perceptions offer controversial depic-
tions of the same object, or they are the outcomes of sensorial organs in
charge of perceiving contrary qualities. Because of that contradictoriness,
the soul is not able to point out determined qualities by them, and so it is
forced to a further inquiry, which is eminently interrogative and critic,
and which implies operations like confronting, comparing, reconsider-
ing. Since achieving distinction is its primary purpose, it is then an incite-
ment for knowledge, and it is apt to awaken the νόησις.

According to the research accomplished in these two dialogues on the
relationship between thought and perception, Plato has attained four relevant theoretical achievements, whose fundamental role played into the
future philosophies (especially the Kant's one) is easily understood:

1. The concept of the cognitive act requires the contribution of two instances, sensation and what is called *idea* (αὐτὸ ὃ ἔστι), viz. the rational
   instance of thought (νόησις);
2. The presence of a structural connection between these two instances;

9 Plat. *Resp.* 524d1-4.

3. The fundamental role of perception as source of knowledge, which in *Republic* is even expressed by the notion of paraclectic perception, namely a perception which consist of a strong stimulation for thought;

4. The permanent role of the rational knowledge, which is determined as a superior kind of knowledge both in *Phaedo* and in *Republic*.

According to the aim of my paper, that ground is the most pertinent from a theoretical point of view for the section of *Theaetetus* that I wish to examine. Now, what kind of new elements does this dialogue bring to the reckoning of the role of perception and thought in the cognitive act and in the determination of their nexus? Concerning the inquiry on the reminiscence theory and the concomitant determination of the notion of idea in *Phaedo*, the theoretical contexts regarding our theme are three: the outstanding diversity of the idea itself from any other corresponding empirical instances, the recognition of such issues as, still, source and origin of knowledge, and the overcoming of the ground of mere sensible perception in favor of the one leading towards the conception of existence of ideas. In *Republic* that issue concerns the epistemological status of mathematical knowledges, which need to let themselves loose from senses – even though they originate from it – in order "to lead upwards" the soul.[10] In this very context, Plato outlines a structured synthesis of the entire gnoseological ground and, from the pattern of αἴσθησις, he grasps to and pulls out the concept of paraclectic sensations to build a coherent progression within the transition from the sensible ground to the ground of νόησις. So, Plato confers to paraclectic perceptions the maximum importance allowed to the sensorial sphere: they consist of a decisive "boost" in leading thought to know something, even though that role means an outcoming from that sphere in order to gain another one. In *Theaetetus* the theoretical context is both similar and different: there the aim is to refute Protagoras' and κομψότεροι's doctrine – these ones are explicitly evoked in this section, when coming to the conclusion that knowledge cannot be based upon πάθη[11] – but, at the same time, by that aim Plato develops his own theoretical consideration. It has two focuses:

---

10 Plat. *Resp.* 525d5-6 (σφόδρα ἄνω ποι ἄγει τὴν ψυχήν).

11 Plat. *Theaet.* 186d2-5: «Then knowledge is not to be found in our bodily experiences (ἐν μὲν ἄρα τοῖς παθήμασιν), but in the process of reasoning about them. For in our reasoning it is possible, apparently, to apprehend being and truth. But in mere experiences, it is not».

on one side the concept of ψυχή, on the other side the notion of αἴσθησις. The inquiry on these two concepts is brought, in *Theaetetus*, to a brand-new level of theoretical analysis: the criticism against Protagoras and the need to refute him lead Plato to that analysis, and it is a further evidence of the relevance of the historical and philosophical elements in analyzing the theoretical pattern of the dialogue. The dialogue with Theaetetus restarts with the reiteration of Theaetetus' thesis, stating that knowledge is αἴσθησις. The question asked by Socrates is supported by a declaration which shows the importance that in this case he annexes to the linguistic distinction which he aims to establish: whether if a man sees black or white, or hears the high-pitched tones or the deep ones, he must not state that eyes and ears are what we perceive "with", but what we perceive "through":

> The easy use of words and phrases and the avoidance of strict preci-sion is in general a sign of good breeding; indeed, the opposite is hardly worthy of a gentleman, but sometimes it is necessary, as now it is necessary to object to your answer, in so far as it is incorrect. Just consider; which answer is more correct, that our eyes are that by which (ᾧ) we see or that through which (δι'οὗ) we see, and our ears that by which or that through which we hear.
> I think, Socrates, we perceive through, rather than by them, in each case.[12]

Scholars have miscellaneously examined these formulas, and this is not the case to sum them all up. Nevertheless, there is an issue to be solved yet: it is not true, as Narcy affirms, that there is no certainty whether there is in Greek a substantial difference between the simple dative and the formula διά + genitive.[13] What we take for granted is that surely Plato perceives the different meaning of the two formulas and vigorously stress-es on it. According to Plato, the formula δι'οὗ expresses the exact compre-hension of what really is the αἰσθάνεσθαι, and transforms a mere instru-mentality concept in a complex instrumentality concept. Whilst the in-

12 Plat. *Theaet.* 184c1-9: – Τὸ δὲ εὐχερὲς τῶν ὀνομάτων τε καὶ ῥημάτων καὶ μὴ δι' ἀκριβείας ἐξεταζόμενον τὰ μὲν πολλὰ οὐκ ἀγεννές, ἀλλὰ μᾶλλον τὸ τούτου ἐναντίον ἀνελεύθερον, ἔστι δὲ ὅτε ἀναγκαῖον, οἷον καὶ νῦν ἀνάγκη ἐπιλαβέσθαι τῆς ἀποκρίσεως ἣν ἀπόκρινη, ᾗ οὐκ ὀρθή. σκόπει γάρ᾽ ἀπόκρισις ποτέρα ὀρθοτέρα ᾧ ὁρῶμεν τοῦτο εἶναι ὀφθαλμούς, ἢ δι' οὗ ὁρῶμεν, καὶ ᾧ ἀκούομεν ὦτα, ἢ δι' οὗ ἀκούομεν; – Δι' ὧν ἕκαστα αἰσθανόμεθα ἔμοιγε δοκεῖ, ὦ Σώκρατες, μᾶλλον ἢ οἷς.
13 NARCY (1994), p. 353, n. 324. On this point, see LURAGHI (2003), p. 70-72.

strumental dative ᾧ means an instrumentality exclusively taken in its determination and punctuality, διά + genitive means always instrumentality, but indicates that the performed operation is led by an agent – by a Subject. Natorp has been the first one to claim that there Plato states the concept of singularity of conscience as a fundamental function of knowledge.[14] Following Natorp, Burnyeat has repeated how Plato aims to establish a radical difference between soul's active and unifying function and the simply instrumental role of sensorial organs, and he reaffirmed that in this section of *Theaetetus* it is first expressed the idea of singularity[15] of conscience in history of philosophy. That interpretation surely owns its legitimacy, but it is affected by a certain degree of generality, and it could not be otherwise. In particular, a point that in this perspective is not considered is that in this section of the dialogue Plato's argument is completely referred to senses.

The need is to explain the phenomenon of perception, and that is clearly stated by Socrates. In fact, the following section includes the two concepts which hold and support that whole page; two concepts that have to be strictly bond together, even though they make up a single theoretical line:

> Yes, for it would be strange indeed, my boy, if there are many senses ensconced within us, as if we were so many wooden horses of Troy, and they do not all unite in one power, whether we should call it soul or something else, by which we perceive through these as instruments the objects of perception.
> I think what you suggest is more likely than the other way.
> Now the reason why I am so precise about the matter is this : I want to know whether there is some one and the same power within ourselves by which we perceive black and white through the eyes, and again other qualities through the other organs, and whether you will be able, if asked, to refer all such activities to the body.[16]

---

14 NATORP (1921), p. 145.
15 BURNYEAT (1998), p. 84. Cf. furthermore BURNYEAT (1976).
16 Plat. *Theaet.* 184d1-6: – Δεινὸν γάρ που, ὦ παῖ, εἰ πολλαί τινες ἐν ἡμῖν ὥσπερ ἐν δουρείοις ἵπποις αἰσθήσεις ἐγκάθηνται, ἀλλὰ μὴ εἰς μίαν τινὰ ἰδέαν, εἴτε ψυχὴν εἴτε ὅτι δεῖ καλεῖν, πάντα ταῦτα συντείνει, ᾗ διὰ τούτων οἷον ὀργάνων αἰσθανόμεθα ὅσα αἰσθητά. – Ἀλλά μοι δοκεῖ οὕτω μᾶλλον ἢ ἐκείνως. – Τοῦδέ τοι ἕνεκα αὐτά σοι διακριβοῦμαι, εἴ τινι ἡμῶν αὐτῶν τῷ αὐτῷ διὰ μὲν ὀφθαλμῶν ἐφικνούμεθα λευκῶν τε καὶ μελάνων, διὰ δὲ τῶν ἄλλων ἑτέρων αὖ τινῶν· καὶ ἕξεις ἐρωτώμενος πάντα τὰ τοιαῦτα εἰς τὸ σῶμα ἀναφέρειν;.

This first argument expresses Plato's background thesis; it allows to give a further account to the already expressed interpretations, and maybe to resolve the interpretative contrast which arises among scholars. Robinson believed that «Plato has here turned his attention away from the world of Forms to the mind of men».[17] Also Reale reads *Theaetetus* as the dialogue in which Plato mostly distances himself from his "metaphysics" of the ψυχή, outlined here in a more «operative-functional»[18] way which would lead to see its meaning closer to that of "mind" rather than that of "soul". Sedley believes that *Theaetetus* shifts within the «cognitive psychology» of historical or "semi-historical" Socrates, who – and I agree with him on that – was totally detached from Platonic metaphysics.[19] Trabattoni's position is different, because he writes that, if in Plato it is possible to find concepts such as "knowledge", "science", "cognition", «there is no such thing to translate as the word "mind" [...], because the Platonic ψυχή is heavily involved with outcomes of metaphysical and ontological character that have really few in common with the modern interest for matters such as "knowledge" or "mind"».[20] Finally, Monique Dixsaut has provided a detailed interpretation of this section, rich in different suggestions, but which, for the examined subject, revolves around two concepts: the soul is here intended as an animating principle of bodies; it implies not knowledge, but feeling.[21]

For my part, I would like to show firstly how the above mentioned argumentation points out two important explicative matters for the thesis it sustains: the first one is that it has to exist a single instance which every sense converges to (συντείνει), the second one is that sense-organs are instruments (ὀργάνων) directed yet unified by such single instance. With this conception, Plato stands against the ancient tradition of Presocratic thought, attested first and foremost by Parmenides and Empedocles, who stood in the opposite perspective and advocated that it is the thought that depends on the combination of the body physical elements. In that perspective, there is no need for a notion such as the soul in order to explain high-complexity phenomena like the thought, nor, *a fortiori*, the sensa-

17 ROBINSON (1950).
18 Cf. REALE (2007), p. 211.
19 Cf. SEDLEY (2004).
20 TRABATTONI (2007), p. 307. We have also to remember ROBINSON (1995), p. X, who claims that even in the psychological contexts the meaning of Plato's ψυχή it is not the same of "mind".
21 DIXSAUT (2002).

tion itself.[22] In fact, this tradition does not provide a dualistic type of opposition between the soul and body, even though in Parmenides as much as in Empedocles it provides the one between intellect and senses. This latter is reached up to Protagoras, who believed that the soul was nothing but perceptions themselves, as doxography informs us quoting *Theaetetus* itself to sustain this proposition.[23] But it is proven by Tertullian's testimony that it is not an element drawn from the *Theaetetus*, because it refers about a soul conceived by Protagoras in a physical sense: Protagoras – just like Chrysippus – located the soul in the chest.[24] The relationship of soul and perceptions has to be intended in terms of a dependence of the first one from the second ones, in a perspective that does not require a real distinction between psychic and physic element – viz. the dualism – but a continuity which also results from the authors of the *Corpus Hippocraticum*.[25] In Protagoras' view, which has surely been under the influence of these last authors, the psychic element is nothing but the subject of senses or, to better say, it is built and determined by them in order to be their outcome.

Vice versa, in this section Plato wishes to express an exactly opposite position; but at the same time, he aims to further inquiry the dualism between body and soul already introduced in his *Phaedo*. Nevertheless, his position on that question in *Theaetetus* is extremely articulated. In fact, he deals with the very advanced thesis of a connection and a synthesis between soul and senses, in order to well define the problem of sensible knowledge. Moreover, the expression συντείνειν εἰς μίαν τινὰ ἰδέαν lets us understand how senseory knowledge is tied to the cognitive contribution of senses, but led by the same directive form, that is, the form which feels. Senses alone do not get any direction, being the least responsible for sensible knowledge. They only have an instrumental function: without explicitly addressing it, the conclusive and rhetorical interrogative presupposes that it is not possible to refer only to the body the entire mechanism of miscellaneous sensations, as Protagoras claims. It seems to me that this page well shows a first outline of those concepts which, starting with Aristotle, and from him to Kant, Hegel and so on, will be the "mat-

---

22 To be seen on the matter BETEGH (2013); SASSI (2016).

23 Cf. Diogenes Laertius IX 51 (=80 A 1 DK): «He would still say that the *psuche* is nothing beyond sensation (μηδὲν εἶναι ψυχὴν παρὰ τὰς αἰσθήσεις), complying to what Plato says in *Theaetetus*».

24 Cfr. Tertull. *De anima* 16 (=80 A 18 DK).

25 SINGER (1992).

ter" and the "form" of knowledge, even though here Plato is only dealing with sensible knowledge, and his argument is totally focused on it. It ought to be considered, as Monique Dixsaut does, that it does not mean that senses are conceived merely as channels transmitting sensible material: «Sentir, ce n'est ni savoir ni même être conscient qu'on sent, mais sentir, par son âme, qu'on sent, grâce à son corps: l'âme ne sent que pour autant que son corps sent, et réciproquement».[26] I think that this notation can be as well overcome by taking a closer look to the concept of συντείνειν that Plato confers to sensations. They are not completely passive, if they can «converge» εἰς μίαν τινὰ ἰδέαν, they also own an active function, which is crucial to grant the encounter and the "convergence" between soul and senses. Even more clearly, if there is a relation and a convergence, it implies a certain degree of activity from both the functions employed. In fact, the meeting of an active soul with completely static and passive senses is simply not possible; at least, these ones have to be somehow predisposed to converge towards such instance or unique function. Nor does Plato ever say that it is the *psuchê* which calls them by itself or which determines them: the senses themselves are the ones who «converge». So, they are conformed in a way that allows them to reach the soul. It is now necessary to notice that in this context it appears an important consideration, which is also to be considered as the demonstrative element of the first argumentation: without that relationship we would be lifeless just like wooden horses, and the senses would be totally unrelated and disunited one another. If things were like this, we would never be able to say that we feel; but only that we hear, we taste, we see, and the general phenomenon of αἰσθάνεσθαι could not be formulated. For this reason, in the passage «soul, or however it has to be called, with which, through these, as of organs, we have the perception of what is sensible» (184d3-5), the term «soul» is the subject both grammatically and logically. But surely it is the "theoretical subject" as well: thanks to it we can conceive the existence of a unified phenomenon like the perception, which is articulated in all of its forms.

That is impossible in Protagoras' perspective. He should only be able to say that we touch with the fingers, see with the eyes, taste with the tongue. Vice versa, the αἰσθάνεσθαι requires a μία ἰδέα which can be called ψυχή or by any other name, whether it would result more appropriate. Plato's reluctance in the exact naming of this instance is explained

26 DIXSAUT (2012), p. 90.

by the new and complex meaning he attributes to the concept of ψυχή,
which receives in this section of *Theaetetus* a double theoretical connota-
tion. In my opinion, that reluctance is due to the fact that, on one side,
he spontaneously conceives the ψυχή as the element which confers life to
a body, and which assures that we are talking about the sensation of an
animated body and not about the sum of senses or unrelated functions;
on the other side, it is due to the fact that he is completely aware of the
new function he gives to the notion of *psuchê*, that is, the same function
identified and expressed by Natorp through the above mentioned Kan-
tian formula. That function is well represented by the expression μία ἰδέα,
which points out the very unifying function of the various sensations, as
well as of the perceived objects, which brands the αἰσθάνεσθαι. Nevertheless, the reason why Plato moved that theoretical step is not the intention
to devise a sort of transcendental notion of Subject (even though, I repeat, it is completely legit to see here outlined – for the first time in the
history of philosophy – that theoretical need), but it is given by the fact
that he is dealing with a traditional theory of αἴσθησις which is widely
diffused in Greek philosophy and which has been well represented by
Gorgias in an anterior time.[27] Not for nothing, the second argumentation
states:

> So tell me: do you not think that all the organs through which you
> perceive hot and hard and light and sweet are parts of the body. Or
> are they parts of something else?
> Of nothing else.
> And will you also be ready to agree that it is impossible to perceive
> through one sense (δυνάμεως), what you perceive through another;

---

27 *De MXG* 979a19-980b8: «In fact – he says – how could one tell with a speech
what he has seen? Or how could it appear to be evident to another one who has
listened to him, but hasn't seen him? As, in fact, sight does not recognise sound,
neither does hearing hear colours, but sounds; and he who speaks says, but not a
colour nor a thing. Of what, therefore, we do not have a concept, how could we
get a concept through discourse or some sort of sign, different from the thing
itself, if not seeing it in the case of a colour, and <hearing it in the case it is a
sound?> Firstly, in fact, he who <speaks> does not say a <sound> neither a colour
but a discourse, so it is not possible to mentally represent a colour, but only see
it, nor represent a sound, but only hear it». Cf. Sext. Emp. *M* 7.81-82. On these
passages see CASSIN (1980), p. 540-552; KERFERD (1984); MOURELATOS
(1987), p. 151-155; CONSIGNY (2001), p. 78-79.

for instance, to perceive through sight what you perceive through hearing, or through hearing what you perceive through sight?
Of course I shall.
Then if you have any thought (διανοῇ) about both of these together, you would not have perception about both together either through one organ or through the other.
No.[28]

The founding principle of this conception is the correspondence between perceptive organ and object: every perception has its perceived object, and nothing else. Therefore, what we perceive with a sense cannot be perceived by any different one: there is no relationship neither between objects perceived, nor among the corresponding sensible faculties. To this perspective belongs Protagoras' conception, who thinks that sensation is always true and that the error is impossible, even if he struggles to overcome the hardships implied by it through the intervention of a corrective instrument which does not alter in any way its epistemological implant: the *logos*. Sophist's logos is able to produce an alteration of status and disposition in man's perceiving. That logos is defined as the «strongest» (κρείττων) or the «most correct» (ὀρθότατος), from the argumentative, logical and rhetorical points of view.[29] His perspective is completely different and more radical that the Plato's one, who means to overcome the mere ground of sensation, though acknowledging its rights, and who argues starting from the proof that thought can grasp a property which is common to two different objects of sense. But it means that this outcome is not achieved through senses, because over them reigns the rule of their mutual separateness and of the two-way correlation, namely a correlation between a determined sense and a determined object of sense. If we limit ourselves to perception it will never be possible to reach an articulate conception of sensation, corresponding to the realness of experience; so, a unifying function must be postulated there, which coincides with the front I have previously defined as «all intern to senses», and this is the

---

28 Plat. *Theaet.* 184e4-185a7: – καὶ μοι λέγε· θερμὰ καὶ σκληρὰ καὶ κοῦφα καὶ γλυκέα δι᾽ ὧν αἰσθάνῃ, ἆρα οὐ τοῦ σώματος ἕκαστα τίθης; ἢ ἄλλου τινός; – Οὐδενὸς ἄλλου. – ᾽Η καὶ ἐθελήσεις ὁμολογεῖν ἃ δι᾽ ἑτέρας δυνάμεως αἰσθάνῃ, ἀδύνατον εἶναι δι᾽ ἄλλης ταῦτ᾽ αἰσθέσθαι, οἷον ἃ δι᾽ ἀκοῆς, δι᾽ ὄψεως, ἢ ἃ δι᾽ ὄψεως, δι᾽ ἀκοῆς; – Πῶς γὰρ οὐκ ἐθελήσω; – Εἴ τι ἄρα περὶ ἀμφοτέρων διανοῇ, οὐκ ἀνδιά γε τοῦ ἑτέρου ὀργάνου, οὐδ᾽ αὖ διὰ τοῦ ἑτέρου περὶ ἀμφοτέρων αἰσθάνοι᾽ ἄν. – Οὐ γὰρ οὖν.
29 On those doctrines, see BRANCACCI (2002); (2010); RADEMAKER (2013); CORRADI (2013).

function recognized to the soul. It is external to senses, but every sense converges towards it; it is itself correlated to senses, but it makes use of them as instruments. The continuation of the argument clarifies this proof in favor of the existence of that function of the soul related to the senses.

> Now in regard to sound and colour, you have, in the first place, this thought about both of them, that they both exist?
> Certainly.
> And that each is different from the other and the same as itself?
> Of course.
> And that both together are two and each separately is one?
> Yes, that also.
> And are you able also to observe whether they are like or unlike each other?
> May be.
> Now through what organ do you think all this about them? For it is impossible to grasp that which is common (τὸ κοινόν) to them both either through hearing or through sight.[30]

This argument is a generalization of the previous one, and aims to demonstrate that a property common to two senses cannot be perceived as a sensorial organ, so it is necessary to admit the intervention of the psychic faculty. The argument is truly not binding since it lacks necessity. In front of the difficulty raised by Plato against Protagoras, Aristotle will argue that not all senses are on the same level, and that it is necessary to distinguish among proper *sensibilia*, which are perceived by a single sense (as for sight happens with color, for smell with odor, for taste with flavor), and common *sensibilia*, which are not exclusively related to a single sense and allow to perceive an object as a whole (they are, as it is known, movement, stillness, number, figure, greatness/size).[31] Aristotle will raise the question concerning the possibility of admitting a sixth sense capable

---

30 Plat. *Theaet.* 185a8-b9: – Περὶ δὴ φωνῆς καὶ περὶ χρόας πρῶτον μὲν αὐτὸ τοῦτο περὶ ἀμφοτέρων ἦ διανοῇ, ὅτι ἀμφοτέρω ἐστόν; – Ἔγωγε. – Οὐκοῦν καὶ ὅτι ἑκάτερον ἑκατέρου μὲν ἕτερον, ἑαυτῷ δὲ ταὐτόν; – Τί μήν; – Καὶ ὅτι ἀμφοτέρω δύο, ἑκάτερον δὲ ἕν. – Καὶ τοῦτο. – Οὐκοῦν καὶ εἴτε ἀνομοίω εἴτε ὁμοίω ἀλλήλοιν, δυνατὸς εἶ ἐπισκέψασθαι; – Ἴσως. – Ταῦτα δὴ πάντα διὰ τίνος περὶ αὐτοῖν διανοῇ; οὔτε γὰρ δι᾽ ἀκοῆς οὔτε δι᾽ ὄψεως οἷόν τε τὸ κοινὸν λαμβάνειν περὶ αὐτῶν.
31 For an elaborate discussion of Aristotle's distinction between proper and common sensibilia, see GRAESER (1978).

of unifying the results of perception by the five senses, but he will discard
this eventuality: we do not need that sense, because everyone of the five
senses already accomplishes thoroughly the perceptive act; it both perceives and has conscience of the perception itself. Unity of perceptions in
its most proper and accurate meaning concerns only common *sensibilia*,
namely the ones perceived by more senses at the same time, which carry
out an unified perception. As it can be seen, this conception is anti-Pla-
tonic *de iure*; it differs from the one drawn up by Plato in *Theaetetus* because it does not start off from the senses – the ones that Plato calls
ὄργανα of soul – but from the sensible data, in which there are included
quality, physical states, mathematical entities. Platonic conception is from
its beginning addressed to demonstrate the existence of an autonomous
and directing function, namely the *psuchê*. Anyway, this third argument
introduces the theory of κοινά, and revolves around the concept of τὸ
κοινόν, which summarily indicates the common property of two senses,
like seeing and hearing, and more generally all the properties common to
two senses or, more precisely, to two sensible objects like sound and sight.
Plato here lists three of them, which are the first three of the κοινά to
whom the rest of the dialogue will dedicate a special and in-depth treaty:
they are the couples be/not be, identical/diverse, alike/unlike. The com-
pletion of the reasoning that Plato cares to build is immediately achieved
through the fourth argument:

> Here is further evidence for the point I am trying to make: if it were
> possible to investigate the question whether the two, sound and
> colour, are bitter or not, you know that you will be able to tell by
> what faculty you will investigate it, and that is clearly neither hearing
> nor sight, but something else.
> Of course it is, the faculty (δύναμις) exerted through the tongue.
> Very good. But through what organ is the faculty exerted which
> makes known to you that which is common to all things; as well as to
> these of which we are speaking – that which you call being and not-
> being, and the other attributes of things, about which we were asking
> just now? What organs will you assign for all these, through which
> that part of us which perceives gains perception of each and all of
> them?
> You mean being and not-being, and likeness and unlikeness, and
> identity and difference, and also unity and plurality as applied to
> them. And you are evidently asking also through what bodily organs

we perceive by our soul the odd and the even and everything else that is in the same category.

Bravo, Theaetetus, you follow me exactly; that is just what I mean by my question.

By Zeus Socrates, I cannot answer, except that I think there is no special organ at all for these notions, as there are for those others; but it appears to me that the soul views by itself directly what all things have in common.

Why, you are beautiful, Theaetetus, and not, as Theodoros said, ugly; for he who speaks beautifully is beautiful and good. But besides being beautiful, you have done me a favour by relieving me from a long discussion, if you think that the soul views some things by itself directly and others through the bodily faculties; for that was my own opinion, and I wanted you to agree.[32]

In that section Plato has fully acquired the distinction between instrumentality of the sentient organ and instrumentality directed by a singular instance, which is same to itself and is provided with a directive function. That last one is the soul, which feels without tasting or seeing or smelling like senses do. Nevertheless, senses are connected to the soul. In fact, the lead of their perceptive acquisitions converges towards it. The soul assures the articulated unity of perceptions, and furthermore allows to perceive two common qualities of a same object. These qualities can be organized

---

32 Plat. *Theaet.* 185b9-e9: – ἔτι δὲ καὶ τόδε τεκμήριον περὶ οὗ λέγομεν· εἰ γὰρ δυνατὸν εἴη ἀμφοτέρω σκέψασθαι ἆρ᾽ ἐστὸν ἁλμυρὼ ἢ οὔ, οἶσθ᾽ ὅτι ἕξεις εἰπεῖν ᾧ ἐπισκέψῃ, καὶ τοῦτο οὔτε ὄψις οὔτε ἀκοὴ φαίνεται, ἀλλά τι ἄλλο. – Τί δ᾽ οὐ μέλλει, ἥ γε διὰ τῆς γλώττης δύναμις; – Καλῶς λέγεις. ἡ δὲ δὴ διὰ τίνος δύναμις τό τ᾽ ἐπὶ πᾶσι κοινὸν καὶ τὸ ἐπὶ τούτοις δηλοῖ σοι, ᾧ τὸ "ἔστιν" ἐπονομάζεις καὶ τὸ "οὐκ ἔστι" καὶ ἃ νυνδὴ ἠρωτῶμεν περὶ αὐτῶν; τούτοις πᾶσι ποῖα ἀπωδώσεις ὄργανα δι᾽ ὧν αἰσθάνεται ἡμῶν τὸ αἰσθανόμενον ἕκαστα; – Οὐσίαν λέγεις καὶ τὸ μὴ εἶναι, καὶ ὁμοιότητα καὶ ἀνομοιότητα, καὶ τὸ ταὐτόν τε και [τὸ] ἕτερον, ἔτι δὲ ἕν τε καὶ τὸν ἄλλον ἀριθμὸν περὶ αὐτῶν. δῆλον δὲ ὅτι καὶ ἄρτιόν τε καὶ περιττὸν ἐρωτᾷς, καὶ τἆλλα ὅσα τούτοις ἕπεται, διὰ τίνος ποτὲ τῶν τοῦ σώματος τῇ ψυχῇ αἰσθανόμεθα. – Ὑπέρευ, ὦ Θεαίτητε, ἀκολουθεῖς, καὶ ἔστιν ἃ ἐρωτῶ αὐτὰ ταῦτα. – Ἀλλὰ μὰ Δία, ὦ Σώκρατες, ἔγωγε οὐκ ἂν ἔχοιμι εἰπεῖν, πλήν γ᾽ ὅτι μοι δοκεῖ τὴν ἀρχὴν οὐδ᾽ εἶναι τοιοῦτον οὐδὲν τούτοις ὄργανον ἴδιον ὥσπερ ἐκείνοις, ἀλλ᾽ αὐτὴ δι᾽ αὐτῆς ἡ ψυχὴ τὰ κοινά μοι φαίνεται περὶ πάντων ἐπισκοπεῖν. – Καλὸς γὰρ εἶ, ὦ Θεαίτητε, καὶ οὐχ, ὡς ἔλεγε Θεόδωρος, αἰσχρός· ὁ γὰρ καλῶς λέγων καλός τε καὶ ἀγαθός. πρὸς δὲ τῷ καλῷ εὖ ἐποίησάς με μάλα συχνοῦ λόγου ἀπαλλάξας, εἰ φαίνεταί σοι τὰ μὲν αὐτὴ δι᾽ αὑτῆς ἡ ψυχὴ ἐπισκοπεῖν, τὰ δὲ διὰ τῶν τοῦ σώματος δυνάμεων. τοῦτο γὰρ ἦν ὃ καὶ αὐτῷ μοι ἐδόκει, ἐβουλόμην δὲ καὶ σοὶ δόξαι.

in a table of properties, common to every object: a research on them would point out that there are not organs arranged to inquire them, because the κοινά are not mere physical qualities, but general notions endowed with a high degree of complexity and abstraction. Plato's conclusion I have quoted at the beginning of this paper is perfectly justified, but it has also a further reach, because Plato declares it only after his discussion on the κοινά, and so takes it into account as well. His conclusion states that there are objects which the soul inquires through body faculties, viz. sensible objects, and that there are "things" or "properties" or "determinations" – naming is not that important: it is not fully established by Plato but it is introduced by me – which the soul inquires by herself through herself. That outcome makes it possible for Plato to perfectly and – dare I say – fully set the matter of sensible and intellectual knowledge. One more step, and we might as well be in the *Erkenntistheorie*. But this step has not been taken anywhere by Plato, because he could not take it, and because this was not his main issue.

Philosophical historiography cannot be realized "backwards", just like a cancerizing movement. Nonetheless, it is righteous when it digs into its sources, and when it questions and examines the diversified present which, from time to time, it assumes as its subject of study. In so doing, it points out the "authenticity" of a certain reflection, although it does not mean that the historian of philosophy uses to disregard the future. As the successive passage shows, philosophical setting and questions of Plato's path led him to other matters. In particular, Plato aims to discuss the question of thought, which the conclusion on the nature of soul achieved in this section is strictly connected to, and which seems to me the further step that Plato takes in regards to the previous determination of the soul, that is, his ending point. It is worthwhile to cite the passage:

And do you define thought as I do?
How do you define it?
As the talk which the soul has with itself about any subjects which it considers. You must not suppose that I know this that I am declaring to you. But the soul, as the image presents itself to me, when it thinks, is merely conversing with itself, asking itself questions and answering, affirming and denying. When it has arrived at a decision,

whether slowly or with a sudden bound, and is at last agreed, and is not in doubt, we call that its opinion.[33]

In accordance with what is partially showed by the conclusion of the previous section – where verbs like ζητεῖν, εὑρίσκω and προβαίνω are employed – the thought is determined by Plato as a "questioning thought", namely as a thought which submits and inquires problems through a continuous and articulated succession of questions and answers. The soul silently addresses these problems by itself, «when it, in itself and by itself, attends to the entities». Thought arises, in a φιλόσοφος φύσις, from contradictions, contrast, antithesis and opposition: that is the theme which is common to *Phaedo*, *Republic* and *Theaetetus*, the works I take into consideration in this paper.

The soul faces these contradictions and difficulties, first of all by converting them into questions. It examines them, by taking all the necessary time to analyze them and to reflect, in order to formulate finally an answer, which is the dissolution of the antithesis and the contrast. The issue of knowledge articulates itself this way with dialectic, as Plato conceives it, defines it and unravels it in the dialogues, and with the theory of ideas. It is not solved in an *Erkenntnistheorie*, but it results in an infinite, as endless, purpose of thinking: because of its constitutive richness and skill in arranging and supporting itself.

---

33 Plat. *Theaet.* 189e4-190a4: – τὸ δὲ διανοεῖσθαι ἆρ᾽ ὅπερ ἐγὼ καλεῖς; – Τί καλῶν; – λόγον ὃν αὐτὴ πρὸς αὑτὴν ἡ ψυχὴ διεξέρχεται περὶ ὧν ἂν σκοπῇ. ὥς γε μὴ εἰδώς σοι ἀποφαίνομαι. τοῦτο γάρ μοι ἰνδάλλεται διανοουμένη οὐκ ἄλλο τι ἢ διαλέγεσθαι, αὐτὴ ἑαυτὴν ἐρωτῶσα καὶ ἀποκρινομένη καὶ φάσκουσα καὶ οὐ φάσκουσα. ὅταν δὲ ὁρίσασα, εἴτε βραδύτερον εἴτε καὶ ὀξύτερον ἐπάξασα τὸ αὐτὸ ἤδη φῇ καὶ μὴ διστάζῃ, δόξαν ταύτην τίθεμεν αὐτῆς. Cf. also Plat. *Soph.* 263e3-264b3 and *Phil.* 38c2-e7. On these passages, DIXSAUT (1997) is crucial.

References

BETEGH, G. (2013). On the Physical Aspect of Heraclitus' Psychology (With New Appendices). In: Sider, D.; Obbink, D. (eds). *Doctrine and Doxography. Studies on Heraclitus and Pythagoras*. Berlin, New York. de Gruyter, p. 227-261.

BRANCACCI, A. (1992). La terza definizione di scienza nel *Teeteto*. In: Battegazzore, A.M. (ed.). *Dimostrazione, argomentazione dialettica e argomentazione retorica nel pensiero greco*. La Spezia. Tirrenia, p. 107-132.

_____ (2001). Antisthène, la troisième définition de la science et le songe du *Théétète*. In: Romeyer-Dherbey, G. (ed.). *Socrate et les Socratiques*. Paris. Vrin, 2001, p. 351-380.

_____ (2002). Protagoras, l'*orthoepeia* et la justesse des noms. In: Dixsaut, M.; Brancacci, A. (eds.). *Platon source des Présocratiques. Exploration*. Paris. Vrin, p. 169-190.

_____ (2010). Dialettica e *orthoepeia* in Protagora. *Méthexis*, 23, p. 53-71.

BURNYEAT, M. (1976). Plato on the Grammar of Perceiving. *The Classical Quarterly*, 26, p. 29-51.

_____ (1998). *Introduction au 'Théétète' de Platon*, trad. fr. par M. Narcy. Paris. Presses Universitaires de France.

CASSIN, B. (1980). *Si Parménide. Le traité anonyme «De Melisso Xenophane Gorgia»*, édition critique et commentaire. Lille. Presses Universitaires de Lille.

CONSIGNY, S. (2001). *Gorgias. Sophist and Artist*. Columbia. University of South Carolina Press.

CORRADI, M. (2013). Τὸν ἥττω λόγον κρείττω ποιεῖν: Aristotle, Plato, and the ἐπάγγελμα of Protagoras. In: VAN OPHUIJSEN/VAN RAALTE/STORK (eds.), p. 69-86.

DIXSAUT, M. (1997). What is It Plato Calls Thinking?. *Proceedings of the Boston Area Colloquium in Ancient Philosophy*, 13, p. 1-27.

_____ (2002). Natura e ruolo dell'anima nella sensazione (*Teeteto*, 184b-186a). In: Casertano, G. (ed.). *Il* Teeteto *di Platone: struttura e problematiche*. Napoli. Loffredo, p. 39-62.

_____ (2012). *Platon. Le désir de comprendre*. Paris. Vrin.

FOWLER, H.N. (1961). Plato. *Theaetetus, Sophist*, with an English Translation, Cambridge (Mass.). Harvard University Press, London. Heinemann.

GRAESER, A. (1978). On Aristotle's Framework of Sensibilia. In: Lloyd, G.E.R.; Owen, G.E.L. (eds.). *Aristotle on Mind and the Senses*, Proceedings of the Seventh Symposium Aristotelicum. Cambridge. Cambridge University Press, p. 69-97.

KERFERD, G.B. (1984). Meaning and Reference: Gorgias and the Relation between Language and Reality. In: Boudouris, K. (ed.). *The Sophistic Movement*. Athens. Athenian Library of Philosophy, p. 215-222.

LURAGHI, S. (2003). *On the Meaning of Prepositions and Cases: The Expression of Semantic Roles in Ancient Greek*. Amsterdam, Philadelphia. John Benjamins Publishing Company.

MIGLIORI, M.; NAPOLITANO VALDITARA, L.M.; FERMANI, A. (eds.) (2007). *Interiorità e anima: la psychè in Platone*. Milano. Vita e Pensiero.

MOURELATOS, A.P.D. (1987). Gorgias on the Functions of Language. *Philosophical Topics*, 15, p. 135-170.

NARCY, M. (1994) (ed.). Platon. *Théétète*, traduction inédite, introduction et notes. Paris. GF-Flammarion.

NATORP, P. (1921). *Platos Ideenlehre. Eine Einführung in den Idealismus*. Leipzig. Mohr (orig. ed. 1903).

RADEMAKER, A. (2013). The Most Correct Account: Protagoras and Language. In: VAN OPHUIJSEN/VAN RAALTE/STORK (eds.), p. 87-112.

REALE, G. (2007), La concezione dell'anima in Platone e le sue aporie. In: MIGLIORI/NAPOLITANO VALDITARA/FERMANI (eds.), p. 211-224.

ROBINSON, R. (1950). Forms and Error in Plato's *Theaetetus*. *The Philosophical Review*, 59, p. 3-30.

ROBINSON, T.M. (1995). *Plato's Psychology*. Toronto. University of Toronto Press (orig. ed. 1970).

SASSI, M.M. (2016). Parmenides and Empedocles on *Krasis* and Knowledge. *Apeiron*, 49, p. 451-469.

SEDLEY, D. (2004). *The Midwife of Platonism. Text and Subtext in Plato's 'Theaetetus'*. Oxford. Clarendon Press.

SINGER, P.N. (1992). Some Hippocratic Mind-Body Problems. In: López Férez, J.A. (ed.). *Tratados Hipocráticos (Estudios acerca de su contenido, forma e influencia)*, Actas del VIIe Colloque International Hippocratique (Madrid, 24-29 de septiembre de 1990). Madrid. Universidad Nacional de Educacion a Distancia, p. 131-143.

TRABATTONI, F. (2007). Si può parlare di "unità" della psicologia platonica? Esame di un caso significativo (*Fedone*, 68b-69e). In: MIGLIORI/NAPOLITANO VALDITARA/FERMANI (2007), p. 307-320.

VAN OPHUIJSEN, J.M.; VAN RAALTE, M.; STORK, P. (eds.) (2013). *Protagoras of Abdera: The Man, His Measure*. Leiden, Boston. Brill.

On Soul-Body "Dualism" in Plato

Franco Trabattoni

I.

It is a commonplace in philosophical historiography that the psychological doctrines of Platonic origin stand in sharp contrast to the Aristotelian ones: the former entail a clear-cut dualism – possibly to be interpreted as a genuine opposition – between soul and body; the latter instead ensure a closer and more realistic harmony between the psychic and physical components of man. In other words, Plato's position would be a weighty and implausible metaphysical hypothesis, whereas Aristotle's position would be a sober and balanced attempt to account for experience. Precisely on the basis of this assessment, Aristotle's psychological doctrines are popular not just among historians of philosophy, but also among many contemporary philosophers, whereas Plato's avowedly dualistic psychology is brushed to the side as a fanciful and unscientific theory, insofar as it consciously ignores experiential data. In the following pages, I aim to at least raise a few doubts with regard to this commonplace.

The theoretical root of the difference between Platonic and Aristotelian psychology would consist in the fact that whereas for Plato the soul is a substance (to use Aristotelian terminology) that is separable – and at times separate – from the body, according to Aristotle it is the form or act of the living organism: since, for Aristotle, form is not really separable from the corresponding matter, although it is separable as a notion, psychological unity is in principle ensured. Precisely for this reason, Aristotle was bound to regard the Orphic, Pythagorean and Platonic doctrine of metempsychosis as absurd. On the other hand, Platonic dualism would seem to raise a theoretical problem that is difficult to solve, and which is made explicit in the words by which Plotinus opens the first treatise of the fifth *Ennead*:

> What is it, then, which has made the souls forget their father, God, and be ignorant of themselves and him, even though they are parts which come from his higher world and altogether belong to it? The

beginning of evil for them was audacity and coming to birth and the
first otherness and the wishing to belong to themselves (V 1 1, tr.
Armstrong).

This problem can be broken down into two different, if connected, aspects. First of all, a Platonist is bound to ask why, from a general metaphysical standpoint, a wholly immaterial and divine entity such as the
soul has become attached to a body. Secondly, it is a matter of taking account of the ethical aspect of this apparently unnatural union: is the
soul's descent into a body to be viewed as something positive, insofar as it
serves the providential purpose of giving life to matter (and hence of animating the world), as the *Timaeus* would seem to suggest? Or is this a fall,
a contamination, possibly the consequence of a transgression, as dialogues such as the *Phaedo* and *Phaedrus* would seem to suggest? Is the nature of the soul in harmony or in contrast with the functions it is meant
to fulfil? More generally, does this double perspective not adumbrate an
ambiguity inherent to Platonic philosophy as a whole, in a way, and
which concerns not just the ontological value and weight of matter and
the body, but also the assessment of the earthly dimension, the meaning
and usefulness of demotic virtues, and the role to be assigned to ethical
reflection and political engagement in Platonic thought? If so-called Platonic dualism is taken at face value, it seems as though the alleged coexis-
tence, on two different levels, of a physical reality and a metaphysical one
is invariably compromised: if this dualism is reinforced as an opposition,
contrast and alternative, it is clear that it will no longer be possible to affirm the full existence of this *and* that reality; rather, it will be necessary
to argue that we either have one thing *or* the other. And since the metaphysical dimension is clearly superior according to Plato, all this is to the
detriment of the body, of earthly life, of relational ethics, and of politics.
Once again, this development is sharply laid out by Plotinus, who claims
that from a Platonic perspective all action is failed contemplation.[1] This
means that action (and hence man's physical operating within the world,
along with ethics and politics) is not only inferior to contemplation but
has no intrinsic positive value; it is merely the negative counterpart to the
one thing that is of some value, and which is therefore worth pursuing:
contemplation.

---

1 *Enn.* III 8.

One of the most crucial Platonic passages dealing with this problem – crucial, that is, not so much for Plato himself as for the systematic use of it made by the subsequent tradition, starting with so-called Middle Platonism – is the famous digression on the philosopher in the *Theaetetus*. Here the aim of human life is seen to coincide with man's assimilation to God (176a8-c2):

> And therefore we ought to try to escape from earth to the dwelling of the gods as quickly as we can; and to escape is to become like God, so far as this is possible; and to become like God is to become righteous and holy and wise. But, indeed, my good friend, it is not at all easy to persuade people that the reason generally advanced for the pursuit of virtue and the avoidance of vice – namely, in order that a man may not seem bad and may seem good – is not the reason why the one should be practised and the other not; that, I think, is merely old wives' chatter, as the saying is. Let us give the true reason. God is in no wise and in no manner unrighteous, but utterly and perfectly [c] righteous, and there is nothing so like him as that one of us who in turn becomes most nearly perfect in righteousness (tr. Fowler).

When taken as a whole, this passage is actually far from identifying the aim of human life with the abandonment of the earthly dimension. Certainly, the first sentence urges man to flee "from earth to the dwelling of the gods" as soon as possible. It is also true that this flight is immediately identified with assimilation to God. However, two significant elements would seem to militate against an interpretation of this passage in ascetic and metaphysical (or exclusively metaphysical) terms. The first element is the clause "as far as this is possible", which Socrates immediately adds. The context is a typically Platonic one where we have a (perfect) model and a copy that imitates it. The clause "as far as this is possible" makes explicit what is actually already implicit in the notion of "similarity". That which is similar to something else resembles it in certain respects but not others,[2] for otherwise the copy and its model would be indistinguishable and would amount to the same thing.[3] Therefore, assimilation to God cannot mean "being identical to God"; rather, it must mean "achieving (or striving to achieve) the highest possible degree of resemblance to him". The easiest way to understand the nature of this resemblance is ap-

---

2 Cf. *Phaed.* 77b-80c: the soul is similar to the Ideas, yet it is not an Idea.
3 Cf. *Crat.* 432b-c.

parently to identify one or more qualities that the model possesses in full, and then establish that the imitator possesses the same qualities to the highest possible degree. For example, if the model is omniscient, omnipotent etc. like the Christian God, assimilation to God must mean becoming as wise, powerful etc. *as possible*. If the essential feature of the model is instead pure contemplation, as Plotinus contends (in agreement with his Aristotelian model), then man must devote his life to knowledge, as far as possible.

However, the Platonic text does not meet these expectations, so much so that it poses a rather challenging problem to Plotinus. Socrates explains that to assimilate oneself to God is to practice virtue, and in particular justice. The problem that this raises for Plotinus lies in the fact that it would seem to undermine the aforementioned relation between action and contemplation. Indeed, the various virtues appear to be intrinsically connected to action; hence, they imply the possession of a body and the presence of the subject within earthly reality. By contrast, he who wishes to make himself similar to God seeks to flee from this reality, to separate himself from matter, the body and all the hindrances created by his needs and desires (in accordance with the *Phaedo* passages we will soon be discussing). The passage from the *Thaetetus*, therefore, seems to imply a subtle yet inevitable paradox: man attempts to assimilate himself to God by a means (the attainment of virtue) that makes it impossible to achieve this aim, since it forces man to cling to certain essential human traits, which give rise to an irresolvable incompatibility with the model to be imitated.

This is not the place to examine Plotinus' solution in detail (I will refer to CATAPANO, 2006). However, it is interesting to note that his suggestion, based on the asymmetry of the relation of resemblance between man and God (whereas the former assimilates himself to the latter, the latter is not similar to the former in any respect), could never work for Plato. The philosopher assigns a crucial role – in cosmology and especially in politics – to the "technical" scheme that posits the necessary existence at all levels of a model which the imitating craftsman (the demiurge, the philosopher-politician) can contemplate, in order to produce copies as similar to it as possible within earthly reality. It is evident, therefore, that the relation of resemblance between the copy and its model cannot work only from the bottom up, as Plotinus would have it, but must also work in the opposite direction, for otherwise the technical paradigm could find no application. This is not a problem for Plotinus, who on the one hand downplays the "technical" and providential role played by the demiurge,[4] but on the other – and most importantly – has no real interest in the political role of philosophy (as already noted, for Plotinus action is nothing but failed contemplation). However, this is hardly acceptable to Plato, who unhesitatingly affirms the centrality of politics, and more generally of the technical activity by which human, earthly and ever-changing matter is providentially and rationally moulded after an external and unmoving divine model.

II.

The crucial role played by politics in Plato's thought is, in certain respects, the decisive factor that makes it necessary to tone down the clearcut dualism between soul and body that would seem to emerge from certain texts – such as the *Theaetetus* digression – that present no doubt ascetic aspects, even apparently extreme ones at times. Indeed, it is hardly a coincidence that many interpreters of the *Theaetetus* have come to regard the digression on the nature of the philosopher as an entirely or partly negative model by which Plato aims to illustrate what philosophy must not – and cannot – be, if it is to maintain an effective connection with the world of ethics and politics (and hence make a successful attempt to counter Protagorean relativism).[5] It is certainly true that the digression presents the philosopher in largely hyperbolic terms. However, this is a conscious emphasis which serves the very opposite purpose from what the interpreters just mentioned suggest. As we have seen, the best way to assimilate oneself to God is to practice virtue. Even more importantly, detachment from the world – a practice which in the digression is no doubt associated with philosophers – is not intended to ensure the achievement of an ascetic lifestyle, or even of a state of pure contemplation. The purpose of distancing oneself from the body and the world is to create the conditions for the attainment of knowledge of the universal, as far as this is possible, which is the natural goal for philosophers. However, it is significant that in a crucial passage of the digression (175c), as a salient example of the universal knowledge to which the philosopher aspires, justice in itself is mentioned: an object whose knowledge is crucial not on

4 See e.g. GERSON (1994), p. 56-57.
5 Cf., with different nuances, RUE (1993), FREDE (1999), MAHONNEY (2004), and LANE (2005).

the level of contemplation (where anything possessing the nature of what is "in itself" would be enough), but rather on the level of action, morality, and politics. The intentionally hyperbolic tone here is designed to stress the merely apparent paradox that action and contemplation, when combined, constitute a function that is algebraically the reverse of the one we would expect. It is not true that the more the philosopher removes himself from the world and from concrete life, the more he detaches himself from ethics and politics. Rather, exactly the opposite is true. According to the technical model, the more knowledge we have of the ideal model of justice in itself, the better we can establish justice in the real world. But if philosophers are to achieve this goal, they must not waste any time enquiring about «the way to the agora [...] where the courtroom is, or the senate-house, or any other public place of assembly» (*Theaet.* 173c-d). Philosophers must «neither hear the debates upon them nor see them when they are published» (173d). Nor will they concern themselves with question such as «What wrong have I done you or you me?» (175c). Whereas according to the ordinary way of thinking all this simply means that the philosopher is inept at practical living (consider the harsh criticism that Callicles directs against Socrates in *Gorg.* 484c-485d), and hence utterly devoid of an aptitude for politics, what Plato is arguing is actually the very opposite. Because the philosopher is the only one to enquire what justice in itself consists in, despite all appearances he is the only real politician.

The same intentional paradox is also to be found in the dialogue which is certainly the text with the most markedly ascetic background – not least for its consolatory nature – namely the *Phaedo*. At the beginning of the dialogue, Socrates must respond to the accusations levelled by his friends, who in the face of the threat of death question the philosopher's alleged happiness (in the *Apology* Socrates had argued that nothing bad can befall the philosopher, either in life or death, 41c-d). He does so by showing that the whole life of the philosopher is an exercise in dying, and that therefore it would make no sense for him to fear death, as only after death it will be possible for him (if at all) to attain the real goal in life, namely the acquisition of knowledge of the Ideas.[6] At first sight, it might seem difficult to find a more unpolitical passage than this in Plato's writing. The philosopher's happiness – as roughly stated also in the *Theaetetus* digression – is nothing but a flight from the world, which is to say his

---

6 Cf. TRABATTONI (2015).

shift to a different and better reality. But what about ethics and politics, then? What about *eudaimonia* and the leading of a good private and public life in this world and in this life? In actual fact, here too – as in the *Theaetetus* – Plato provides plenty of clues to suggest to the reader that he is highlighting what is only an apparent paradox. Socrates concludes that it is absurd for the philosopher to fear death.

> 'Then is it not,' said Socrates, 'a sufficient indication, when you see a man troubled because he is going to die, that he was not a lover of wisdom but a lover of the body? [68c] And this same man is also a lover of money and of honor, one or both?'
> 'Certainly,' said he, 'it is as you say.'
> 'Then, Simmias,' he continued, 'is not that which is called courage especially characteristic of philosophers?'
> 'By all means,' said he.
> 'And self-restraint – that which is commonly called self-restraint, which consists in not being excited by the passions and in being superior to them and acting in a seemly way – is not that characteristic of those alone who despise the body [68d] and pass their lives in philosophy?' (68b8-c12, tr. Fowler).

After that, as is widely known, Socrates develops a series of arguments to clarify the difference between common virtues (what we might call demotic virtues) and truly philosophical ones. The opportunity to switch from the topic of death to that of virtue is offered in a perfectly natural way by the evident connection between death and courage. Yet this is not enough to justify the insertion, at this particular point in the text, of a treatment of virtues that breaks up the linear unfolding of the dialogue: 1) Socrates is about to die; 2) he must show that death is not a bad thing for him; 3) he does so by showing that philosophy is an exercise in dying; 4) however, he must also show (as Cebes asks him to do, for else the whole argument would not hold) that man, or at any rate his soul, survives death. How does the "digression" on virtue fit within this scheme? In reality, the situation mirrors, if only in a reverse way, what we find in the *Theaetetus*. In the *Theaetetus* an ethical and political context (Socrates has just noted that Protagorean relativism struggles to justify the actual political praxis of cities) is interrupted by a digression with "ascetic" overtones, whereas the exact opposite occurs in the *Phaedo*: a highly ascetic context is suddenly interrupted by an ethical and political digression. My thesis is that both cases offer the same explanation, if only in inverted terms: when what is at issue is the need for philosophy, and hence philosophers, on the ethical and political level (which in the *Theaetetus* is justified by the ethical-political inadequacy of relativism), Plato draws attention to the paradox according to which philosophy can play a political role precisely insofar as it is an ascetic practice; when what is at issue is the ascetic nature of the philosopher, Plato feels the need to warn the reader that this nature of the philosopher not only does not detach him from ethics and politics, but that on the contrary it makes him the only person competent in such matters (*Phaedo*). What is particularly significant, in my view, is precisely the "digression" in the *Phaedo*. In this dialogue Plato faces a truly challenging task, since the forced circumstances of Socrates' death sentence present the problem in an extreme form. The enquiry risks slipping into an alternative that makes any attempt at mediation difficult, if not impossible. How is it possible to show that the philosopher is happy even after death, if not on the basis of the hypothesis that the real life is not "this one" but "another one"? And if the real life is a different one, how can we hope to preserve the ethical and political vocation of the philosopher, which Plato unambiguously affirms and recalls again and again? Hence the sudden reference to virtues. It is as though Plato were trying to tell his readers: I have just explained that the distinguishing trait of the philosopher is the exercise of dying; however, this should not be taken to suggest that philosophy has no relevance on the ethical-political level; on the contrary, it is possible to show that only the disposition I have described makes the ethical and political virtues what they are, for otherwise they would be only a pale imitation (the same principle is reaffirmed by Socrates later on, at 83e). Divine or philosophical virtues, in other words, encompass human virtues, in the sense that human virtues only become real virtues if they have divine virtues as their model.[7]

---

7 Of course, the hypothesis I have put forward is only acceptable if the section of the *Phaedo* concerning virtues is not interpreted as being inevitably removed from the one featured in the *Republic*, and hence as useless on the political level (as suggested for instance by FREDE, 1999). As I have already discussed this problem in TRABATTONI (2007), I will refer the reader to this essay for a more detailed analysis.

III.

This state of affairs finds various expressions in Plato's writing: the well-known identification between the philosopher and the politician in the *Republic* and *Seventh Letter*; the need to uphold the political profile of the philosopher against accusations of ineptitude, as in the *Gorgias* and *Republic* (esp. 473e-474a e 487b-d; but let us not forget that this is also the avowed purpose of the myth of the cave, namely to identify *apaideusia* as the cause of philosophers' lack of recognition among ordinary people); and, finally, the only apparently ambiguous nature of Socrates "the philosopher", who in the *Apology* affirms to have never engaged in politics (31c-32e), but then in the *Gorgias* claims to be the only Athenian of his day to have practised the *true* art of politics (521d). However, politics is not the main concern. In its apparent conflict with theory (or contemplation, if we prefer), politics only serves as an example to illustrate the dialectical and functional nature of all forms of Platonic dualism, where a pair of terms are distinguished from one another (insofar as they can be separated) and asymmetrically placed on two different levels, yet at the same time never stand to one another as mere alternatives. The distinctions between real and ideal, action and theory, politics and philosophy, body and soul, do not constitute a binary and parallel system in Plato, whereby we must take either this side or that, and in choosing one thing must abandon the other. For Plato, the real is not real (i.e. cannot be understood as real) without a reference to an ideal model; there can be no action without theory, and no politics without philosophy; most importantly, we are not forced to choose the body to the detriment of the soul and vice-versa, since it is precisely by virtue of the separability of the body that the soul can take a leading role with respect to the human being, who is composed of soul and body, so as to promote and ensure his proper functioning (not merely as a soul but as a composite of soul and body). The less man engages in action and the more he practices contemplation, the more competent he becomes in politics. Likewise, the more the soul distances itself and becomes separate from the body, with its desires and needs, the more it is capable of leading the body (so as ensure a good life for individuals and communities, insofar as this is possible).

In other words, to get back to the question raised at the beginning of the present essay, I would argue that it is incorrect to draw a contrast between Aristotle's psychology and Plato's, as though the former sought to realistically account for the psychophysical harmony of man, and the lat-

ter portrayed man as being torn between two different and alternative
drive, whereby no positive outcome may be reached unless one sacrifices
the inferior and weaker element. On the contrary, according to Plato it is
precisely the relative separation between soul and body that provides the
most suitable empirical illustration of the psychophysical harmony of
man, including all his physiological, psychological, and ethical functions.
For Plato, this separation is not a way to show the essentially metaphysical nature of man, as opposed to what he actually is in his current and
concrete condition (according to the famous image of man as an embodied soul); rather, from an empirical and rational perspective, it is the most
realistic way to correctly describe man as he actually is, with all his plans,
desires, and aspirations. Had Plato been given the chance to counter the
Aristotelian conception of the soul, his most significant objection would
not have been – as arguably most scholars suggest – that the soul as the
"form of the body" impoverishes the divine nature of man by making
him inextricably bound to matter. Rather, he would have argued that the
idea of the soul as the form of the body does not adequately explain the
make-up of man. I will now adduce some arguments in support of this
thesis.

Let's start by asking some questions. When in the *Phaedo* Socrates in-
vites his friends to become as detached from the body as possible, what
exactly does he mean? And what does this advice imply? What is its ultimate purpose? The actual separation of soul and body?

These questions find an answer in another important passage of the
Phaedo, in which Socrates explains why it is dangerous for us not to do
our best to minimise the demands imposed by our material nature. Right
from this moment, it is important to stress the fact that in any case the
separation could not be a complete one, given that if man is to continue
to exist as a man he must ignore the physiological needs of his organism
(even though he can choose to meet these needs to the smallest possible
extent, as Socrates recommends). We will return to this point shortly. For
the time being, it is important to examine the final part of the section:

> 'The lovers of knowledge, then, I say, perceive that philosophy, taking
> possession of the soul when it is in this state, encourages it gently and
> tries to set it free, pointing out that the eyes and the ears and the oth-
> er senses are full of deceit, and urging it to withdraw from these, ex-
> cept in so far as their use is unavoidable, and exhorting it to collect
> and concentrate itself within itself, and to trust nothing except [83b]

itself and its own abstract thought of abstract existence; and to believe that there is no truth in that which it sees by other means and
which varies with the various objects in which it appears, since everything of that kind is visible and apprehended by the senses, whereas
the soul itself sees that which is invisible and apprehended by the
mind. Now the soul of the true philosopher believes that it must not
resist this deliverance, and therefore it stands aloof from pleasures
and lusts and griefs and fears, so far as it can, considering that when
anyone has violent pleasures or fears or griefs or lusts he suffers from
them not merely what one might think – for example, illness or loss
of money spent [83c] for his lusts – but he suffers the greatest and
most extreme evil and does not take it into account.'
'What is this evil, Socrates?' said Cebes.
'The evil is that the soul of every man, when it is greatly pleased or
pained by anything, is compelled to believe that the object which
caused the emotion is very distinct and very true; but it is not. These
objects are mostly the visible ones, are they not?' (83b5-c9, tr. Fowler).

In my view, the key point of this passage is as follows. Socrates does not
argue that excessively or chiefly concerning oneself with the body is a bad
thing merely on the basis of a dualistic contrast, whereby the body and
care of it would be "bad", but the soul and the care of it would be "good".
The problem with souls overly attached to the body does not lie in the
fact that they are incapable of freeing themselves from the body (besides,
in the *Phaedo* Socrates warns his readers that suicide is not a legitimate
option), but rather in the fact that in such a way they end up believing
that the body, i.e. that which is material, is the thing that exists in the
most evident and truest way (ἐναργέστατόν τε εἶναι καὶ ἀληθέστατον). But
in actual fact – and this is the point that Socrates is trying to make – the
reality which exists in the most evident and truest way is not sensible reality but intelligible reality (hence the soul, which has the latter as its object, is clearly superior to the body). Therefore, according to the Socrates
of the *Phaedo*, both the body and the soul exist, yet in an asymmetrical
relation. As the truest reality is that of the soul, it follows that care of the
soul is a far more worthwhile pursuit than care of the body. The point is
that according to Plato both the existence of body and soul and the superiority of the latter over the former imply separation. The empirical data
we must account for are first of all the actual separation between impulses, desires and physical needs on the one hand, and values and goals of a

spiritual nature, on the other; and, secondly, the superiority – in terms of the complete fulfilment of human nature – of the goods of the soul over those of the body. If this is the case, then the most effective theoretical model is the one distinguishing soul and body as two different and separable objects. Naturally, it may be objected that the analysis of the experience mentioned here is incorrect, and that therefore the dualistic theoretical model has not been adequately justified. This might be true from a general perspective; but it was far from obvious for the poetic and philosophical tradition of the Greeks, from Homer to Socrates and the Socratics: for the most prevalent perception was that expounded by Plato, which sees the soul and body as two different things of unequal value. In any case, this is not the real point at issue. What matters is the fact that for Plato psychological dualism is justified – regardless of the correctness of one's argument – by the need to account for experience, and not by the desire to assign human nature different traits from those it actually possesses.

According to Plato, the fact that the soul is superior to the body and separable from it implies that it can also exist on its own, which is to say in a disembodied and purely spiritual condition. This discloses a potentially very weighty metaphysical background; hence the efforts made by contemporary scholars to downplay this aspect of Platonic thought – for example, by reducing it to a metaphor. In my view, this "reduction" is untenable, or at any rate methodologically incorrect. But, again, this is not what matters here. The reduction just mentioned is usually carried out in order to safeguard the interest of Platonic philosophy in "this world", the world which actually exists – and its pertinence to it – particularly as regards ethics, politics, anthropology, and so on. But this is an ill-founded concern. The possibility that the soul might lead a better life in disembodied form is a side effect of the separability of soul and body required by our analysis of experience. Therefore, the fact that the the best condition for man is to become all soul and no body in no way changes the fact that the separability of the soul is the precondition for man to lead a good life already in this world. The life of the disembodied soul, as the life of a bodiless soul, is no doubt a form of life unknown to us, one utterly different from the life we experience. While the death *of man* is nothing but the separation of soul and body (as we read in the *Phaedo*), the life *of man* consists in the soul's animation of the body. The life of the separate soul, then, is a different thing; as such, it in no way undermines the intrinsic unity of soul and body in the living mortal being. The unity of soul and body would be compromised if the soul could lead the kind of life it leads in the body even without it. In such a case, the body would be superfluous – it would be nothing but a burden. But the life of disembodied souls is the life of gods, not men. Hence, for Plato the separability of the soul constitutes both the basis for a future super-human and disembodied life, and the most effective explicative and guiding model to understand and regulate the life of man in his present condition, understood as the soul's animation of the body.

IV.

In support of the thesis I have put forward in the previous pages, namely that for Plato the marked dualism between soul and body is chiefly required as an explicative model to account for experiential data, I will shortly be discussing a problem which Plato raises again the *Phaedo*: the so-called doctrine of the soul as harmony. This will also allow us to carry out an interesting comparison with the Aristotelian position. Against the doctrine of the soul as harmony (of the body), which Simmias presents in the *Phaedo* as an objection to the thesis of the immortality of the soul championed by Socrates, the text puts forward three different arguments.[8] Here we are concerned with only one of them, the argument expounded at lines 94b4-95a2:

> 'Well,' said Socrates, 'of all the parts that make up a man, do you think any is ruler except the soul, especially if it be a wise one?'
> 'No, I do not.'
> 'Does it yield to the feelings of the body or oppose them? I mean, when the body is hot and thirsty, does not the soul oppose it and draw it away from drinking, and from eating when it is hungry, and do we not see the soul opposing the body in countless other ways?'
> 'Certainly.'[9]

---

8 See TRABATTONI (1988).
9 In the *Republic* (439c-e) the same argument is used not to show the independence of the soul from the body, but to uphold the idea of the tripartition of the soul. But this issue does not concern us. If what is at issue here is the autonomy of the soul with respect to the body, the problem does not apply at all to a soul responsible for all the vital functions of man.

'Did we not agree in our previous discussion that it could never, if it
be a harmony, give forth a sound at variance with the tensions and
relaxations and vibrations and other conditions of the elements
which compose it, but that it would follow them and never lead
them?'

'Yes', he replied, 'we did, of course.'

'Well then, do we not now find that the soul acts in exactly the opposite way, leading those elements of which it is said to consist and opposing them in almost everything through all our life, and tyranniz-
ing over them in every way, sometimes inflicting harsh and painful
punishments (those of gymnastics and medicine), and sometimes
milder ones, sometimes threatening and sometimes admonishing, in
short, speaking to the desires and passions and fears as if it were distinct from them and they from it, as Homer has shown in the
Odyssey when he says of Odysseus:[10]

He smote his breast, and thus he chid his heart:

"Endure it, heart, you have born worse than this."

Do you suppose that, when he wrote those words, he thought of the
soul as a harmony which would be led by the conditions of the body,
and not rather as something fitted to lead and rule them, and itself a
far more divine thing than a harmony?'

'By Zeus, Socrates, the latter, I think.'

'Then, my good friend, it will never do for us to say that the soul is a
harmony; for we should, it seems, agree neither with Homer, the divine poet, nor with ourselves' (tr. Fowler).

Socrates' reasoning is quite straightforward. As, on the level of experience, it is possible for the human will to counter the desires and stimuli
of the body, within man there must be a subject responsible for this opposition; not only that, but this subject must also be independent from
the body, for otherwise it would be incapable of offering any opposition
at all. Therefore, supposing that the subject in question is the soul, the
soul cannot be a harmony (or agreement) of bodily elements, for in such
a case all its operations would merely be the forced consequence of the
arrangement of bodily parts. The eventuality we experience on the empir-

---

10 XX, vv. 17-18 (Odysseus, who has just returned to Ithaca, conceals his indigna-
    tion at the sight of the amorous exchanges between his maid servants and the
    suitors).

ical level of the soul disobeying the body and ordering it to act against its
own wishes would never occur.

A comparison with Aristotle proves interesting in this respect. Aristotle too in the first book of *De anima* offers some arguments to refute the
doctrine of the soul as harmony, but these are not pertinent to our enquiry. Rather, it is significant that at the end of his refutation Aristotle in
a way seems to question the result achieved by posing the following
question:

εἰ δ'ἐστὶν ἕτερον ἡ ψυχὴ τῆς μίξεως, τί δή ποτε ἅμα τῷ (τὸ) σαρκὶ εἶναι
ἀναιρεῖται καὶ τὸ (τῷ) τοῖς ἄλλοις μορίοις τοῦ ζῴου.

I have left these two lines untranslated because the Greek is uncertain.
This (already according to Alexander of Aphrodisias[11]) makes at least two
different interpretations possible, which partially depend on the variants
I have added in brackets. I will present them in Ross' versions:[12]

(1) "If the soul is not a ἁρμονία, why is it that when the mixture which
    constitutes flesh is destroyed, that of the other parts is destroyed with
    it?".
(2) "If the soul is not a ἁρμονία, why is it destroyed when the flesh is de-
    stroyed?".[13]

Before addressing the textual problems, let us consider the meaning of
each translation. The sentence occurs within the context of a series of objections that Aristotle raises against the doctrine of the soul as harmony.
Therefore, the most natural way to understand it would be as an exten-
sion/integration of the previous critical observations. Yet it is difficult to
see how this could be the case. What we have is a hypothetical sentence
that starts with the conditional clause "if the soul is not a harmony", and
then introduces a factual element that ought to refute the hypothesis: if x
is not true, how do we explain y? Therefore, the conclusion ought to be
that x is true (namely, that the soul is a harmony). This is precisely the
opposite of how the sentence must be interpreted if we accept translation
(2). Besides, this version is hardly unproblematic, for it seems to introduce a sort of foreign body into an argument that is heading in a very dif-

---

11 *Ap.* Philop. *in de An.* 153, 3ff. An overview of the positions adopted by the an-
    cient commentators is provided by HICKS (1907), p. 271-272.
12 ROSS (1961), p. 197.
13 Among the ancient commentators, the first translation is accepted by Simplicius
    and Philoponus, the second one by Themistius.

ferent direction. It is easy to understand why already the ancient commentators took a second possibility into account, namely the one based
on translation (1). Apparently, there is little difference, because the hypothetical structure remains the same; hence, it seems natural for the conclusion to support rather than disprove the doctrine of the soul as harmony. But let's consider the complex justification of translation (1) provided
by Alexander (via Philoponus). The sentence in his view refers to what
Aristotle has stated in the previous lines (408a10-18), and in particular to
his argument that if the soul were a mixture, given that different combi-
nations of elements are possible, we would have different souls. Alexander takes this conclusion to mean that the doctrine of the soul as harmony necessarily implies the existence of multiple souls (ἐκ τοῦ τὴν ψυχὴν
ἁρμονίαν λέγειν συμβαίνειν πολλὰς ψυχὰς ἔχειν τὸ ζῷον, Philop. *in de An.*
152, 34-35). But if we argue that, precisely because the soul is a harmony,
all the mixtures (both that of the flesh and those of all the other parts)
perish together, this implies the singularity of the soul: for else, this si-
multaneousness would be unaccountable. Therefore, the doctrine of the
soul as harmony would seem to be compromised, because on the one
hand it must grant the multiplicity of souls (given the multiplicity of mixtures), while on the other it must also grant the unity of the soul, since all
the mixtures perish together.[14]

This does not strike me as a very plausible explanation, for more than
one reason. First of all, the argument would be adduced too late, since
the discussion of the multiplicity of souls had already been brought to an
end a few lines before, after which the debate had taken a different turn
(the focus had shifted to Empedocles' doctrine).[15] Secondly, if Aristotle
truly meant to say what Alexander believes, he would hardly have given
the sentence a hypothetical form. Rather, he would have argued along the
following lines: given the structural multiplicity of mixtures, the doctrine
of the soul as harmony implies the plurality of souls; bodily mixtures perish together; hence, if the soul were a harmony, it would have to be simul-

14 Philop. *in de An.* 152, 3-10: εἰ γὰρ μὴ εἴη, φησίν, ἡ ψυχὴ ἁρμονία ἀλλ'ἕτερόν τι τῆς
    μίξεως, διὰ τί τῆς μίξεως τῆς σαρκὸς φθειρομένης καὶ ἡ τῶν λοιπῶν μορίων
    συμφθείρεται μῖξις; εἰ γὰρ τοῦτο, δόξειεν ἂν μία μῖξις εἶναι πάντων τῶν μορίων καὶ
    οὐ πολλαί· διὰ τί γὰρ τῇ μιᾷ πᾶσαι συμφθείρονται; οὕτω δὲ καὶ ἡ ψυχὴ μία ἔσται
    καὶ οὐ πολλαί, εἰς ὃ ἄτοπον ἀπάγεσθαι ἐδόκει ὁ λόγος ὁ λέγων τὴν ψυχὴν ἁρμονίαν
    εἶναι. ὥστε εἰ μιᾶς μίξεως ἀναιρουμένης ἀναιρεῖται τὸ ζῷον, μία ἄρα καὶ ἡ ψυχὴ
    ἁρμονία οὖσα.
15 408a18-24.

taneously one and many. In this reasoning, the second premise carries an absolute meaning, so it makes no sense to make it conditional upon the hypothesis that the soul is a harmony. If the soul were not a harmony, wouldn't the various bodily mixtures perish together anyway? Finally, the sentence we are discussing has a clearly contrastive sense, as is shown by the opening δέ.

It thus seems to me that the only acceptable meaning is the one expressed by translation (2). The fact that this is a kind of aside that is not taken any further does not strike me as a problem, since Aristotle frequently interrupts or attempts to problematise his argument: a feature that probably reflects the aporematic nature of his thought, as well as the dialogical-dialectic dynamics inherent in teaching. After having refuted the doctrine of the soul as harmony, Aristotle note the problem of the compatibility of what he has just stated with his own views: if, as Aristotle's philosophy suggests, the soul perishes the very moment it is stripped of "the mixture which constitutes flesh and that of the other living parts", it would seem as though the theory according to which the soul is the harmony of the body represents the most natural and effective explanation for what has just been argued, namely that the soul perishes together with the body. Hence Aristotle's question: why, despite this, is the soul not a harmony? In other words, notwithstanding all the objections already raised, Aristotle here would be displaying a somewhat sympathetic attitude towards the notion that the doctrine of the soul as harmony is the explanation most compatible with the soul's dependence upon the body. Giancarlo Movia has rightly noted that «of all his predecessors' doctrines, that of the soul as harmony is the one closest to the Aristotelian thesis of the unity of soul and body».[16]

Let's see how all this might be compatible with the text. I will here continue to follow Ross' commentary. In his view, translation (1) would require τῷ at line 25 and τό at line 26 (although it would also be compatible with the presence of τό in either position). By contrast, translation (2)

---

16 MOVIA (2001), p. 262 («fra tutte le dottrine dei predecessori, quella dell'anima-armonia è la più vicina alla tesi aristotelica dell'unità dell'anima e del corpo»). Cf. Philop. 151, 9-10: Ἐκτιθέμενος τὴν δόξαν τῶν λεγόντων ἁρμονίαν εἶναι τὴν ψυχὴν ἔλεγε πιθανὸν εἶναι τοῦτον τὸν λόγον.

would require τῷ in either case. Here is breakdown of the three possibilities, accompanied by the respective translations:

(a) τῷ at line 26 and τό at line 25:
     "together with the mixture which constitutes flesh, also that of the
     other material parts is destroyed" (tr. 1).
(b) τό in both cases:
     "the mixture which constitutes flesh and that of the other material
     parts are destroyed together" (tr. 1).
(c) τῷ in both cases
     "[the soul] is destroyed together with the mixture which constitutes
     the flesh and that of the other material parts" (tr. 2).

This breakdown is consistent with the fact that both HICKS (1907) and
HETT (1936), who adopt translation (2), choose to insert the article τῷ in
both positions (the same translation is provided by LAURENTI (1973),
which does not give the Greek text). However, Ross disagrees with this interpretation, probably based on the fact that whereas the manuscripts are
more or less equally divided in their reading of line 25, almost all of them
favour τό at line 26. Therefore, Ross chose to print τό at line 26 but for
line 25 adopted τό in his 1956 *editio minor* and τῷ in his 1961 *editio major*.
Evidently, though, the meaning in his view does not change, because
whereas (1) is compatible with either variant, (2) necessarily requires τῷ
at line 26, and hence must apparently be ruled out. The translation featured in the *editio major* is consistent with (1). ROSS (1961) is followed by
MOVIA (2001), whereas CORCILIUS (2017) adopts ROSS (1956); both
scholars, in keeping with the Greek text they give, choose translation (1),
as BODEÜS (1993) does in his French translation (without the Greek).

    The situation, to my mind, is quite clear. Some of the most respected
translations of last century chose the textual variant that practically entails
version (2), evidently on the grounds that this seems like the more natural
version and the one more in keeping with the hypothetical-dialectic nature of the sentence. Later, other authors and commentators, starting
with Ross, deemed the philological factors more cogent, namely the insufficient and weak attestation of τῷ at line 26; hence, they chose to leave
τό in that position, which led them to accept translation (1). It thus seems
as though we are dealing with a typical exegetical aporia: the variant that
seems more natural in terms of meaning is the less probable one as far as
the reconstruction of the text is concerned.

In my view, the problem can be solved by proposing a fourth possibility, based on a different reading of the text according to (b), namely:

(b') τό in both cases:
   "together [with the soul], the mixture which constitutes flesh and that of the other material parts are destroyed" (2).

This would solve all problems. The question that Aristotle is suddenly raising, possibly as a kind of annotation inserted in the text in view of future considerations, might be taken to be the following: while there are good reasons to reject the doctrine of the soul as harmony, one must also bear in mind that the most natural position for someone wishing to demonstrate the simultaneous passing away of soul and body is a theory similar to – or partly overlapping with – that of the soul as harmony. And the Aristotelian conception of the soul as the form of the body would indeed appear to be a theory of this sort (as shown, in particular, by the interpretation provided by Alexander of Aphrodisias[17]).

Given all this, we can now draw some conclusions. Had Plato known the Aristotelian doctrine according to which the soul is the form of the body, he would probably have countered it with an objection similar to the one Socrates raises against Simmias in the *Phaedo*. He would not so much – or merely – have argued, as throngs of later Platonists were to do (Atticus, Plotinus, Porphyry, etc.[18]), that it is philosophically and metaphysically outrageous to deny that the soul is a substance which is separate, imperishable, divine, and so on. Rather, he would have argued that the theory according to which the soul is the form of the body is inadequate on the scientific and explanatory level, since – just like the doctrine of the soul as harmony, towards which Aristotle significantly shows some indulgence – it fails to duly account for the psychological and ethical elements which de facto characterise man and his actions within the world.

---

17 See Alex. Aphr. *De an.*, 24-26.
18 «Platon war kein Platoniker» (GADAMER, 1985-1991, p. 508).

References

BODEÜS, R. (1993). Aristote. *Traité de l'âme*. Paris. Flammarion.

CATAPANO, G. (2006). Plotino. *Sulle virtù, I 2 [19]*. Pisa. Pisa University Press.

CORCILIUS, K. (2017). Aristoteles. *Über die Seele. De anima*, Übersetzt, mit einer Einleitung und Anmerkungen. Hamburg. Felix Meiner.

FREDE, D. (1999). *Platons "Phaidon". Der Traum von der Unsetrblichkeit der Seele*. Darmstadt. Wissenschaftliche Buchgesellscharft.

GADAMER, H.G. (1985-1991). *Gesammelte Werke II*. Tübingen. Mohr Siebeck.

GERSON, L. (1994). *Plotinus*. London, New York. Routledge.

HETT W.S. (1936). Aristotle. *On the Soul, Parva naturalia, On Breath*. Cambridge (Mass.). Harvard University Press, London. Heinemann.

HICKS, R. (1907). Aristotle. *De anima*, with Translation, Introduction and Notes. Cambridge. Cambridge University Press.

LANE, M. (2005). 'Emplois pour philosophes': l'art politique et l'étranger dans le politique à la lumière de Socrate et du philosophe dans le *Théétète*. *Les Études Philosophiques*, 3, p. 325-345

LAURENTI, R. (1973). Aristotele. *Dell'anima*. In: Giannantoni, G. (ed.). Aristotele. *Opere*, vol. IV. Bari. Laterza.

MAHONNEY, T. (2004). Is Assimilation to God in the *Theaetetus* Purely Otherworldly?. *Ancient Philosophy*, 24, p. 321-338.

MOVIA, G. (2001). Aristotele, *L'anima*, Milano. Bompiani.

ROSS, D. (1956). *Aristotelis de anima*. Oxford. Clarendon Press.

_____ (1961). Aristotle. *De anima*, Edited with Introduction and Commentary. Oxford. Oxford University Press.

RUE, R. (1993). The Philosopher in Flight: The Digression (172c-177c) in Plato's *Theaetetus*. *Oxford Studies in Ancient Philosophy*, 11, p. 71-100.

TRABATTONI, F. (1988). La teoria dell'anima-armonia nel *Fedone*. *Elenchos*, 9, p. 53-74.

_____ (2007). Si può parlare di "unità" della psicologia platonica? Esame di un caso significativo (*Fedone*, 68b-69e). In: Migliori, M.; Napolitano Valditara, L.; Fermani A. (eds.). *Interiorità e anima. La* psychè *in Platone*. Milano. Vita e Pensiero, p. 307-320.

De An.I 1, 403a25 and the *lógoi énuloi*: An Heraclitean Heritage in Aristotle's Psychology

Giuseppe Feola

I. The Problem

> εἰ δ'οὕτως ἔχει, δῆλον ὅτι τὰ πάθη λόγοι ἔνυλοί εἰσιν
> if this be so, the attributes [of the soul] are evidently forms or notions realised in matter.
> (*de An.* I 1, 403a24-25).[1]

Aristotle seals in this way the preliminary discussion, in the first chapter of the treatise *On the Soul*, of the relation of the psychic affections or attributes of the soul (πάθη) to physical bodily affections. The psychical affections had been characterized, some lines before, as something «inseparable» (ἀχώριστον, 403a15) from body, since they are «always conjoined with a body of some sort» (ἀεὶ μετὰ σώματός τινος ἐστιν, 15-16); i.e.: since we do not observe any psychical affection that happens without a concomitant affection of the body, and since «all are attended by some particular affection of the body» (18-19, ἅμα γὰρ τούτοις πάσχει τι τὸ σῶμα).

As a result of this, the affections of the soul would be "forms realised in matter" or "enmattered forms". Aristotle specifies this characterization by giving us an example of how we should define an affection or change in the soul (i.e. of how we should define an enmattered form):

> τὸ ὀργίζεσθαι κίνησίς τις τοῦ τοιουδὶ σώματος ἢ μέρους ἢ δυνάμεως ὑπὸ τοῦδε ἕνεκα τοῦδε.
> anger [is] a movement in this body or part [of the body] or power [of the body] produced by *a* in order to produce *b* (403a26-27).[2]

where *a* and *b* are the efficient and the final cause that are the parameters for the formal definition of the passion we are defining; while the body,

---

1   Unless otherwise stated, quotes from the *De anima* refer to Ross' text: ROSS (1961). English translation of quotes from the *De Anima* are from HICKS (1988).
2   Here the English translation is of my own, and not Hicks'.

or the bodily part, or the bodily power (the physio-chemical power which is contained in some determinate physical substance or compound, as e.g. the corrosive power of the gastric liquids or the heat of the blood[3]) in which *a* induces the affection in order to produce *b*, is the substrate that behaves as the matter for the form.

The characterization we are here given of the kind of definition that is required for the affections of the soul is explicitly presented by Aristotle as normative: i.e. it is presented as a model to which the definitions of the affections of the soul in general should conform. The reason for such a normativity (we are told) lays in the fact that all the affections of the soul are enmattered reasons. We can therefore say that the characterization of the psychic affections as "enmattered reasons" produces both the epistemic model to which their definitions should conform and the ontological model on which this epistemic model relies.

It is thus clear that it would be important to understand the meaning and the semantic overtones of the lemma "enmattered reason" in order to understand Aristotle's psychobiology.[4]

In this article, I will propose a lexical analysis that could give us a key to the meaning of this famous phrase. The result of the lexical analysis could (I hope) give us in the future a more complete understanding of the relationship between matter and form in Aristotle's psychology; the problem of the relationship between matter and form is something I do not want to face here, for many reasons, and above all because it would require a metatheoretical analysis of all Aristotle's theories about living beings.

3 The parallelism with "body" and "bodily part" makes me think that here "δύναμις" does not have the commonest sense in Aristotle, of "psychic power" or "function" (in which case the δύναμις should pertain to the 'psychic' and formal level of the definition, and not to the somatic and material level), but rather the rarer, but anyway present, meaning of "physio-chemical power", e.g. of a plant or of another body of organic origin: cf. Xen. *Cyr.* 8.8, 14; *Œconomicus* 16, 4; Thphr. *HP.* 8.11, 1.

4 Since we do not have resolved this problem yet, I have not paraphrased the lemma "enmattered forms" with any other expression, as e.g. "reasons in matter", which is its usual rendering in English: at this point, we do not know yet whether Aristotle means *reasons in matter* or *reasons that have matter inside of themselves*.

II. A Peculiar "Void" in Critical Literature

On account of what we have now said, we could expect that the famous sentence should have been the object of accurate analyses. We can notice, indeed, that the whole debate about the meaning of Aristotle's psychology and its relation to XX century functionalism[5] was a debate about the meaning we should assign to that phrase: i.e., it was a debate about the theoretical consequences of the idea that the affections of the soul are enmattered forms. Quite strangely, scholars have taken for granted that we already knew what Aristotle meant by "enmattered forms": the "enmattered forms" were presumed to be *"forms or abstract notions"* (these are the commonest renderings of λόγος) that are "embedded in matter", i.e. such as that their nature always entails a physiological realization. The debate was only (or almost only) about the identification and evaluation of the theory that Aristotle produced, in the central books of the *Metaphysics* and, with specific focus on the nature of living beings, in the *De anima*, as a further development of this sketchy characterization of the passions of the soul as "enmattered forms".

But this expression "λόγος ἔνυλος" does not pertain to Aristotle's technical language (in this case, the adjective ἔνυλος should appear far more often in the *corpus*), nor to the lexicon of other professionals of knowledge of that time (e.g. doctors), nor to the lexicon of the Attic literary prose. It is a *hápax*; it is an expression with a high degree of originality, which Aristotle inserts in a very important point of the discussion, clearly in order to emphasize the importance of something he refuses to describe by using a more standard language (either his own technical jargon, or the jargon of other scientific disciplines, or the standard language of his time's prose, or the literary language of the poets).

It is clear, therefore, that it would be important to understand what Aristotle meant by such a strange wording: for it is this *quid* which, clearly, is the central idea of which the whole hylomorphic theory is the theoretical development.

---

5 We can say that almost every book or article about Aristotle's definition of the soul and of the soul's affections is automatically a book or article which, explicitly or implicitly, deals with the interpretation of this passage: therefore, it would be quite pointless to mention just a few titles. Anyway, we can surely say that BURNYEAT (1992), p. 15-26, and NUSSBAUM/PUTNAM (1992), p. 27-56 have played a very important role in the debate about how our passage should apply to the case of sense-perception.

III. Looking at 403a25 in the Frame of the Whole De anima

First of all, let us see what we can infer from the context. The famous sentence occurs in the middle of the exposition of a problem for those who want to investigate the nature of the soul. In ch. I 1, Aristotle exposes a series of these problems; and a long piece, from 403a3 to 404a19 (more than a whole Bekker page), is devoted to the exposition of the following *aporía*: are the affections (or the passions) of the soul (403a3, πάθη τῆς ψυχῆς: we will see how ambiguous is this wording) «common to the owner [of the soul] too» (403a3-4, πότερόν ἐστι πάντα κοινὰ καὶ τοῦ ἔχοντος)?[6] In other words: Aristotle would like to know whether they are common to the soul and the ensouled body, «or whether any of them are peculiar to the soul itself» (403a4-5, ἢ ἔστι τι καὶ τῆς ψυχῆς ἴδιον αὐτῆς). The consequences of the answer to this question would be very relevant: if every affection of the soul is shared with the body, the soul does not have any feature that it can continue to have when the body is absent, and therefore the soul would cease to exist with the death of the body; what is at stake is the immortality of the soul, which was so important for Plato.[7]

Aristotle, here, does not answer the question; he just notices that all the affections of the soul[8] «seem» (ἔοικε, 403a16) «to occur with the body» (ἔιναι μετὰ σώματος, 16-17),[9] and that all «are attended by some particular affection of the body» (a18-19, *loc. cit.*). Moreover, the bodily conditions can affect our psychic reactions to external stimuli, e.g. by fa-

---

6   In this case the translation is of my own, and I am not following Hicks' translation.

7   The overall sense of this passage seems quite clear, and Ross's paraphrasis seems adequate: «He is dealing with the question whether there are any attributes which belong to the soul as such, not to a besouled or living being. If there is any form of acting or suffering (being acted on) that belongs to soul as such, the soul can exist without the body; if not, not» (ROSS, 1961, *ad* 403a10-16, p. 168). Ross's paraphrasis follows quite faithfully Hicks's one (1988, *in* 403a10-27, p. 195), and is in its turn followed by POLANSKY (2007), *in* 403a3-24, p. 50. GABBE (2016), understands the passage in a slightly different way: the point that Aristotle would be stating against Plato would not be the inseparability of the soul's affections from the body, since Plato too credited the body with some role in the production of the emotions (that are the kind of affections of the soul that Aristotle here mentions); what Aristotle would be arguing here (according to GABBE, 2016, p. 42) is that Plato's interactionist dualism cannot explain the unity of soul and body that is so clear in the case of the passions.

8   By this, he means what we call "emotions": see the list at a17-18.

9   Here too I depart from Hicks' rendering.

cilitating an angry or fearful reaction when our body is already in a disposition that is similar to the disposition which is typical of angry or fearful reactions (a19-24).

It is on the basis of these remarks that Aristotle concludes that «the affections of the soul are enmattered reasons», and goes on in the way we already saw: by stating that the definition of the passions/affections of the soul should conform to the paradigm he gives for anger: 'passion p is a motion m in the body b, on account of a and for the sake of b' (see 403a26-27, *loc. cit.*).

The relation between *súnolon*, matter and form is specifically addressed in books VII-IX of the *Metaphysics* and in book II of the *Physics*, and I think that in the *De anima* Aristotle uses the hylomorphic theory without the ambition of giving a new general description of it: for the sake of a study about hylomorphism, Aristotle's biology and psychology are fundamental in order to understand its main applications and the scientific questions that required its formulation; but it is not in the *De anima* (I think) that we should search for the main formulation of hylomorphism, nor for its philosophical justification.

In particular, Aristotle seems here to be taking for granted (and therefore not to be willing to discuss) some points that are quite obvious for the readers of *Physics* and *Metaphysics*: that natural phaenomena need an adequate matter in order to be concretely realized (they are "forms in matter"), and that it is precisely on account of this fact that the definitions of living beings should always include some reference to matter (they are "forms that have matter in themselves"). Aristotle, in *De anima*, assumes without debate both these points (that are discussed in the other two works); and this holds true notwithstanding the value (whatever value) we credit to the phrase "enmattered form" in our passage.

It remains nevertheless true that such an inclusive explanation does not match our impression that such a peculiar wording, with such a degree of originality from the lexical point of view, should have a very precise meaning and a sense the author carefully pondered about: a sense which we should understand.

For this reason, I will now leave for some moments the field of the historical and philosophical analysis and I will move to that of lexicography.

IV. Meaning of "énulos"

The phrase "λόγοι ἔνυλοί" must have perplexed the ancient readers too, if no less than two manuscripts, *Parisiensis 1853* and *Parisiensis 386*, read ἐν ὕλῃ,[10] which is clearly to be refused as *facilior*, and which is a patent effort to substitute an unusual word with a very common sentence. Anyway, λόγοι ἔνυλοί is testified by Themistius, Simplicius, Philoponus and Sophonia.[11] Ross does not give any explanation about its meaning, and he simply refers to Hicks's explanation[12] (which we will see soon). Polansky prefers to read ἐν ὕλῃ.[13] But, as I already said, choosing ἐν ὕλῃ would violate the principle of preferring, *cæteris paribus*, the *lectio difficilior*: therefore, I cannot share Polansky's choice.

Perhaps it will aid to start from the meaning of the adjective.

As an example of usage of ἔνυλος, Bonitz[14] refers just to this single passage.[15] An interpreter notices a semantical and grammatical analogy with ἔνυδρος: this is Hicks (*ad* 403a25, p. 199), who suggests that the possible meanings of ἔνυλος would be parallel to the meanings that (according to Hicks) Bonitz testifies for ἔνυδρος. But Bonitz does not give two meanings of this adjective: rather, he lists two groups of entities that Aristotle describes as ἔνυδρα:

- in a larger group of cases, ἔνυδρος refers to living beings that live *in water*; in these cases, the adjective clearly means (*1*) "contained in water, immersed in it";[16]
- in the other group,[17] the occurrences of the adjective refer to places and geographic spaces; in all these cases, we can understand the adjec-

---

10 Cf. ROSS (1961), critical apparatus 403a25.
11 Cf. *ibidem*.
12 Cf. ROSS (1961), *ad* 403a25, p. 168.
13 Cf. POLANSKY (2007), *ad* 403a24-b19, p. 56.
14 BONITZ (1955), s.v. ἔνυλος.
15 LIDDELL/SCOTT/JONES (1996), s.v. ἔνυλος, adds some instances from Iamblichus and Proclus, two authors that surely had our passage of the *De anima* in mind.
16 Cf., e.g., *Hist. An.* I 1, 487a15ff.; for a very clear instance of the relation between ἐν and the root of "water" in these cases, see *Juv.* 6, 470b2-4: opposition ἔνυδρα [...] ἐν τῷ ἀέρι; 15, 474b25: opposition ἔνυδρα [...] ἐν τῇ γῇ.
17 *Mete.* I 14, 351a34, 35, b25, 352a22; *Hist. An.* VIII 2, 589a19.

tive as in (*1*) (these places are immersed in water[18]) or (as Hicks understands) (*2*) "that has water in it" (those places contain water).

Now, it is clear that the regions that contain a lot of water can also be conceived as regions that are immersed "in water": so, all the occurrences of group 2 can be conceived as well as occurrences of group 1 too; and, in the light of the great superiority in number of the occurrences where meaning 1 is the only affordable one, I think that the most viable understanding of the occurrences of the group 2 is the one which absorbs this group into the group 1.

Therefore ἔνυδρος would mean (in all its occurrences) "immersed in water"; and, if it is true that ἔνυλος was coined on the model of ἔνυδρος, then ἔνυλος will mean "immersed in matter".

But, after all, we do not have any linguistic proof that ἔνυλος was coined on the model of ἔνυδρος. And, from a general point of view, the adjectives of the form "ἐν + root of the noun" do mean in some cases "which is in *x*", and in other cases "full of *x*"[19]. So, in principle, the two interpretations of ἔνυλος given by Hicks would remain plausible despite (or, rather: on account of) the fact that there seems not to be any good reason to call for a parallelism with ἔνυδρος.

V. Meaning of "páthos"

What about the meaning of πάθος in our sentence? It seems obvious that there is a connection with πάθη τῆς ψυχῆς in 403a3, which can mean both "passions of the soul" (current meaning of πάθος in the IV sec. B.C.) and "affections of the soul" (technical sense of πάθος: cf. *Cat.* 8, 9a28ff.). I think that such an apparent ambiguity is not an ambiguity at all: Aristotle is trying to consider the relation between the soul and its passions as a particular case of the relation between substance and attributes.

---

18 See e.g. Louis, that in *Hist. An.* VIII 2, 589a19, translates «couvertes d'eau».
19 Cf. ἔνθεος, which has always only this second meaning.

VI. *Meaning of "lógos"*

The verb λέγω has two basic meanings.[20] The first, which is the only one which is attested in Homer, is (I) "to collect", "to choose"; and therefore "to count sthg as a member of a set" (cf. Hom. *Od.* IV, 452); then "to count"; "to enumerate"; finally, "to expose point by point". The other one, post-Homeric only, is (II) "to speak", "to say"; it is easy to understand how the second one could stem from the first: in every discourse we follow a 'thread', which is an ordered and countable collection of words, concepts, etc.

Consequently, for λόγος we have (II) "discourse" (e.g. the discourse of the orator); (I*a*) "calculation";[21] (I*b*) "relation between x and y".[22] The meaning I and II conflate in Aristotle,[23] since Aristotle borrows his own notion of *discoursive rationality* from Plato, who had excluded from it the exercise of rhetoric in order to connect it as tightly as possible to the paradigm of geometry; and geometry, in Plato's and Aristotle's time, used to solve problems by "breaking" the geometric figures in more simple elements so as to be able to reconstruct them as particular kinds of "relations" between such elements: in the same fashion, Plato proposes to understand the definitory practice as an art of resolving the notion of the *definiendum* in more simple and fundamental concepts, whose appropriate relationship would show its structure.[24] As a consequence, in Aristotle λόγος means (in the majority of the cases) "relation between notions or between concepts";[25] in a relevant subset of the occurrences, these notions are mathematical abstractions.

---

20 I give up here the question of whether it is just one verb with two meanings or we have to do with two verbs with a common origin and connected meanings.

21 Cf. e.g. Hdt. III, 142, 5 (λόγον διδόναι χρημάτων: "to render an account of the money").

22 Already in Æsch. *Sept.* 518-519. Aeschylus did not show, in its linguistic choices, any particular interest in scientific neologisms; so, I think we should exclude that this usage of λόγος in Aeschylus could result from some re-usage, on Aeschylus' part, of the mathematical lexicon.

23 Cf. BONITZ (1955), s.v. λόγος.

24 Cf. Plato, *Soph. passim.*

25 Clearly aligned to this meaning is also the usage of λόγος that immediately comes to memory: the λόγος as "notion" of the object of science: the *lógos* of *man* is *rational animal*, which is a relation (an essential predication, in this case) between the universals *animal* and *rational*.

VII. Meaning of "lógos énulos"

Which are the results of our lexicographical analysis? What are the *lógoi énuloi*? (*1*) the "reasons in matter" or (*2*) "reasons that have matter in themselves"?

In the *corpus* we can find evidence for both interpretations: *Metaph.* Z 7, 1033a4-5 (ὁ δὴ χαλκοῦς κύκλος ἔχει ἐν τῷ λόγῳ τὴν ὕλην: «The brazen circle, then, has its matter in its formula»),[26] favours 2; but, *pace* Ross (*ad* 403a25, p. 168) it is not decisive at all, since in our passage, just after a few lines (403b3), we can read that the *lógos*, in order to have objective reality, should be «in such a matter» (ἐν ὕλῃ τοιᾳδί); if textual proximity bears some weight in disambiguating terms, interpretation *1* is the most obvious one, in the light of the whole passage: it is as if Aristotle, after he realized that he had just used an unusual word (perhaps a word he himself invented in that moment), had thought it would be good to explain its meaning by using a paraphrase.

It seems, therefore, that the *lógoi énuloi* are the "reasons in matter"; but this meaning does not exclude the correlative fact that such a matter "in which" are the *lógoi*, can (from another point of view) be comprised in the *lógoi* themselves, because they have to embed a reference to it.

At this point, having resolved by strictly philological methods the problem of the meaning of "*énulos*", we can reconsider the analogy between "*énulos*" and "*énudros*": is there really a semantic parallelism between the two adjectives? If yes, which is the philosophical relevance of this parallelism?

VIII. Heraclitean Heritages. Heraclitus on Water and Dis-course

As a matter of fact, there *is* a cogent motif for accepting Hicks's suggestion about the relation between "*énulos*" and "*énudros*": this motif is the link which held, in the imagery of the Greek thought before Aristotle, between the concepts of "liquid/water" and "material substrate" of change. Changeability is often, in Pre-Socratic thought and in Plato, represented

---

26 Aristotle, *Metaphysics*, trans. ROSS, The Internet Classical Archive: http://classics.mit.edu//Aristotle/metaphysics.html, 16 iii 2018; the notion of the brazen circle is *circle made out of bronze*, a notion in which a reference to bronze is comprised.

as something 'liquid'. Apart from Plato, who, in describing the unordered principle upon which the One should impose its order, mentions the "Sea of dissimilarity" (τὸν τῆς ἀνομοιότητος [...] πόντον, *Pol.* 273d6-e1), the most straightforward example is obviously Heraclitus. Who, besides having composed the aphorism according to which «you cannot step twice into the same river»[27] (ποταμῶι γὰρ οὐκ ἔστιν ἐμβῆναι δὶς τῶι αὐτῶι, DK 22 B 91; cf. B 49a too), which is mentioned by Plato, *Crat.* 402a8-10, is also the philosopher who introduced the word "*lógos*" in philosophy:

> τοῦ δὲ λόγου τοῦδ᾽ ἐόντος ἀεὶ ἀξύνετοι γίνονται ἄνθρωποι καὶ πρόσθεν ἢ ἀκοῦσαι καὶ ἀκούσαντες τὸ πρῶτον· γινομένων γὰρ πάντων κατὰ τὸν λόγον τόνδε κτλ.
>
> This *lógos*, which is always real, is not understood by men; neither before they hear to it nor after they have heard: since everything happens in accordance with this *lógos* etc. (22 B 1 DK).

According to Heraclitus, the *lógos* in primary sense is the relation that binds together the parts of Nature in a consistent Whole;[28] in a derivative sense, the *lógos* is his own (of Heraclitus) discourse,[29] that declares and reveals the *lógos* which rules the Nature.

Heraclitus discourse declares that there is a nexus that binds together the many parts of Nature and guides them through their various interactions: moreover, in his fragments we more than once find an attention to the numerical ratios in which those interactions are articulated (22 B 31 DK); in many cases, the literary style of the fragment seems to focus on the numerical ratios between the parts of the sentence (cf. 22 B 30 DK). From a general point of view, from his fragments we can extract an idea of *lógos* as "relation": either as a relation between the parts of the speech, or as a relation that binds together in a single Cosmos the various parts of Nature; in Aristotle's terms, we could say: the *lógos* is, according to Heraclitus, the form of the cosmos; it has, on the cosmic level, the role that, in Aristotle's thought, the form will have in the little cosmos which the single living being is.

---

27 All translations of fragments of Heraclitus are here from BURNET, https://en.wikisource.org/wiki/Fragments_of_Heraclitus, 16 iii 2018.
28 Cf. 22 B DK *passim*, and above all 1 and 2.
29 In DK 22 B 1 cit., τοῦδ᾽ can refer both to the cosmic *lógos* with which the fragment deals and to the discourse that Heraclitus is here beginning to utter (this fragment is the *incipit* of the treatise).

According to the doctrine "everything is in flux", the world is a set of everchanging elements that produce a harmony in virtue of obeying the *lógos*, which, to each single element, in each single time, assigns some definite (and continuously changing) role.[30]

Aristotle assumes a similar stance, about living nature, in *Long.* 3, 465b25-27: «hence all things are at all times in a state of transition and are coming into being and passing away. The environment acts on them either favourably or antagonistically»[31] (διὸ πάντα ἀεὶ ἐν κινήσει ἐστί, καὶ γίνεται ἢ φθείρεται. τὸ δὲ περιέχον ἢ συμπράττει ἢ ἀντιπράττει); and afterwards he adds: «[the] animal is by nature humid» (τὸ ζῷόν ἐστι φύσει ὑγρόν, 5, 466a18).[32] In *de Gen. An.* IV 4, 772b19, too, we find a comparison between the living natures and the behaviour of liquids: the growth of the embryo, during which the form gets specified out of the matter of the mother's womb, is compared to a whirlpool in a river with its definite motion pattern which gets differentiated from the flux of the whole river («as the whirlpools in the rivers», καθάπερ ἐν τοῖς ποταμοῖς αἱ δῖναι, trans. of my own). So, if *"énulos"* recalls *"énudros"* (we cannot have any certainty, but it seems to me that Hicks's intuition was justified), we can explain the strange phraseology of Aristotle, here, as an implicit reference to the fact that the soul expounds its casual power in the flux of the metabolism, as a general form or project that dictates the ways and times of the various phenomena of the life of the organism, and that the phenomena of life are forms of rationality that are intrinsic to their matter, while each is a particular expression of this general order.

---

30 Cf. 22 B DK *passim*. The verb used by Heraclitus in describing the act of the Intelligence (γνώμη) that ruled «everything through everything» (πάντα διὰ πάντων) is ἐκυβέρνησε, «steered» (B41). The Whole is conceived as a sea, a sea which follows a route, as if it would sail through itself.

31 Translation by ROSS, *The Internet Classics Archive*: https://en.wikisource.org/wiki/On_Longevity_and_Shortness_of_Life .

32 Comparisons between the living nature and the behaviours of liquids are found also elsewhere in the *corpus*: cf. e.g. *de Part. An.* II 1, 647b2-4.

IX. *The Interpenetration of Matter and Form*

At this point we can well make a digression, and ask ourselves up to which point, in hylomorphism, the interpenetration of matter and form arrives.[33]

In the frame of Aristotle's psychology, every theory, about whichever function or affection of living beings, must be such that the function or affection in question should not be explainable only in terms of the material components of the body and of their interactions; it must be such that the function or affection should require the presence of material components; it must be such that the nature of these material components should be relevant for the realization of the function/affection.

What is not clear, is up to which level in the bottom the nature of the material components should be determined by the hypothetical necessity of realizing that form: in other terms, Aristotle does not tell us up to which level of detail the form puts its constraints on the features of the matter. At the deepest level of all, it is clear that the necessity of implementing the form can reach only the point of determining the ratios in which the simple bodies and their elementary qualities get mingled in producing the physical features that are necessary for the realization of a given tissue for the sake of the functions of the organ of which the tissue is part;[34] but it cannot require the presence of elementary bodies that are

---

33 A tentative classification of the exegeses offered about this point is to be found in RORTY (1992), p. 7-13; cf. especially p. 9, where Rorty classifies the interpreters in three categories: (1) those that hold that every kind of soul is an enmattered form in the sense that every psychic activity implies a material change; (2) those that hold that every kind of psychic activity implies a physical change but add that there is no direct correlation between types and/or tokens of psychic activities and types and/or tokens of material changes (every kind of psychic activity could, in principle, be instantiated in whichever kind of matter); (3) those that hold that Aristotle's interest is not in the relation between form-soul and matter but in the relation between form-soul and synolon: and therefore, since the synolon is different in each species, the relation between the synola and the forms will be different too. I think that we could well find also a lot of other criteria for classifying the various positions, that in the last forty years multiplied.

34 For instance, the organs of sight require to be nourished by the purest blood, for this is the blood that contains the highest degree of heat (*de Part. An.* II 10, 656b3ff.). The general principle that the physical composition and the qualities of the blood are differentiated, in the various animal species, for the sake of the way of life of each species, is stated in *de Part. An.* II 2, 647b29ff.

different from the four bodies described in the *De generatione et corruptione*.[35]

Moreover, I think that it is highly implausible that Aristotle could have thought that the realization of a generic function as sight requires a high level of detail in the definition of the organs: for he calls "eyes", ὄμματα (whose meaning is "organs of sight"[36]), both the eyes of the invertebrates and of the vertebrates (cf. *de Part. An.* I 13, 657b30ff.) whose difference, not only in macroscopic structure, but also in the tissues, is very clear also to observers that do not have a magnifying glass.[37]

But what should we say about a function which is as specifically defined as "seeing that particular shade of blue"? Such a function should be conceived as a subspecies of sight which is defined by its proper object: a colour which is different from all other colours.[38]

---

35 ACKRILL (1977), p. 175, thinks that the four simple bodies are too remote to be considered as matter of the living beings. CODE/MORAVCSIK (1992), p. 133 and 138ff. hold a similar position. But *Metaph.* Λ 5, 1071a13-14 explicitly states that earth, water, air and fire are the matter of each single specimen of man. An extensive answer to this puzzle, which calls for the distinction between many levels of matter can be found in WHITING (1992).

36 The identity of an organ lays in its function: cf. *Metaph.* Z 11, 1036b30-32, and *Mete.* IV 12, 390a10-15, where the example that is chosen is the eye, whose identity is given by the fact of being the instrument of sight. This point is fundamental for all the functionalist interpretations of Aristotle's psychology, whose "archetype" is NUSSBAUM/PUTNAM (1992), p. 35, n. 17: «For Aristotle, the organic parts of animals […] are *functionally defined*: the heart is whatever performs such and such functions in the animal» (p. 35).

37 As a matter of fact, Aristotle notices that the eyes of insects and some vertebrates are hard, differently from those of the majority of vertebrates (657b34). The principle of the multiple realization is implied by *de Part. An.* II 1, 647a20-21, and is thus commented on by NUSSBAUM/PUTNAM (1992), p. 33: «The same activity can be realized in such a variety of specific materials that there is not likely to be *one* thing that is just what perceiving red *is*, on the material level». COHEN (1992), too, accepts this line of reasoning: «the same psychic state may have different material realizations. In animals made of flesh, for example, the organ of touch is flesh; in other animals it is the part "analogous to flesh"» (p. 59).

38 Aristotle defines all the five senses on the basis of their proper objects: cf. *de An.* II 7-11, and SORABJI (1979), *passim*; it is very clear, on this point, the *incipit* of the discussion about touch, where the problem about the unicity or multiplicity of touch is explicitly connected with the problem of the variety of the species of tangible items (11, 422b17ff.). From this same principle should follow that the lowest species of sense-perceptions should be as many as the species of sense-objects.

Will not the physical structure and composition of the tissues of the eye of some species make that same species more or less able to perceive some colours than other colours? If so, the physical structure of the eye would be a major factor in the definition of the power of sight of that species. Well, Aristotle does not explicitly expound this argument about the eye; but he explicitly expounds it about the organ of touch, the flesh, and about the blood – the substance that, according to the *De partibus*, is the matter from which all the tissues and organs of the animal, *in primis* flesh, get formed: *de Part. An.* II 4, 651a13-15, states clearly that the nature of the blood (ἡ τυῦ αἵματος φύσις), is the cause (αἰτία), for the animals, of many effects that are relevant for the temper (κατὰ τὸ ἦθος) and for the power of sense-perception (κατὰ τὴν αἴσθησιν).[39]

And this is obvious, since one fundamental corollary of the doctrine of sense-perception as a "mean", i.e. as the presence of a physiological structure whose physical features would be "intermediate" between the features of the sense-objects,[40] is that the sense-organ is not able to spot sense-objects that have the same physical feature of the external sense-organ itself.[41] The animals whose fleshes (or the analogous) would differ in bodily constitution will have different blind-spots and will therefore be sensible to different degrees of heat and moisture.

But this conclusion could perhaps be threatened by observing that in principle nothing excludes that the same shade of blue or the same degree of heat can be perceived by eyes or fleshes that have different anatomical features, if these different anatomies are equally performing and if they embody the same "mean".

If this be so, the determination of the matter by the hypothetical necessity imposed by the form would never reach the ultimate point: the same form could always (at least in principle) be realized in different matters.

And this is why I believe that, in Aristotle's biology, the same function or form, identically defined on the basis of its object (not only on a generic level as e.g. "sight" or "touch", in which case the possibility of multiple

---

39 Aristotle states over and over again that the accurateness of sense-perception hangs on the physical composition of the blood: cf. *de Part. An.* II 2, 648a3-10; II 4, 650b19ff.; IV 10, 686a6-11. OPPEDISANO (2009) focuses on this point.

40 That the sense-organ must have physical features that are intermediate between the features of the sensible items is explicitly said in *de An.* II 11, 424a1ff. I expounded my interpretation of the *mesótēs* theory in FEOLA (2014) to which I refer for more details.

41 Cf. *de An.* II 11, 424a1-16.

realization is obvious; but also, e.g. as the power of seeing a particular shade of blue which corresponds to a precise ratio between black and white[42]) can (in principle) be realized in many different matters, if these matters share the qualities and features that allow the realization of that form:

> ὁ μὲν γὰρ λόγος ὅδε τοῦ πράγματος, ἀνάγκη δ᾽ εἶναι τοῦτον ἐν ὕλῃ τοιᾳδί, εἰ ἔσται·
>
> the *lógos* of the thing, if it is to be, must be realized in a matter with some determinate qualities (403b2-3: tr. of my own).

The adjective τοιᾳδί, which would *prima facie* seem to prove with a direct textual evidence my thesis, can be interpreted in two different ways, which, if applied to our problem, would lead to two opposite conclusions: it can be meant as "matter of some determinate species", in which case Aristotle would be denying the possibility of multiple realization; or else it can be meant as "matter with some determinate qualities", in which case he would be saying that the form requires the presence of a matter whichever that is endowed with the relevant features.[43] Luckily, the same doctrine is reformulated in II 2, 414a26, where we find, this time without ambiguity, that the actuality (ἐντελέχεια) of each thing must be realized «in the appropriate matter» (ἐν τῇ οἰκείᾳ ὕλῃ): this time the Greek sentence is quite clear in specifying that the relevant point is the appropriateness of matter to the realization of form.

Thus, both textual evidences and the reasons we deployed till now bring us to conclude that in hylomorphism the form puts some constraints on the matter that is apt for its bodily implementation, but such

---

42 As it is well known, Aristotle thought that all the colours derive from the many ratios, that are infinite in number, in which black and white can mix to each other (cf. *Sens.* 3, *passim*).

43 Ross' paraphrasis, according to which the *lógos* (which is understood by Ross as the "definition of the thing") «must be embodied in a particular kind of matter, if it is to exist» (1961, p. 164, *ad* 403a29) seems to me to leave the question open, because it substitutes the ambiguity of the Greek with a similar ambiguity in English; HICKS (1988), p. 202, *ad* b3, understands the passage in the sense that the form requires "the appropriate matter", and seems thus to favour the multiple realization; it is a merit of Hicks (*ibid.*) to recall II 2, 414a26, which I think is resolutive. POLANSKY (2007), *ad* 403a24-b19, p. 58, favours multiple realization: «since many different sorts of plants and animals have psychical functions, there is considerable flexibility in the sort of matter capable of supporting such functions».

constraints never reach the point of always and completely forbidding the possibility of multiple realization.

Moreover, another line of reasoning about this point seems particularly compelling to me: Aristotle acknowledged that also the same physical instance of the same form (the same living item) can get realized in matters that, from one point of time to another, are numerically different: this is proved by the attention he pays, in works as *De longitudine et brevitate vitæ*, *De juventute et senectute*, *De vita et morte* e *De respiratione*, to the phenomenon of continuous replacement of matter in the body, due to metabolism. So, the replacement of matter in the same living being, due to metabolism, is a good proof that Aristotle's theory accepts, at the deepest level of the organism's composition, the principle of multiple realization.

X. Conclusions

In the critical discussion about the matter-form relation, what is most emphasized by the interpreters is the role of matter as a condition of possibility for the realization of form. This aspect is clearly pivotal and crucial for articulating the concept of hypothetical necessity.

But, on the basis of the lexical analogy between "*énulos*" and "*énudros*", and of the Heraclitean tones in our Aristotelean passage, I think we can conclude that what Aristotle wants to stress here, by calling the affections of the soul "*lógoi énuloi*", is another aspect of the matter-form relation: the role of form as principle of permanence during change, and as a factor that regulates the change.[44]

It is precisely the nomological value of the form in change that implies (and explains) that other role of the form: the role of form as the antecedent of the "if ... so" which grounds the hypothetical necessity; what is in change has matter, and what has matter must obey to some relations that regulate the relation between form and matter. The role of form as a

---

44 This aspect of Aristotle's hylomorphism is acutely stressed by FURTH (1988), who describes the living beings as "knots" of greater level of complexity of form in the flux of the sublunary world and as «highly convoluted but relatively stable eddies in the general commingling-and-separation» (p. 172). Worth of remembering is the attempt of theoretical synthesis and, within some limits, also of formalization, of the doctrine of the nomological role of the form in the change of living beings, that Furth proposes in the end chapter of his book (pp. 268-284).

factor that rules and regulates the change explains the fact that matter (whose presence is directly entailed by the possibility of change), if it has to implement that form by passing through that given change, has to satisfy some precise binding conditions: the conditions that are dictated by the form.[45]

Let us see (again) the example of *lógos énulos* provided by Aristotle:

> τὸ ὀργίζεσθαι κίνησίς τις τοῦ τοιουδὶ σώματος ἢ μέρους ἢ δυνάμεως ὑπὸ τοῦδε ἕνεκα τοῦδε.
> Anger [is] a movement *m* in this body or part [of the body] or power [of the body] produced by *a* in order to produce *b* (403a26-27).

In describing all this as a "*lógos*", Aristotle affirms, first of all, that *a, b, m* must bear some definite relation to each other ("in order to", "produced by"); and, by adding "*énulos*", he states that such a relation is realized, immersed, in a matter. If this relation is not immersed in a matter, we cannot have any instance of anger, because anger is the reaction of an organism to some environmental stimulations, whose biological meaning is provided by the fact that the organism must react to some changes in the environment (e.g. a beat on the nose) by beginning some other changes (e.g. by disposing its own body in an attitude of defence against eventual other beats and, if necessary, by preventing them by putting the enemy in a condition of harmlessness).

An affection like anger is a step endowed with a definite role in a process (a reaction of defence) among the many processes that constitute the life of the animal (i.e. in the sum of the processes that involve the animal in a mutual relation with its environment). These are the processes that determinate and regulate the reactions that allow the organism to effectively answer to the environment, in this way allowing the organism itself to proceed toward its specific goals. Animals, as all natural beings, are beings structured by nature in order to be immersed in a continuously changing (and challenging) environment. In Aristotle's words,

> αἰσθητὸν γάρ τι τὸ ζῷον, καὶ ἄνευ κινήσεως οὐκ ἔστιν ὁρίσασθαι, διὸ οὐδ' ἄνευ τῶν μερῶν ἐχόντων πώς.
> for an animal is something perceptible, and it is not possible to define it without reference to movement – nor, therefore, without reference to the parts' being in a certain state. (*Metaph.* Z 11, 1036b28-30;

---

45 For a detailed analysis of the concept of "hypothetical necessity" cf. COOPER (1985).

tr. by W.D. Ross, http://classics.mit.edu/Aristotle/metaphysics.7.vii.ht
ml, 16 iii 2018).

References

ACKRILL, J.L. (1977). Aristotle's Definition of Psuche. In: Barnes, J.; Schofield, M.; Sorabji, R. (eds.). *Articles on Aristotle, 4. Psychology and Aesthetics*. London. Duckworth, 1979, p. 65-75.

BONITZ, H. (1870). *Index Aristotelicus* (secunda editio). Berlin. Reimer (reprint: Graz. Akademische Druck und Verlangsanstalt, 1955).

BURNET, J. (ed.) (1900-1907). *Platonis opera*. Oxford. Clarendon Press.

_____ (trans.) (1920). *Early Greek Philosophy*. London, A.&C. Black Ltd; the Internet Classical Archive: https://en.wikisource.org/wiki/Fragments_of_Heraclitus, 16 iii 2018.

BURNYEAT, M.F. (1992). Is an Aristotelian Philosophy of Mind Still Credible? In NUSSBAUM/RORTY (1992), p. 15-26.

CODE, A.; MORAVCSIK, J. (1992). Explaining Various Forms of Living. In: NUSSBAUM/RORTY (1992), p. 129-146.

COHEN, S.M. (1992). Hylomorphism and Functionalism. In: NUSSBAUM/RORTY (1992), p. 57-73

COOPER, J. (1985). Hypothetical Necessity. In: Gotthelf, A. (ed.), *Aristotle on Nature and Living Beings. Philosophical and Historical Studies. Presented to David M. Balme on His Seventieth Birthday*. Pittsburgh. Mathesis, p. 151-167.

DIELS, H.; KRANZ, W. (1934) (eds.). *Die Fragmente der Vorsokratiker*, vol. I. Berlin. Weidmannsche Buchhandlung.

FEOLA, G. (2014). Aristotele sull'intenzionalità elementare: la sensazione dei 'propri' e la teoria della 'medietà'. *Documenti e studi sulla tradizione filosofica medievale*, 25, p. 1-28.

FURTH, M. (1988). *Substance, Form and Psyche: an Aristotelian Metaphysics*. Cambridge. Cambridge University Press.

GABBE, M. (2016). Aristotle on the Metaphysics of Emotions. *Apeiron*, 49 (1), p. 33-56.

HICKS, R.D. (ed.) (1907). Aristotle. *De Anima*, with translation, introduction and notes. Cambridge. Cambridge University Press (repr. by Ayer Company, Salem, 1988).

HUDE, C. (ed.) (1908), *Herodoti Historiae*. Oxford. Clarendon Press.

LIDDELL, H.; SCOTT, R.; JONES, H.S. (1996). *A Greek-English Lexicon (with a revised supplement)*. Oxford. Clarendon Press.

LOUIS, P. (ed.) (1956). Aristote. *Les parties des animaux*, texte établi et traduit. Paris. Les Belles Lettres.

_____ (ed.) (1964). Aristote. *Histoire des animaux*, tome I, livres I-IV, texte établi et traduit. Paris. Les Belles Lettres.

NUSSBAUM M.C.; PUTNAM, H. (1992). Changing Aristotle's Mind. In: NUSS-BAUM/RORTY (1992), p. 27-56

_____; RORTY, A.O. (eds.) (1992). *Essays on Aristotle's* De Anima. Oxford. Clarendon Press.

OPPEDISANO, C. (2009). Sensazioni e percezioni in Aristotele. *Rivista di estetica* 42, p. 117-139.

PECK, A.L. (1942, 1990). Aristotle. *Generation of Animals*. Cambridge (Mass.), London. Harvard University Press.

POLANSKY, R. (2007). Aristotle's *De Anima*, Cambridge. Cambridge University Press.

RORTY, A.O. (1992). *De Anima*: its Agenda and its Recent Interpreters. In: NUSS-BAUM/RORTY (1992), p. 7-13.

ROSS, W.D. (1924, 1966). Aristotle's *Metaphysics*, a revised text with introduction and commentary. Oxford. Clarendon Press; The Internet Classical Archive: http://classics.mit.edu//Aristotle/metaphysics.html, 16 iii 2018

_____ (1928). *The Works of Aristotle Translated into English*. Oxford. Clarendon Press. The Internet Classical Archive: http://classics.mit.edu/Aristotle/metaphysics.7.vii.html , 16 iii 2018.

_____ (1955). Aristotle. *Parva naturalia*, with introduction and commentary. Oxford. Clarendon Press.

_____ (1961). Aristotle. *De anima*, edited, with introduction and commentary. Oxford. Clarendon Press.

SORABJI, R. (1979). Aristotle on Demarcating the Five Senses. In: Barnes, J.; Schofield, M.; Sorabji, R. (eds.), *Articles on Aristotle, 4. Psychology and Aesthetics*. London. Duckworth, 1979, p. 76-92.

WHITING. J. (1992). Living Bodies. In: NUSSBAUM/RORTY (1992), p. 75-91.

Physiology and the Exemplar:
Aristotle on Recognition and Moral Progress

Roberto Medda

Aristotle's moral philosophy has been often considered as a form of exemplarism. The *phronimos* is a benchmark for the citizen of the *polis* and in particular for the youth. However, this is just part of the picture, because Aristotle does not use a keyword we would expect him to use, *paradeigma*, nor does he spell out a theory of moral development in the adult. Moreover, it will be necessary to bridge the gap between the role of exemplars in Aristotle's ethics and the cognitive capacities that enable an agent to interpret another subject's conduct as a standard for himself or herself. In this respect, considering the psychophysiological background of exemplarism will be of the utmost importance. *Phantasia* will play a prominent part, because of its mimetic potential towards the virtuous. The importance of *phantasia* has been already acknowledged in a recent work by Jessica Moss,[1] but what is striking in Aristotelian scholarship is that it is very difficult to find a unified account of physiology, psychology and ethics. My contribution here, of course, is more a path of research than a complete programme, but it may be helpful to establish what is missing. On the one hand, the scholar has access to excellent works on motivation that encompass psychological and physiological aspects of the phenomenon of intentional movement;[2] on the other hand, when talking about ethics, while there is a certain resistance to speak of psychology, with notable exceptions,[3] physiology is for the most part neglected. What can be well described as a bias against psychology is explained by Moss as a fear by interpreters to entangle Aristotle's ethics with «arcane, empirically falsifiable, or otherwise suspect» details of his psychology. However, in defending Aristotle's psychology, the author confirms the bias against

---

1 MOSS (2012).
2 CORCILIUS (2008) and CORCILIUS/GREGORIC (2013).
3 HANKINSON (1990) and MOSS (2012).

physiology,[4] somewhat losing the unity of the Stagirite. I will try to apply this method to the recognition and the role of exemplars in Aristotle, a topic much debated in contemporary ethics.

I.

A well-established branch of today's moral reflection is known as virtue ethics. In one way or another, the authors referring to this option resort to ancient philosophical models in order to challenge deontologism and utilitarianism (or, broadly construed, consequentialism), considered the paradigms to overcome.[5] The aim of this paper is not to discuss virtue ethics in itself, or the many varieties thereof that have been conceived, but rather to assess how some of these modern authors use Aristotle on some specific points in order to elaborate original ethical theories. In particular, it is interesting to note that Aristotle's *phronimos* has been recently used by ZAGZEBSKI (2017) as a model – admittedly, only one of the models – for her exemplarist moral theory. Reading *Eth. Nic.* VI 6, 1141a20-1141b8, she claims that the *phronimos*, in opposition to the *sophos* («often useless in practical matters»), «can be used as a touchstone for moral decision making».[6]

The author also considers Plato. Plato's ethics certainly had exemplars too. In the first place, Socrates takes centre stage in of many Platonic dialogues and represents the model of the philosopher in a city in turmoil. The picture that emerges from many of the dialogues (*Apology*, *Crito* and others, but in particular the *Republic*) is one of great complexity, but the outcome is a peculiar twist of the traditional *paideia* towards a mathematical and intellectual search for a stable truth. In Zagzebski's opinion, Plato in some sense uses Socrates to convey a set of values through an admirable exemplar.[7] However, it can be said that Plato does not spell out a theory of motivation that can be easily framed within the ethics of virtue. The ideal city is certainly a paradigm (*Resp.* 592b) and so are the virtuous citizens that live in that city (435a-b), but Plato tends to identify just ac-

---

4   MOSS (2012), p. XV: «Aristotle's moral psychology as I will interpret it is, *physiological details aside*, very much a going one» (emphasis is mine).
5   HURSTHOUSE (1999), p. 4; CARR/ARTHUR/KRISTJÁNSSON (2017), p. 3. This idea can be traced back to ANSCOMBE (1981).
6   ZAGZEBSKI (2017), p. 2.
7   ZAGZEBSKI (2017), p. 67.

tions as those that establish and nurture a just trait of the character, rather than arguing that a just character leads to just actions.[8] In that respect, shaping desires from a very young age is more important than considering motivation in the adult, and this is one of the reasons why establishing the correct *curriculum studiorum* is so important in the architecture of the *Republic*. Aristotelian focus instead noticeably shifts to deliberation, choice and context-based psychological drives, which are more appealing to the advocates of virtue ethics.

If one wants to recognize exemplars in Aristotle's philosophy the task might be both easier and more difficult at the same time. It is easier because, in his *Ethics*, the excellence of the *phronimos* is clearly the model for any ethical progress. *Phronêsis* and the *phronimos* are not thoroughly discussed until Book VI of the *Nicomachean Ethics*. This is meaningful in the structure of the work. At the beginning we find the goal of ethical life, human good, which is happiness. In Aristotle's opinion happiness is an activity of the soul that fulfils the highest capacities a human being can exercise, namely rational activities performed at their best. The necessary habitual state of the soul for flourishing as a human being is virtue and Aristotle deals with virtue in books II and IV. In the middle of this discussion there is a detailed study of voluntariness, deliberation and choice: this book (III) suggests that practical knowledge can never be separated from action. After that, there is an important analysis of justice, and only in the sixth book does the philosopher tackle the question of practical wisdom, *phronêsis*. All the pieces scattered throughout the preceding books are now put together in a single concept and in a single individual: wisdom and the wise person. If happiness is an activity, wisdom is a *hexis*, a stable possession of a soul, more precisely «a true state involving reason, a practical one, concerned with what is good or bad for a human being» (VI 5, 1140b5-6). In particular, this state concerns the capacity of choosing correctly what is good in each situation. Wisdom is the architectonic practical virtue: in a passage at the end of book VI (1144b32-1145a2) Aristotle states that natural virtues can be found individually or severally in a person, but if a person is to be termed virtuous in the strict sense then he must possess all the virtues. I cannot go into detail on virtues and wisdom, but Aristotle has a clear idea of how a wise person should be:

---

8 These observations are drawn by WHITE (2015). Cf. also COOPER (1984) for an account of motivation in Plato.

εἰ δ'⁹ ὑγιεινὸν μὲν καὶ ἀγαθὸν ἕτερον ἀνθρώποις καὶ ἰχθύσι, τὸ δὲ
λευκὸν καὶ εὐθὺ ταὐτὸν ἀεί, καὶ τὸ σοφὸν ταὐτὸ πάντες ἂν εἴποιεν,
φρόνιμον δὲ ἕτερον· τὰ γὰρ περὶ αὐτὸ ἕκαστα τὸ εὖ θεωροῦν φησὶν εἶναι
φρόνιμον, καὶ τούτῳ ἐπιτρέψει αὐτά.

Moreover, if what is healthy or good is different for people and for
fish, but what is white or straight is always the same, everyone would
say that what is theoretically wise (*sophon*) is the same, while what is
practically wise (*phronimon*) is different. For when someone considers
well the particular things that concerns him they call that practically
wise, and will entrust such matters to him (*Eth. Nic.* VI 7,
1141a22-26).

The distinction between the object and the kind of knowledge gained by
an intellectual grasp or by a practical cognition is sharp, and so is the resulting action of the knower; however, as I said, the task of finding what
is the concrete model for wisdom is easy because what Aristotle says
seems legitimate in general terms, but difficult because in Book VI he
rarely mentions examples that can be credited with such complete virtue
and he gives us very few hints of what one should do in particular contexts.[10] The difference with the treatment of Book IV on particular virtues
is startling. Every virtue, and every excess and defect relative to each

9 I follow here the text of the *codex* Marcianus 213 (εἰ δ') – instead of the other
   manuscripts, which have εἰ δὴ – as Rackham and many modern translator do
   (e.g. Natali, Irwin, Reeve). These remarks are in any case not greatly relevant in
   the present context. More important is the understanding of the text after the
   ano teleia. In the whirl of emendations proposed, I adopt Bywater's text, which
   remains, in my opinion, the most economical and intelligent option, writing τὰ
   instead of the first τὸ found in the manuscripts. Also notice that, for the sake of
   intelligibility, I did not translate into the neutral gender, but Aristotle uses it because immediately afterwards he mentions that some "wise" animals share a sort
   of capacity to foresee the future (*dunamis pronoêtikê*).

10 It is true that Aristotle says that «we suppose (οἰόμεθα) that Pericles and the like
   to be practically wise» (*Eth. Nic.* VI 5, 1140b7-8). However, as the text makes
   clear, they are representative of that kind of wisdom that is political, in so far as
   they are able to conduct an *oikos* and political affairs, while «it is held to be practical wisdom especially the one that is concerned with oneself, the individual (ἡ
   περὶ αὐτὸν καὶ ἕνα)» (*Eth. Nic.* VI 8, 1141b29-30). If this is true, οἰόμεθα should
   be taken as a sign of an *endoxon*: see also IRWIN (1999), 242. The same can be
   said for *An. Post.* II 13, 97b15-25, where Aristotle mentions Alcibiades (besides
   Achilles and Ajax), and Lysander and Socrates as examples of two sorts *megalopsuchia*: the salient traits that mark them out seem to be not to tolerate being dis-
   respected on the one hand and indifference towards good or bad fortune on the

virtue, is accompanied by examples. In addition, Aristotle says that in his own language, Greek, not every excess or defect has a name, but that the philosopher should consider them because they occur (or, in some cases, may occur) in real life practices. Therefore, whereas in his study of particular virtues *endoxa* (opinions accepted by a relevant audience) and dialectical discussion have a place, when it comes to *phronêsis* we seem to be on a more theoretical level, a philosophical project, I would say. It is not surprising that when Aristotle in Book VII tackles the issues of ethically foul behaviour (*akolasia* – intemperance – and *akrasia* – lack of self-control) he again uses the method of Book IV, even with trivial examples, such as the opportunity of tasting sweet food (e.g. *Eth. Nic.* VII 3, 1147a29-35) or the drunken reciter of Empedocles' verses (*Eth. Nic.* VII 3, 1147b12). Regarding the *phronimos*, we are left with incomplete information because a new path leading to practical wisdom is being traced by Aristotle.

The lack of exemplars also emerges from the absence of the word *paradeigma* in Book VI. Aristotle does not use *paradeigma* for several reasons. The most relevant one is the necessity to downplay the centrality this word had in Plato's ontological and epistemological philosophy. *Paradeigmata* are the Forms, and when Aristotle, as in *Metaph.* A 9, 991a26, criticizes Platonic *eide*, he says that the relation between model and copy applied to Forms and sensible entities is a mere use of empty words (κενολογεῖν) and of poetical metaphors (μεταφορὰς [...] ποιητικάς). Thus Aristotle denies the application of the word *paradeigma* to general/particular relations, but he uses a different meaning of the word, namely that which expresses the relation between particular and particular. In *An. Pr.* II 24, Aristotle sketches out the theoretical framework for the concept and provides us with a clear illustration. It is evil to make war on one's neighbours. Just as the war the Thebans visited on their neighbours – the Phocians – was evil, so the war the Athenians wish to wage against their neighbour – Thebes – is evil. The basis for an example is similarity. In one case in the past the fight against neighbours was a failure, so one should always avoid this kind of war. This is plainly a very weak argument to establish the general point, because the proof relies on a single case. Induction has the same structure, but considers all known cases.

other. Again, the discussion looks doxastic and far from the positive treatment of *megalopsuchia* in *Eth. Nic.* IV 3 and *Eth. Eud.* III 5. About Pericles, see also AUBENQUE (1963), p. 51-56.

Nonetheless, examples come in handy for rhetorical discourse. In *Rhet.* II 20 they are described as persuasive means to end a speech, in particular deliberative speeches. In this genre the orator must persuade the listener to take a correct decision, and general statements are often insufficient to persuade. An example is a valid testimony (μάρτυρος) to make the point more realistic and viable. As a matter of fact, it helps to chart a future course of events on the basis of past occurrences that the listener can represent to themselves. We will see below that this continuity of experience is grounded in our cognitive capacities, in particular memory, and therefore in *phantasia*. But let us set *phantasia* aside for a moment and sum up the role of exemplars in Aristotle's ethical philosophy.

The starting point of the Stagirite's practical reflection is that the subject always acts here and now, in a specific situation (*Eth. Nic.* II 7, 1107a29-33). The particulars (καθ' ἕκαστα) are non-reproducible and contingent and this fact bears important consequences for Aristotle's theory of action. The exercise of one's reason is not sufficient for a successful result (even the *phronimos* is fallible after all),[11] because one cannot master all the causal connections that contributed to one's action or those that will be generated in the world as a result. Therefore, the role model of the *phronimos* has to be dynamic and context-based. The fact that we cannot find exemplars for perfect virtue, but only for particular virtues, is not a major problem in his theory. Examples, after all, work from particular to particular, from the action of a given wise man to my own particular experience: they are similar, but never identical.[12]

This poses some problems to virtue ethicists and accounts for Zagzebski's shift from endorsing the Aristotelian theory as a kind of exemplarism to say that she is «not suggesting that Aristotle intended to offer an exemplarist moral theory».[13] In order to meet the requirements for an exemplarist theory, Aristotle should concede to the single action of the *phronimos* a normativity it does not possess. The agent implements a course of conduct because of his own character, which may differ from another's needs, desires, personal history, public role. As a consequence, Aristotle shows very little interest in the "reverse engineering" of a just action performed by the wise for the sake of moral development. This seems to be

11 Cf. DREFCINSKI (1996).
12 As a general remark, this is meant to be a direct challenge to the so-called "Socratic intellectualism" (e.g. *Eth. Nic.* I 1, 1095a6), in which theoretical knowledge is a sufficient condition for just actions.
13 ZAGZEBSKI (2017), p. 23.

in contrast with some neo-Aristotelian reconstructions. For example, Merritt, following Hursthouse, thinks that self-evaluation and self-discrepancy in respect to the *phronimos* play a great role in the moral development of a mature agent.[14] The subject evaluates the distance between himself and the exemplar and is constantly engaged in a process of adjusting his conduct towards a "desired self". The scholar then just leaves Aristotle and turns to contemporary psychology in order to show how *thinking* as a virtuous person can be attained. In Aristotle, as I will try to show in the next section, the recognition of the *phronimos* is not a question of perception or of a purely intellectual act. Moreover, Aristotle does not adopt a first-person or an aspirational perspective, but rather seeks a criterion to discern who is practically wise or not.

Coming back to *Eth. Nic.* VI 7, 1141a22-26, one important characteristic of the *phronimos* is the correct consideration of the particular matters in relation to him, which we *entrust* to him. Aristotle is clearly not referring to personal interest: after all, what would be the point of handing over decisions about another human being's welfare, which resides in him in the first place? Actually, the wise man's peculiar trait is to deliberate well not on particular fields of application (κατὰ μέρος) – this is what the possessor of a *technê* does – but on the good life in general (ὅλως) (1140a25-28). Just like we do not permit ourselves to explain to ants or bees how should they live, because they have in themselves the *telos* towards which their acts are organized, similarly the *phronimos* shows what a flourishing life is and everyone in the community should then promote this kind of life. Aristotle's project is political no less than ethical: «political art and wisdom are the same disposition, but their being is not the same» (VI 8, 1141b23-24) and «presumably one's own good cannot exist without household management, nor without a political community» (1142a9-10). In stressing that there are several species of "political wisdom" – related, but different from what is primarily called wisdom – Aristotle wants to establish that the *phronimos* must be conceived as a fulfilled individual but also that he guarantees public trustfulness and reliability. This is why Aristotle says that we entrust to «Pericles and people of that sort» decisions over what is good for a human being.

Then, we will likely shape a pedagogy in order to form more citizens like them, though the impact on already formed characters will be limited. In addition, even if we consider the *phronimos* as an actual model for

---

14 MERRITT (2009), p. 33-36.

the adult agent, some features seem to be beyond the reach of a person with an engrained character, because they act as second nature in the wise. What has been deliberated should be carried out quickly, whereas practical calculation can be slow (*Eth. Nic.* VI 9, 1142b4-5; 1142b26-27), although good deliberators strike us for their prompt reactions. «Sometimes, in virtue of representations or thoughts in the soul, just as if seeing them (ὥσπερ ὁρῶν), one calculates and deliberates future things with reference to things which are present» (*de An.* III 7, 431b6-8), just like geometers do with figures in search of a proof (*Eth. Nic.* III 5, 1112b20-21).[15] The visual analogy makes clear that the deliberation of a *phronimos* tends to be effortless and typically fast, in particular when circumstances require it (and this is often the case for political decisions). This picture leads to the issue at stake from the outset: for several reasons the *phronimos* is not a prescriptive model for moral development of the adult. The conditions of his action are unique, the character that expresses the choices is entrenched in the agent in a way that an admirer cannot easily imitate and the focus on the public relevance of the actions of the *phronimos* stresses how Aristotle suggests more an ethics between less or more morally successful peers, rather than an ethics of aspiration and progress.

II.

Even when these restrictions are given, it is difficult to deny any exemplarity to the wise. But how can a *phronimos* be a model if the conditions of his choices and actions cannot be reproduced? The question is connected with a broader issue, that of the teachability of virtue, a central theme for the Sophists and for Plato (e.g. *Protagoras* and *Meno*). From the Stagirite's standpoint it is not possible to convey the content of virtue through general statements concerning virtue, but, as Myles Burnyeat wrote in the seminal paper *Aristotle on Learning to Be Good*, «what Aristotle is pointing to is our ability to internalize from a scattered range of particular cases a general evaluative attitude which is not reducible to rules or precepts».[16] So to understand moral development one should first take

---

15 This analogy is present to NATALI (1989), p. 174 and 178, n. 72 and has been thoroughly explained by CATTANEI (2009).
16 BURNYEAT (1980), p. 72.

a step back to the process of habituation,[17] and then to the psychological structure of our learning and recognition.

Concerning this last point, teaching the content of virtue is impossible because every action must be calibrated to the situation. However, one can evaluate a course of conduct and regard it as exemplar. One of the main drives that has been considered central for moral progress is the concept of *zêlos*, "emulation".[18] In *Rhet.* II 11, Aristotle describes emulation – the counterpart of envy, treated in the preceding chapter – as follows:

> εἰ γάρ ἐστιν ζῆλος λύπη τις ἐπὶ φαινομένῃ παρουσίᾳ ἀγαθῶν ἐντίμων καὶ ἐνδεχομένων αὐτῷ λαβεῖν περὶ τοὺς ὁμοίους τῇ φύσει, οὐχ ὅτι ἄλλῳ ἀλλ' ὅτι οὐχὶ καὶ αὐτῷ ἔστιν (διὸ καὶ ἐπιεικές ἐστιν ὁ ζῆλος καὶ ἐπιεικῶν, τὸ δὲ φθονεῖν φαῦλον καὶ φαύλων· ὁ μὲν γὰρ αὑτὸν παρασκευάζει διὰ τὸν ζῆλον τυγχάνειν τῶν ἀγαθῶν, ὁ δὲ τὸν πλησίον μὴ ἔχειν διὰ τὸν φθόνον), ἀνάγκη δὴ ζηλωτικοὺς μὲν εἶναι τοὺς ἀξιοῦντας αὑτοὺς ἀγαθῶν ὧν μὴ ἔχουσιν, <ἐνδεχομένων αὐτοῖς λαβεῖν>· οὐδεὶς γὰρ ἀξιοῖ τὰ φαινόμενα ἀδύνατα (διὸ οἱ νέοι καὶ οἱ μεγαλόψυχοι τοιοῦτοι).

> For if emulation is a sort of distress at the apparent presence among others like him by nature of things honoured and possible for a person to acquire, a distress present not because another has them but because the emulator does not (for this reason emulation is good and belongs to good people, whereas envy is bad and belongs to bad people; for the one, through emulation, prepares himself to secure the good things in question, while the other, through envy, prepares himself to stop his neighbours from having them), [if emulation is this] it is then necessary that those are emulous who deem themselves worthy of the good things they do not have, (if it is possible for them to attain them). For no one deems himself worthy of things manifestly impossible. For this reason the young and the high-minded are inclined to emulation (*Rhet.* II 11, 1388a32-b3).

There are many crucial points for our discussion in this passage. In virtually every definition of the affections of the soul (πάθη τῆς ψυχῆς) there is cognitive content and a desiderative component. In the present situation,

17 Cf. LEUNISSEN (2012) (2017).
18 E.g. ZAGZEBSKI (2015); IRWIN (2015) argues against the relevance of the concept in Plato and Aristotle.

distress (λύπη) is the precursor of a desire to attain the same goods that others have and I am in a position to attain, but in the definition of *zêlos* there is also a cognitive evaluation. When Aristotle says that the presence of valuable goods in other people is «apparent» (ἐπὶ φαινομένῃ παρουσίᾳ) he means that the agent evaluates this presence as real and manifest, given his understanding of the environment.[19] This representation is entrusted to a faculty that links perception and reason: *phantasia*.[20] The agent reacts to the stimulus in so far as it is recognized not just as pure information, but as something that concerns him.

Let us linger over Aristotle's general attitude towards this kind of phenomenon for a moment. The needs of contemporary philosophy tend to privilege the psychological side of the Aristotelian description and overlook the physical explanation given by the philosopher, in order not to get entangled in his somewhat whimsical physiological account of motivation and self-motion. However, Aristotle would reproach anybody attempting this operation for being like the dialectician, who describes what is essentially psychophysical, like anger, only by the macroscopical causal antecedents from which springs the affection and by the changes that the subject will carry out in his environment, while totally neglecting the material facet of the process.[21] Thus we shall pay proper attention to the hylomorphic nature of passions, emotions and intentional acts in Aristotle.[22] In brief, the philosopher had in mind a cardiocentric system. The incoming stimuli received by the peripheral sense organs are trans-

---

19 Other examples can be found in the *Rhetoric* for the definitions of anger («a desire, accompanied by distress, for *apparent* retaliation because of an *apparent* slight directed without justification towards oneself or those near to one», *Rhet.* II 2, 1378a30-32) and pity («a certain distress at an *apparent* evil, destructive or distressful, happening to one who does not deserve it, and which someone might expect himself or one of his own to suffer, and this when it *appears* close at hand», *Rhet.* II 8, 1385b13-16). The definition of anger is notoriously vexed: I follow Kennedy's translation (KENNEDY, 2006) with modest adjustments. For a textual appraisal see WISSE (1989), p. 69.

20 For a discussion of other occurrences of *phainesthai* and its cognates in the *Rhetoric* see MOSS (2012), p. 75-84.

21 *De An.* I 1, 403a24-b16. The importance of this methodological remark has been well argued by CHARLES (2008) and (2009), and recently defended by MINGUCCI (2015), in particular p. 55-112.

22 This has been accomplished by CORCILIUS/GREGORIC (2013) for a general model of animal motion and by GREGORIC/KUHAR (2014) for the physical details. For an older, but still enlightening view on the topic cf. also MANULI/VEGETTI (2009).

mitted through the blood vessels (or a different system of channels, the *poroi*) to the heart, where the information arrives and then lies deposited.[23] In the first sensorium a thermic alteration takes place. The heating or chilling in the heart arising from perception enhances or disrupts the internal equilibrium and can be considered as the material counterpart of pleasure and pain. Then a consequent expansion or contraction of the *symphyton pneuma* eventually triggers the tension or relaxation of *neura* (sinews or tendons) that move the organic parts in reaction to the environment.[24]

Implausible as it may seem, this model meets several major Aristotelian demands within his psychological model. The paramount importance of the blood and of the heart reconciles the need for a dynamic[25] and virtually ubiquitous bodily system with the possibility of having an *arche* of intentional and voluntary motions, a cornerstone of his ethics (e.g. *Eth. Nic.* III 1, 1110a15-18). In addition, the system I briefly sketched out expresses both cognitive and desiderative elements of motivation in a way that can account for its psychophysical nature. This should be taken into consideration by those who want to propose an Aristotelian model of moral progress. In general, those positions suppose a rational agency that can typically master the impact of the environment on the agent and thus pick out the best candidates for emulation. However, the structure of character and intentional acts in Aristotle is a little more complicated than this. Firstly, some acts supposedly originate from perception of what is naturally good or bad for the animal or the human being: given the right internal conditions, the animal discriminates between what is wholesome or harmful and acts accordingly.[26] Secondly, and more de-

---

23 The involvement of physical alteration in perception is at the centre of a wide debate that cannot even be summarised here (cf. CASTON, 2005 and ZUCCA, 2015, p. 119-197). For my present purpose, I shall maintain that perception requires to be at least accompanied by a physical alteration. A further complication is that the question of the transmission from peripheral organ (in particular the distal ones) to the heart is not properly addressed by Aristotle, leaving open the possibility that there are two candidates: the blood or the *pneuma*.

24 This is, in my opinion, the scheme underlying *MA* 8, 702a17-19.

25 Of course Aristotle did not conceive blood circulation as we do since Harvey, but nonetheless hematic fluids are not static for him, since they carry the nourishment from the heart to the periphery. Cf. GREGORIC (2007), p. 44-45.

26 This is the interpretation given by CORCILIUS/GREGORIC (2013), and opposed to that put forward by MOSS (2012), who implies that in every desire there is an additional evaluative cognition.

cisively, the greater part of our behaviour relies on a "second nature". The elder, the expert and the wise develop a habitual state of foreseeing future outcomes of the present situation with the «eye of the soul» in order to plan a successful course of conduct (*Eth. Nic.* VI 13, 1144a23-36) and for this reason we believe in their undemonstrated claims no less than in actual demonstrations (*Eth. Nic.* VI 12, 1143b11-14). In general, the habitual state of our character is conceived by Aristotle as so rooted and stubborn that an inattentive observer might be tempted to consider that the actions flowing from an evil character are involuntary, albeit that it was possible for him not to have developed this kind of character in the first place (*Eth. Nic.* III 5, 1114a3-21). And even if in sleep the perceptive and desiderative parts are incomplete in their activities, the residual movements cause better *phantasiai* in good people than those of bad ones, unless a physical impairment occurs (*Eth. Eud.* II 1, 1219b24-26).

Given the context of the passage, this last remark looks like a casual observation, but it is more important than it may seem at first glance. The persistence of the quality of character also shows when the *hêgemonikon*, the ruling part of our soul, and the perceptual activities are at rest, pointing at something different – the architecture of character itself, that I identify with *phantasia*. The effort of commentators in the last four decades on this psychological capacity has been impressive and it is impossible to summarize it here. However, I would like to stress two important features of *phantasia* that are relevant for our discussion. *Phantasia* is a «kind of weak perception» (*Rhet.* I 11, 1370a28), or, better, a movement arising from perception (*de An.* III 3, 428b10-17). It accounts for the persistence of the cognitive content of perception being the psychophysical precipitate of perceptual instances: the *phantasma* imprints itself on the first sensorium like a signet-ring on wax (*Mem.* 1, 450a30-32).[27] A new trace becomes part of a network of others establishing mutual relations[28] and, in particular, *phantasia* gives us the possibility of comparing previous experiences of similar objects to build up coherent representations of

27 This is meant to be more than a simile, since internal conditions are said to affect fixation, definition and continuity over time of a mnemonic trace (*Mem.* 1, 450a32-b11) and to influence recollection of information from past experience (*Mem.* 2, 453a20-b7).
28 Thanks to this, it is possible to recollect one thing associating it with different ones, that have a certain degree of similarity, contrariety or proximity (*Mem.* 2, 451b16-22).

them.[29] Recognizing what appears to us through perception as worthy of emulation can be a rational assessment, but often it simply relies on the representation of similar cases, on how I usually react to similar situations, and on what I am expected to do in such cases by my social environment. This is the first use of *phantasia* in agency: it constitutes the texture of our cognitive world and enables the subject to make consistent the features of contingent particulars. Representative capacities merge the history of one's actions and feelings and the assessment of others' behaviour in order to perform a new action. The future outcome of this action can be predicted by comparison with similar contexts previously stored in our memory. In the particular case of emulation, *phantasia* suggests to the agent that he can attain the same goods if he reproduces what made his role model able to attain the benefits he desires. In this sense *phantasia* can be considered the spark that triggers distress regarding the current condition of the agent, and therefore leads him or her to act accordingly.

There is a second feature of *phantasia* that can be useful in the present context. Representative capacities help the agent to separate the recognition of a particular conduct from its axiological relevance. In a key passage of *De memoria* (1, 450b11-451a2), Aristotle says that the knower can have cognitive detachment from the way in which things appear to him, and this makes it different from belief, which requires our assent and emotional commitment.[30] One can regard the *phantasma* either as something coming from the external world or existing by itself, just as we can regard a portrait as denotative of the person depicted or as a figure painted on canvas. The latter way of representing the content allows the subject to attribute to it values that come from past experiences and future expectations (449b9-30), or even from rational intervention. In the example of the portrait we might attribute aesthetic significance to the painting, and in the ethical case, we might evaluate the action of other people as just or unjust, appropriate for the situation or not, moderate or excessive, etc. Thus, thanks to *phantasia* a subject can contrast and compare different courses of conduct and consider them viable for himself or not: this is the preliminary stage before mature rational wish (*boulêsis*) and deliberative processes (*bouleusis*).

---

29 Cf. FREDE (1992).
30 Cf. ZUCCA (2018), p. 78-79.

III.

Let us consider in more detail the consequences for character and ethical development. Moral progress begins well before rational capacities are fully fledged and Aristotle is certainly aware of this fact. In particular, the intelligence of the youth is sharp and receptive of teachings in mathematics and sciences that require abstraction, but they lack the experience of particular cases, whose gathering requires a fair amount of time: you will never meet a young *phronimos*.[31] Despite this fact, the philosopher's optimistic vision of the natural character of the young[32] combined with a good upbringing are sufficient to ensure the acquisition of mature virtue in adulthood. Looking at the candidates, *phantasia* seems a promising cognitive capacity that can turn out to be useful in the process. It is something between perception and reason, so it is available before the complete intellectual maturation of the young, and it meets the requirements for the reproduction of courses of conduct considered good by people we trust, like members of the family, experts in particular fields or recognized individuals in society. This is the reason why Aristotle believes in the importance of one's social environment for ethical progress. Values kick in in one's life years before reason can scrutinize them, so it is fundamental to give the correct shape to our interpretation of perceptive data from a very young age.[33]

As we have seen, *zêlos* implies *phantasia*, but it is not in virtue of *zêlos* that we become responsive to the noble *per se*, since emulation concentrates on the goods acquired and in that respect, under the wrong guidance, an ability to attain the goal, regardless of its righteousness (i.e. *deinotês*, "cleverness": *Eth. Nic.* VI 12, 1144a23-26), might work as well. This is why the young are inclined to *zêlos*: they are inexperienced in the humiliations of life and are confident in their future, and thus they think they deserve great things, like the high-minded (*Rhet.* II 12, 1389a29-32). The adult *megalopsuchos* has however an altogether different character. He deems himself worthy of the greatest honours because his ambitions match the excellence of his character. Honour is not pursued in itself, as

31 *Eth. Nic.* VI 8, 1142a11-20.
32 See the favourable description at *Rhet.* II 12.
33 Even when the agent is adult, actions based on representations are more efficient than those based on rational evaluation, because the former are quicker and the agent is more confident, while the latter are better for problems or conditions with which the agent is not familiar.

it is only a kind of ornament (κόσμος τις) and prize (ἆθλον) for virtue (*Eth. Nic.* IV 3, 1123b35-1124a3) or, rather, complete virtue (*Eth. Nic.* IV 3, 1124a26-29). In this sense, the high-minded is the only one really entitled to aspire to great things, also because he has the right sense of detachment towards external goods (*Eth. Nic.* IV 3, 1124a12-17).

In conclusion, *zêlos* proves to be a limited instrument for education. It indulges the natural inclinations to the noble of the young, but without the correct attitude it can degenerate towards a formal adherence to the model, bringing first (honours and social recognition) what should come last, after the acquisition of a virtuous character. On the other hand, the nature of emulation unveils the underlying constituent of a noble upbringing: *mimêsis*.[34] In *Poet.* 4, 1448b4-10 imitation is said to be connatural to human beings, and in particular to the child, who develops his or her earliest understanding while enjoying the activity of imitation. The subject, thanks to the cognitive detachment given by *phantasia*,[35] can bask in the contemplation of the most dreadful things represented by the artist (*Poet.* 4, 1448b10-24). *Mimêsis*, though, does not limit itself to cognitive pleasure; it is also realized «by actively engaging in *mimêsis* of others»,[36] whose actions are taken as exemplar. The subject can isolate the relevant features of the character admired and apply himself to re-enact them. And partly because of its very nature, partly because of the exposure to good models, which are welcomed by the community, the young will be in a position to imitate the appropriate exemplar. However, *mimêsis* will form a disposition, a tendency to perform noble actions, but they will remain like the figure of the animal portrayed in relation to the real thing, even if the child's competence of discrimination of a just conduct will only gradually be formed.

Mimêsis has a further advantage. Sometimes a noble action implies a certain degree of actual pain and our rationality tells us to endure this pain in order to achieve a future greater goal (*de An.* III 10, 433b7-10). Imitating these kinds of acts at a young age, apart from the pressure of the context, will likely minimize the impact of immediate pains and pleasures and stimulate the rational evaluation of the conduct. The switch to mature virtue will be accomplished when the adult called to action, after being exposed to such models in his childhood, does not merely carry

---

34   This position is convincingly argued by FOSSHEIM (2006).
35   Again, *Mem.* 1, 450b11-451a2.
36   FOSSHEIM (2006), p. 122.

out the correct course of conduct but takes increased pleasure in doing so because he is acting in accordance with his true nature. Under the cognitive side, the subject moves from *phantasia* about what is good to an unchanging belief, accompanied by a rational desire for it.[37]

We have seen who can be an exemplar in Aristotle's opinion. In theory, the *phronimos* is the best candidate, because the virtue he possesses is complete and covers all kinds of particular virtues. Being more realistic, it is better to emulate models of particular virtues because Aristotle's *phronimos* is hard to find in contemporary society, and even when he associates historical individuals to *phronêsis*, it seems that the philosopher bears in mind prominent political figures that cover only the public projection of practical wisdom. However, since virtue is not inborn nor is it sufficient to gain a theoretical knowledge of what is just or unjust, the interpreter must somewhat overcome Aristotle's reticence about moral development. One of the candidates, *zêlos*, proves to be insufficient for explaining the phenomenon, or, at least, to be a subset within the mimetic powers of the soul. In any case, *phantasia* seems to be the psychophysical cognitive engine in the process of ethical flourishing. Aristotle chooses it because it accounts for the transition to rational evaluation that the mature agent must have to be virtuous without postulating any discontinuity in the subject's experience.

---

37 The question whether our appraisal of the environment in adulthood can change is still open. VAKIRTZIS (2015) holds that a selective, interpretative mimesis plays an important role in character friendship, which can restructure our behavioural patterns when faced with the friend's conduct. In a forthcoming paper, I will try to show that accidental changes can also interfere with our characters, MEDDA (forthcoming).

References

ANSCOMBE, G.E.M. (1981). Modern Moral Philosophy. In: Id. (ed.). *Ethics, Religion and Politics: Collected Philosophical Papers*, Vol. III. Oxford. Blackwell, p. 26-42 (orig. ed. 1958).

AUBENQUE, P. (1963). *La prudence chez Aristote*. Paris. Presses Universitaires de France.

BURNYEAT, M.F. (1980). Aristotle on Learning to Be Good. In: Rorty, A.O. (ed.). *Essays on Aristotle's Ethics*. Berkeley. University of California Press, p. 69-92.

CARR, D.; ARTHUR, J.; KRISTJÁNSSON, K. (2017). *Varieties of Virtue Ethics*. London. Macmillan.

CASTON, V. (2005). The Spirit and the Letter: Aristotle on Perception. In: Salles, R. (ed.). *Metaphysics, Soul and Ethics: Themes from the Work of Richard Sorabji*. Oxford. Clarendon Press, p. 245-320.

CATTANEI, E. (2009). L'immaginario geometrico dell'uomo che delibera. Schemi di esercizio della φαντασία βουλευτική in Aristotele. In: Fermani, A.; Migliori M. (eds.). *Attività e virtù. Anima e corpo in Aristotele*, Atti del convegno di Macerata (24-26 marzo 2004). Milano. Vita e Pensiero, p. 43-82.

CHARLES, D. (2008). Aristotle's Psychological Theory. *Proceedings of the Boston Area Colloquium in Ancient Philosophy*, 24, p. 1-29.

_____ (2009). Aristotle on Desire and Action. In Frede, D.; Reis, B. (eds.). *Body and Soul in Ancient Philosophy*. Berlin, New York. De Gruyter, p. 291-307.

COOPER, J.M. (1984). Plato's Theory of Human Motivation. *History of Philosophy Quarterly*, 1, p. 3-21.

CORCILIUS, K. (2008). *Streben und Bewegen: Aristoteles' Theorie der animalischen Ortsbewegung*. Berlin, New York. De Gruyter.

_____; GREGORIC, P. (2013). Aristotle's Model of Animal Motion. *Phronesis*, 58, p. 52-97.

DREFCINSKI, S. (1996). Aristotle's Fallible *Phronimos*. *Ancient Philosophy*, 16, p. 139-154.

FOSSHEIM, H.J. (2006). Habituation as *Mimesis*. In: Chappell, T.D.J. (ed.). *Values and Virtues: Aristotelianism in Contemporary Ethics*. Oxford. Clarendon Press, p. 105-117.

FREDE, D. (1992). The Cognitive Role of *Phantasia* in Aristotle. In: Nussbaum, M.C.; Rorty, A.O. (eds.). *Essays on Aristotle's "De Anima"*. Oxford. Clarendon Press, p. 195-225.

GREGORIC, P. (2007). *Aristotle on the Common Sense*. Oxford. Oxford University Press.

_____; KUHAR M. (2014). Aristotle's Physiology of Animal Motion: On *Neura* and Muscles. *Apeiron*, 47, p. 63-90.

HANKINSON, R.J. (1990). Perception and Evaluation: Aristotle on the Moral Imagination. *Dialogue*, 29, p. 41-64.

HURSTHOUSE, R. (1999). *On Virtue Ethics*. Oxford. Oxford University Press.

IRWIN, T. (1999). Aristotle. *Nicomachean Ethics (Second Edition)*, translated, with introduction, notes, and glossary. Indianapolis, Cambridge. Hackett.

_____ (2015). *Nil Admirari?* Uses and Abuses of Admiration. *Proceedings of the Aristotelian Society*, 89, p. 223-248.

KENNEDY, G.A. (2006). Aristotle. *On Rhetoric. A Theory of Civic Discourse*,Second Edition, translated, with introduction, notes. New York, Oxford. Oxford University Press.

LEUNISSEN, M. (2012). Aristotle on Natural Character and Its Implications for Moral Development. *Journal of the History of Philosophy*, 50, p. 507-530.

_____ (2017). *From Natural Character to Moral Virtue in Aristotle*. Oxford. Oxford University Press.

MANULI, P.; VEGETTI, M. (2009). *Cuore, sangue e cervello. Biologia e antropologia nel pensiero antico*. Pistoia. Petite Plaisance (orig. ed. 1977).

MEDDA, R. (forthcoming). Accidentalità e alterazioni del carattere in Aristotele. In Cattanei E.; Sanna M. (eds.). *L'universalità e i suoi limiti. Meccanismi di inclusione ed esclusione nella riflessione filosofica dall'antichità al mondo contemporaneo*. Roma. Edizioni di storia e letteratura.

MERRITT, M. (2009). Aristotelean Virtue and the Interpersonal Aspect of Ethical Character. *Journal of Moral Philosophy*, 6, p. 23-49.

MINGUCCI, G. (2015). *La fisiologia del pensiero in Aristotele*. Bologna. Il Mulino.

MOSS, J. (2012). *Aristotle on the Apparent Good: Perception, Phantasia, Thought, and Desire*. Oxford. Oxford University Press.

NATALI, C. (1989). *La saggezza di Aristotele*. Napoli. Bibliopolis.

VAKIRTZIS A. (2015). Mimesis, Friendship, and Moral Development in Aristotle's Ethics. *Rhizomata*, 3, p. 125-142.

WHITE, N. (2015). Plato and the Ethics of Virtue. In: Besser-Jones, L.; Slote M. (eds.). *The Routledge Companion to Virtue Ethics*. New York. Routledge, p. 3-15.

WISSE, J. (1989). Ethos *and* Pathos *from Aristotle to Cicero*. Amsterdam. Hakkert.

ZAGZEBSKI, L. (2015). Admiration and the Admirable. *Proceedings of the Aristotelian Society*, 89, p. 205-221.

_____ (2017). *Exemplarist Moral Theory*. New York. Oxford University Press.

ZUCCA D. (2015). *L'anima del vivente. Vita, cognizione e azione nella psicologia aristotelica*. Brescia. Morcelliana.

_____ (2018). The Method of Aristotle's Inquiry on φαντασία in *De Anima* iii 3. *Méthexis*, 30, p. 72-97.

What is Aristotle's Active Intellect?

Diego Zucca

In what follows, I consider perhaps the most controversial lines in the Aristotelian *corpus*, namely, *De Anima* III 5 (430a10-25). To examine the *vexata quaestio* concerning the nature and ontological status of the so-called Active Intellect (AI), I first very briefly present the main traditional interpretive options and then offer an alternative option that appears to be compatible with all that Aristotle says in *de An*. III 5 and avoids some well-known difficulties of other classical readings. To achieve this, I divide the text into points and take each of the main interpretations at face-value through determining which of them best satisfies these points, and to what extent.

Part I: The Active Intellect Introduced

I.1 What III 5 Says

To address the matter directly, let us start from the enigmatic text of *de An*. III 5 (430a10-25):[1]

10 Ἐπεὶ δ'ὥσπερ ἐν ἁπάσῃ τῇ φύσει ἐστὶ τι τὸ μὲν ὕλη
11 ἑκάστῳ γένει (τοῦτο δὲ ὃ πάντα δυνάμει ἐκεῖνα), ἕτερον δὲ
12 τὸ αἴτιον καὶ ποιητικόν, τῷ ποιεῖν πάντα, οἷον ἡ τέχνη
13 πρὸς τὴν ὕλην πέπονθεν, ἀνάγκη καὶ ἐν τῇ ψυχῇ ὑπάρχειν
14 ταύτας τὰς διαφοράς· καὶ ἔστιν ὁ μὲν τοιοῦτος νοῦς τῷ πάντα
15 γίνεσθαι, ὁ δὲ τῷ πάντα ποιεῖν, ὡς ἕξις τις, οἷον τὸ φῶς·
16 τρόπον γάρ τινα καὶ τὸ φῶς ποιεῖ τὰ δυνάμει ὄντα χρώ-
17 ματα ἐνεργείᾳ χρώματα. καὶ οὗτος ὁ νοῦς χωριστὸς καὶ

---

1 This is the text established by TRENDELENBURG (1833); ROSS (1961) expunges ὥσπερ and τι at line 10, and the lines 19-22 (τὸ δ'αὐτό [...] νοεῖ), he (following Torstrik) opts for ἐνέργεια instead of ἐνεργείᾳ at line 18: such choices are mainly due to philosophical interpretation, which is what is at stake in this paper. This is why I prefer to start from the more preservative text.

18 ἀπαθὴς καὶ ἀμιγής, τῇ οὐσίᾳ ὢν ἐνέργεια· ἀεὶ γὰρ τιμιώτε-
19 ρον τὸ ποιοῦν τοῦ πάσχοντος καὶ ἡ ἀρχὴ τῆς ὕλης. τὸ δ'
20 αὐτό ἐστιν ἡ κατ' ἐνέργειαν ἐπιστήμη τῷ πράγματι· ἡ δὲ
21 κατὰ δύναμιν χρόνῳ προτέρα ἐν τῷ ἑνί, ὅλως δὲ οὐδὲ χρόνῳ,
22 ἀλλ' οὐχ ὁτὲ μὲν νοεῖ ὁτὲ δ'οὐ νοεῖ. χωρισθεὶς δ'ἐστὶ μόνον
23 τοῦθ' ὅπερ ἐστί, καὶ τοῦτο μόνον ἀθάνατον καὶ ἀΐδιον. οὐ
24 μνημονεύομεν δέ, ὅτι τοῦτο μὲν ἀπαθές, ὁ δὲ παθητικὸς
25 νοῦς φθαρτός, καὶ ἄνευ τούτου οὐθὲν νοεῖ.

Translation (I introduce letters for the sake of clarity):

> But since, (**a**) as in all of nature there is something that is the matter
> of each kind (and this is potentially all those things), while some-
> thing else is the cause, i.e., it is productive, because it makes them all
> as falls to a craft in relation to the matter, (**b**) of necessity these differ-
> ences must be present also in the soul. (**c**) And there is a sort of intel-
> lect, such as to become all things, and another sort such as to make
> them all, (**d**) as a kind of a positive state such as light. For in a certain
> way light too makes colours that are in potentiality colours in actuali-
> ty. (**e**) And it is this intellect which is separable and impassive and un-
> mixed, being it its essence in actuality. For (**f**) what acts is always su-
> perior to what is acted upon, as too the principle is to the matter.
> Now (**g**) actual knowledge is the same as the thing, but in the indi-
> vidual potential knowledge is prior in time, though generally it is not
> prior in time either. But (**h**) it is not the case that sometimes it thinks
> and sometimes it does not. However, (**i**) it is only as separated, that it
> is just what it is, and (**l**) this alone is deathless and eternal, though
> (**m**) we do not remember, because this is impassive, whereas the pas-
> sive intellect is perishable and (**n**) without this does not think noth-
> ing.

Let us simply list what Aristotle says about AI: any interpretation of what
AI is should provide a candidate that can be at least plausibly characterized as Aristotle characterizes AI *apertis verbis*. I will first focus on 1-10 –
each number corresponds to a letter in the translation – leaving aside (b)
and (g), which I will consider later.

Features AI is credited with:

1) It is related to the 'passive' intellect as *technê* is related to its matter
    (*a*);

2) It is *productive* of all things that the other (kind of) intellect becomes
    (c);
3) It is like light, which makes potential colours into actual colours *(d)*;
4) It is (not only) separable, impassive, unmixed (but also) *in actuality*
    by its own essence *(e)*;
5) It is *superior* to the other intellect, as the active principle is always su-
    perior to the passive one *(f)*;
6) It is not the case that sometimes it thinks and sometimes it does not
    think *(h)*;
7) Only as *separated*, is it essentially what it is *(i)*;
8) Only this intellect is *deathless* and *eternal (l)*;
9) We do not remember, because it is impassive, while the passive intel-
    lect is corruptible *(m)*;
10) Without it *nothing thinks (n)*.

Other elements to account for:

(b): the active/passive difference needs to also be present *in the soul*;
(g): actual knowledge is identical with the object known and is in general
     prior to potential knowledge (even though potential knowledge is
     temporally prior in the individual).

I.2 Aristotle's View of Human Intellect in de An. before III 5[2]

The introduction of AI follows the inquiry on human intellect (III 4), i.e.,
on «the part of the soul by which the soul knows and understands»
(429a10-11). Whether it is separable or not is to be established, as well as
whether it is separable only conceptually-definitionally or also spatially,
and how understanding comes about. Similarly to perception, intellection is supposed to consist in being acted upon by its objects (νοητά), and
so it is characterized as impassive, receptive of the form and potentially
identical with it (a14-17). But the analogy with perception is also a contrastive one: as intellect can know *all* things – rather than just receiving
certain kinds of sensible forms as perception does – it must be *unmixed*,
such that its own nature could not be anything else than absolute *poten-*

---

2 Here I only consider III 4: other references to νοῦς in the first book are embedded
   in dialectical and doxographical reconstructions, so it is not obvious that they are
   definitive theoretical commitments on Aristotle's part.

tiality or capacity (a18-22). Thus, its impassivity must be different from that of perception: the latter is grounded in certain bodily features that work as *ratios* in the respective bodily organs, and that a) enable a sense to receive-become *different* forms (a sense cannot become itself, this is why sight cannot perceive transparency: the eye-jelly already *is* transparent), and b) limit the range of perceivable forms to a certain type (e.g., colours impacting on the transparent eye, sounds impacting on the "silent" ear) and entail the existence of "blind spots" even within the type the sense is sensitive to (e.g., we cannot literally hear silence). Intellection has no blind spots and no limitations concerning its possible contents, so νοῦς has no positive nature, neither can it be grounded in a dedicated bodily organ (a20-29). Separability[3] and unmixedness explain why receiving "intense" νοητά[4] strengthens the noetic capacity, whereas perceptions that are too intense impair the sense by disturbing its internal, bodily *ratio* (a29-b6).[5] Perception is dependent on present bodily stimulation, while intellect can retain the received forms and exercise/re-actualise them *by itself* (b7-9). This "spontaneity" makes possession of the forms compatible with νοῦς remaining a pure capacity, as it still can "become" everything, including the already received and possessed forms (by spontaneously re-actualizing them). This freedom enables it to think *itself* (b9-10), thus entailing the possibility of self-understanding.

Aristotle has already credited the human intellect with a number of features. Like perception, it is *receptive* of forms, potentially *identical* with them, and *impassive*, while unlike perception it is *unlimited* as a potentiality, *separable* and *without organ*, *peculiarly* impassive, as it is *"spontaneous"* and so capable of preserving its absolute potentiality even when possessing certain forms.[6] Finally, its spontaneity enables it to grasp and know *itself*.[7]

---

3 On separation and its meanings in Aristotle's psychology, see FINE (1984), MORRISON (1985), MILLER (2012).

4 The more abstract and far from sensibility a νοητόν is, the more intense it is. The more you understand, the more you become able to understand.

5 See *de An.* II 8, 425a27-b8.

6 This difference from perception has been already suggested in *de An.* II 5, 417b20-26: universals are "in a way" in the soul.

7 At b9 Ross follows the emendation of Bywater who changes καὶ αὐτὸς δὲ αὐτὸν to καὶ αὐτὸς δι'αὐτοῦ, which would mean that νοῦς is able to think *by* itself, rather than just *itself*. But the emendation would make the passage redundant, as spontaneity has been introduced above, at b7.

After a very difficult passage on the relation between sensibility and the noetic grasp of essences (429b10-22), two puzzles are addressed. 1) If νοῦς is impassive and unmixed (thus a 'negative' nature with no positive forms in common with anything), but thinking is being acted upon, how can νοῦς think/grasp anything at all, given that X can be only acted on by a Y that has something in common with X (a22-26)? 2) How could νοῦς think of/understand *itself*?[8] If it is a νοητὸν simply due to its own nature (*per se*), then all νοητά will share this nature so everything intelligible will have νοῦς![9] It will otherwise share some feature with νοητά that makes it thinkable (*per aliud*) as the other νοητά. In sum, self-thinkability entails either an absurd panpsychism or – in fact like Puzzle 1 – the negation of unmixedness. The 'solutions' of the puzzle deserve a much deeper analysis,[10] but they are worth mentioning even in brief, as they may be helpful in understanding what AI is later. As to the first puzzle, intellect is nothing at all until it thinks – it is absolute, content-less plasticity and pure potentiality even *of itself* – just like a writing tablet without anything written on it. The tablet does not have to be *like* the contents of the words or propositions we can write on it, or like the letters those words and propositions are made of.[11] Noetic contents are abstract, and their reception is unlike the bodily alteration of the like by the like (e.g., the eye-jelly's chromatic assimilation), even if receiving them may well *involve* such bodily alterations (the contents are received onto the tablet through physical impressions on the wax tablet's surface). Perceptual contents are thus physically assimilated by the senses in a way conceptual contents are not, even if no concept can be acquired without the subject acquiring certain relevant perceptual contents. Once at least *some* noetic contents are received, then νοῦς is genuinely present as a positive capacity, which the

---

8　The second puzzle is an application of the first puzzle to a special object: νοῦς itself.

9　Such a panpsychist consequence echoes that discussed in Plato's *Parmenides*, 132b10-c8.

10　To my knowledge, the deepest analysis of these puzzles is to be found in LEWIS (2003); see also DRISCOLL (1992), POLITIS (2001), MILLER (2012), ch. 4.3, SISKO (2001), p. 185-189, GREGORIC/PFEIFFER 2015.

11　The wax-tablet analogy concerns the different ways propositional contents and perceptual contents respectively "impress" our cognitive soul; it recalls Plato's *Philebus'* image (39a-b) of a *scribe* and a *painter* cooperating into our soul. More generally, the Aristotelian use of the wax analogy concerning both perception (II 12) and intellection (III 4) clearly parallels Plato's *Theaetetus* (191c8-195a9).

138   *Diego Zucca*

subject can exercise at will, but mastering a concept[12] is a dispositional ability that does not undermine the unlimited nature of thought. On the contrary, intellect may still *become* both the contents already acquired and those still to be acquired, so it can still become everything. As to the second puzzle, when thought objects are without matter, that which thinks and that which is thought are the same *simpliciter*[13] rather than just in form, but in enmattered particulars the intelligibles/universals are only potentially present. It is thinking itself that actualises its thought objects through "extracting" them from their matter, so although things need not have intellect in them for them to be thought (no panpsychism), νοῦς can think itself without sharing alien elements into its nature, which would ground its and everything else's intelligibility (no negation of unmixedness). Indeed, it can think itself and become a νοητὸν *for* itself "indirectly", i.e., only when it has received other νοητά.[14] The idea can be illustrated as follows. Knowing X is becoming X without already being X; our intellect can become itself without contradiction, insofar as it (spontaneously) becomes (but also actualises) an intelligible other than itself, such that it can grasp itself as the capacity of becoming/knowing anything. It *is* the capacity of actualizing universals both in itself and in the worldly particulars, so in becoming something else it may understand itself as the capacity to become *anything* else, namely a "negative" and unlimited nature. So far, so good for the νοῦς *aporiai*. We are now ready to come back to our AI in III 5.

---

12 Although νοῦς is responsible for conceptual activity in general, its cognitive excellence is grasping the essences. See FRONTEROTTA (2016); BURNYEAT (2008), p. 24-25.

13 But as we will see (cf. note 65), it is accidental sameness.

14 Noetic self-cognition happens to be ancillar and collateral (ἐν παρέργῳ, *Metaph.* Λ 9, 1074b35-36) to the first-order cognition of other noetic objects. Only by 'becoming' something else does our νοῦς *become this becoming*, namely, itself.

PART II: The Interpretations at Face-Value: Pros and Cons

II.1 The Divine Interpretation (DI)

DI comes in many forms, but classical DI, as defended by Alexander of Aphrodisias[15] and prevalent among contemporary scholars[16] is broadly an *externalist* interpretation, which identifies AI with a particular substance: God or the Divine Mind characterised as νόησις νοήσεως in *Metaph.* Λ (8, 1074a34). AI is conceived of as *transcendent* of human individual souls/ intellects and as separated from them. Let us start from the predicates DI most straightforwardly satisfies. God is separated, impassive, unmixed and *in actuality* by its own essence, as for point (4)(e).[17] As for point (5)(f) it is *superior* to the other intellect (ours) as the active principle is always superior to the passive one, since as a pure actuality it is ontologically superior to anything that is partially passive and potential. God does not of course think intermittently, so point (6)(h) is satisfied. As it is separated,[18] God is essentially what it is: by being a pure essence without matter and

---

15 See Alexander, *de An.*, 88, 16-89, 22 Bruns; *de Int.* (*Mantissa*, II), 106, 19-109, 10 Bruns.

16 DI probably goes back to Theophrastus (see BRENTANO, 1867, p. 5ff., MORAUX, 1978) and is argued for by FREDE (1996), CASTON (1999), BURNYEAT (2008), among many others.

17 At line 18 we have ἐνέργεια in Ross' text, instead of ἐνεργείᾳ. This emendation made by TORSTRIK (1862) on the basis of Simplicius is theory-laden, as it depends on the latter favouring DI: God *is* actuality indeed (cfr. *Metaph.* Λ 9, 1075a1-5, 1074a33-34). We can in any case make sense of ἐνεργείᾳ as a characterization of God from the point of view of our sublunary world.

18 χωρισθείς can be given a *temporal*, a *causal*, an "*aspectual*" or a *hypothetical* reading. The first (*when* it is separated) does not fit with DI but fits with what I will call the Human Interpretation (see *infra*); the second (*since-*, *insofar as* it is separated) does; the third (*when taken* as something separated) fits with the interpretations I will call Social Interpretation and Content Interpretation, as we will see (see *infra*), but much less with DI. The fourth (*if* it is separated: SILLITTI, 2016) looks implausible to me, in this assertive context. CASTON (1999), p. 207-211 accommodates the third option within DI by giving to χωρισθείς a *taxonomical* meaning: X is separable from Y if it can be instantiated without Y's being instantiated. God as Intellect is an example of intellect without nutritive and perceptual soul, so νοῦς is separable from the other souls insofar as at least one instance of it does not require the presence of other souls, just as the nutritive soul is separable from the perceptual soul because it is instantiated alone in plants. This account is quite appealing, but it entails that the same *kind* [νοῦς] has mortal instances (our intellects) and eternal instances (God=AI): but, in a passage quoted

ontologically separable from the world, God fits well with point (7)(*i*). There is also no doubt that God is deathless and eternal, which addresses point (8)(*l*).

Let us come back to (1)(a) and (2)(c): does God *make* all things our intellects become (i.e., 2), and is God to these things as art is to its appropriate matter (i.e., 1)? Apparently not. First, God is not a productive cause but makes everything move as a final cause,[19] and as our intellects become what they receive, i.e., the intelligibles, in the DI God would be said to produce all νοητά. However, this does not seem to be a job for the Aristotelian God, which only thinks itself without either knowing or (even less) producing contents other than itself. Art is a productive principle through which an artist imposes a form onto a suitable matter, but God is not such a productive principle. We may stretch the meaning of (1) and say that the Unmoved Mover causes the sublunary world to move and the species to reproduce, so that it is a kind of indirect cause of our intellection of the species.[20] Could Aristotle suggest such a loose (and even faltering) analogy, assimilate a productive principle such as art to a final cause such as God, and then equate a direct causal relationship, as art is to matter, to such a remote causal relation as that of God with νοητά ? This seems extremely unlikely, so points (1)(a) and (2)(c) are *not* satisfied by DI.

(3)(d) explains (2)(a), as AI makes all things – that our "passive intellect" (=PI) become – «as a kind of disposition, such as light», which indeed actualizes colours in potentiality. AI is to PI is thus what light is to

by Caston as decisive (II 2, 413b24-27) where it is said that νοῦς is a different kind of soul, separated as the eternal is from the perishable: a) the subject is νοῦς *and* theoretical δύναμις: it cannot be God, as there is no δύναμις in God; and b) the passage is highly hypothetical and non-committal, as it says that nothing is clear about the matter and this *seems* (*prima facie*) to be a different, separate kind of soul. As I will argue, only the *content* of our intellectual power will be confirmed to be eternal and identified with AI. See *infra*.

19 CASTON (1999), p. 216-223 argues at length that God as a final cause is genuinely productive, but not in the ordinary sense in which *moved* movers are productive (as 'efficient' causes and through contact). Yet, this non-ordinary but genuine sense of being productive is not the way *art* is productive. Art and knowledge are not productive in themselves indeed, the desire of that who possesses the art or knowledge is (see *de An.* Γ 10, 433a18-20; *Eth. Nic.* VI 2, 1139b5-37).

20 This is the way Alexander (*de An.* 88.54-89.26 Bruns) accommodates the passage, followed by FREDE (1996), p. 387, CASTON (1999), p. 216-222, and many others.

colours. We may suppose that just as light[21] makes colours both *visible* (first actuality) and *seen* (second actuality)[22] through illuminating the transparent *media* (air, water), so AI is responsible for making the objects of PI *thinkable* and *thought*. Again, it is difficult to credit God with the causal role or power to actualize our intellects, as this weighty analogy suggests (see *infra*), given that it only thinks itself; God may well be relevant for our contemplation and thought in a 'moral' sense, as an *exemplum* and a regulative idea, but this is a different issue. Thus, Point (3)(d) also appears to trouble DI.

Let us consider (9)(m). *What* is it that we do not remember? *Why* do we not remember, and what connection with God could such a phenomenon have? Depending on how we read ὅτι, we can either obtain: "we do not remember, *because* AI is impassive whereas the passive intellect (PI) is perishable";[23] or "we do not remember *that* AI is impassive [...]". For the first reading – whatever account we give to the relation between our not remembering and the mortality of our intellects – it is hard to show how the radical impassivity of God[24] could ever *cause* or *ground* our not remembering (the issue of *what* we do not remember must be addressed anyway, not only within DI: see *infra*).[25] For the second that-clause reading, it has been suggested that μνημονεύομεν may have an "urban" sense, something like "let's not forget it!".[26] Aristotle would then be telling us that we should keep in mind that God is radically impassive, unlike our affectable intellects that are perishable. Through this ingenuous interpretation, DI could make sense of (9), but to me, assuming the adoption of a dialogical-colloquial tone in such a solemn and

---

21 Light is the actuality of the transparent as such (*de An.* II 7, 418b9-11).
22 On this point, See KOSMAN (1992).
23 τοῦτο at line 24 must denote AI, as it is contrasted with παθητικὸς νοῦς.
24 I add "radical" because PI is also said to be impassive (e.g. 429b23): clearly, the impassivity of AI contrasted with the mortality of PI must be of another kind than the impassivity PI has already been credited with. PI is παθητικὸς with respect to AI, but impassive with respect to the passivity of perception (which – as an *alteratio perfectiva* – is impassive on its own with respect to standard alterations). We have three kinds of cognitive impassivity (one of them is absolute) and two kinds of cognitive passivity (two of them – PI and perception – are compatible with *relative* impassivity).
25 On this passage, cf. FRONTEROTTA (2007).
26 CASTON (1999), p. 214; cf. also WEDIN (1988), p. 179-181.

assertive context[27] is highly implausible. Thus, in my view point (9)(m) is at best only *poorly* satisfied by DI.

(10)(n) can be construed in many ways, including a) without AI, PI thinks nothing[28] b) without AI, nothing thinks[29] c) without PI nothing thinks and d) without PI, AI thinks nothing. The first two options are textually and also philosophically more reasonable than the latter two, which are plainly incompatible with DI. Advocates of DI may argue that without God not only would natural species be absent – as (1) and (2) infer – but also any human desire to know would not be moved towards inquiry, learning and contemplation. Therefore, not only would any object of PI not be there (νοητά such as essences and species), but no actualization of PI would be there either, without the Object that moves all in the sublunary cosmos as imitated and beloved. If God moves everything, it also moves thinking subjects towards thinking and knowing, even though thought as such is not a movement but a perfect state. This reading does make sense of (10), but some perplexing issues remain. God is a condition of thinking, but not just *qua* thinking, rather insofar as thinking as a human activity causally depends on our desire to understand. Again, I would say that Point (10)(n) is *poorly* satisfied, and only if the interpretation is stretched.

The remaining points (b) and (g) can now be evaluated in terms of DI. Initially (b) appears to be a problem for DI: the principle of the difference between active and passive/potential, which holds in Nature (and in art), is also said to hold *in the soul* (ἐν τῇ ψυχῇ), but the difference between God and our intellect is not *in* our soul. The soul is just one of the *relata*, the other being transcendent and separated from us. It is true that the act of the mover is *in* the patient,[30] so even the difference between agent and patient may be thought to reside in the patient, but although the idea that God is *in* our soul as a mover may sound familiar to us, it

---

27 CASTON (1999), p. 214-215, provides many examples of the "urban" use of μνημονεύω: but significantly they all come from Platonic *dialogues*, where a conversational rhetoric is deployed, for obvious reasons. Here in III 5 we face a totally different register.

28 HICKS (1907), p. 509-510, summarises the debate about the four options and convincingly argues for a).

29 For example, ROSS (1961), among many others.

30 Alexander, perhaps because he perceives the difficulty, paraphrases ἐν τῇ ψυχῇ with ἐπὶ τοῦ νοῦ (*de An.* 88.22 Bruns).

does not sound Aristotelian at all.[31] The expression ἐν τῇ ψυχῇ can be alternatively interpreted, perhaps not in the most natural way,[32] as referring to the general *domain* of psychological kinds.[33] As with natural things, there is matter/capacity and an active principle, and similarly there are two kinds of intellect, PI and AI. In any case, these possible ways of accommodating (b) appear somewhat *ad hoc*, so I would take it as *poorly satisfied* by DI. Point (g) appears to interrupt the discourse and looks out of place, and indeed it occurs also elsewhere,[34] which is why Ross has expunged it, so it is problematic in itself and not just for DI. When contrasting God with our intellects, what is the point of saying that actual knowledge is identical with its object, temporally posterior at the level of individuals but temporally prior in general? Before knowledge is actualized in us, it is in potentiality in our νοῦς, which is a *tabula rasa* in the first place (see *supra*), but God always knows itself in- and as absolute actuality, as it is eternal. Therefore, if we take knowledge in general, actuality comes before potentiality even temporally, because God does not come after *any* individual intellect and its self-knowledge comes before individuals' knowledge of the world. This would be a strange and too condensed and opaque comparison between God's self-knowledge and our knowledge of the world: an option that cannot be ruled out but, again, renders (g) only *poorly satisfied* by DI.

More generally, DI is unsatisfactory because the introduction *ex abrupto* of God as a *deus ex machina* within a psychological discourse is quite mysterious in itself: what is the explanatory job of introducing God, and how does it shed light on the machinery of cognitive psychology? Why is there an unannounced shift from psychology to theology, and then an unexplained return to psychology in III 6?

In sum, DI *can* account for (4), (5), (6), (7) and (8), does *not* account for (1), (2) and (3), and *poorly* accounts for (9), (10), (b) and (g).

---

31 In particular, God is a final cause, final causes are not *into* the items that move towards them.

32 For the meanings of ἐν, see *Phys.* IV 3, 210a14-24.

33 BURNYEAT (2008) suggests that ἐν τῇ ψυχῇ must be as generic as its term of comparison ἐν ἁπάσῃ τῇ φύσει. See CASTON (1999), p. 205-207.

34 *De An.* III 7, 431a1-3.

II.2 *The Human Interpretation (HI)*

The HI is an *internalist/immanentistic* reading, in which AI is regarded as a part/function/aspect of our individual soul, just as PI is. Historically, HI has had many advocates,[35] and some among contemporary scholars.[36] The general idea – disregarding its many versions – is that our individual intellectual soul consists of an active part acting upon a passive part. We can thus attempt to read III 5 from the perspective of the HI.

An active part of our soul can act upon a passive/receptive part (PI as defined in III 4, scc *supra*), so that PI receives from AI the forms in the same way that suitable matter is informed by art. Thus (1)(a) is at this point satisfied, although *i*) how the two parts cooperate remains obscure, and *ii*) nowhere else in the *corpus* are *two* co-operating intellects (or intellectual powers) even mentioned. Such an active part would actualize the passive one by playing an active role – for example, by abstracting/extracting the universals from empirical contents retained in perceptive soul as φ αντάσματα[37] – so it would make sense to say that AI makes all that PI becomes as light makes colours actual, as in (2)(c) and (3)(d), which are thus satisfied. AI can well be separable, impassive and unmixed, just as PI has already been said to be (see *supra*: Part I.2), but it is difficult to maintain that a part of our soul is by its own essence *in* actuality (in the dative-reading) or, even worse, simply actuality (in the nominative-reading).[38] Each part of the cognitive soul in Aristotle's psychology is a capacity that may or may not be actualized, so how is it that we are not continuously conscious of AI's essentially actual and supposedly uninterrupted activity, for example when we are asleep? This objection makes both (4)(e) and (6) (h) highly problematic. However, for (5)(f), there is no problem: AI would be superior to PI as an active principle is superior to a passive one. If AI is an immortal part of the human soul – perhaps our most real self – we get the most natural reading of (7)(i): indeed, the passive aorist χωρισθ εὶς could be given temporal meaning, i.e., "having been separated". After death AI is separated from the body and is essentially what it is. Of

---

35 For example, Theophrastus *apud* Themistius (*Paraph. De An.* 107.30-108.35); Philoponus (*De Int.* 57.70-74); Thomas (*In de An.* 742-43, *De Un. Int.* IV).

36 See RIST (1966), GERSON (2005), SISKO (2001); see also ROSS (1961), BRENTANO (1977), TRENDELENBURG (1833), *ad loc.*

37 This is the suggestion by Thomas, *In Aristotelis librum de anima commentarium*, book III, lectio 10, c. 736.

38 See *supra*, n. 1.

course, we cannot deny the embarrassing tension between the idea of an immortal part of our soul and the theoretical framework of Aristotle's psychology, but such a tension also concerns Aristotle's somewhat anti-naturalist characterization of PI, so it cannot disqualify a reading of AI. However, with (8)(l) things get much worse for HI: AI is not just death-less but also *eternal*. Eternity also concerns the past, not just the future like immortality, and thus it follows that our *individual* AI pre-exists our birth and come to inhabit our body at a certain point.[39] This "metempsy-chosis-assumption" is something that Aristotle considers insane and refus-es point blank.[40] Thus, HI does not satisfy (8)(l).

However, (9)(m) can be accommodated. As a function of sensibility,[41] remembering is essentially embodied, therefore our real, immortal self will not remember its mortal life once separated from the body (and pre-sumably from PI, which is corruptible as it is rooted in φαντάσματα[42]). The most plausible readings of (10)(n) are easily satisfied in HI: without AI, PI thinks nothing – or nothing thinks – if receiving the universals re-quires an active function of "making" them. Finally, (b) is done the most justice by HI, and in fact HI has been put forward as an argument in favour of (b):[43] the difference between AI and PI being *in* the soul clearly favours an internalist reading of AI. Again, (g) is troubling for HI: if AI is to PI as actual knowledge is to potential knowledge, AI is prior *simpliciter* to PI but PI is temporally prior in the individual. Thus, if AI *is* in the in-dividual as for HI, AI is at a time prior and posterior to PI! Thus, (g) is not satisfied by HI, unless it is excised from III 5 as Ross does.

Some interpretive attempts have been recently made to articulate a de-flactionary version of HI,[44] i.e., to regard AI and PI simply as two cogni-

39 I do not enter into the debate about *de Gen. An.* II 3, 736b28, where νοῦς is said to come «from without» (θύραθεν) and to be divine. Themistius and BURNYEAT (2008) suggest that *teaching* and *experience* are νοῦς' external movers. CASTON (1999), p. 215-216, appeals to Aristotle's sexist embryology (the *form* of the embryo comes from the father's semen, and its matter comes from the mother's menses). In any case, the passage need not be referring to a pre-existence of our intellect to our biological life.
40 See *de An.* III 3, 407b20-26.
41 See *Mem.* 1, 45012-25.
42 No thought without φαντάσματα, so without perception, so without body (III 8, 432a4-10).
43 See Themistius (*In de An.* 102.30-103.19), Thomas (*De Un. Int.*: IV, 83), ROSS (1961), *ad loc.*
44 See WEDIN (1989), (1993); BARNES (1979).

tive functions of our intellect introduced to explain our ability to think, thus making psychological sense of (1), (2) and (3). From this view, PI explains the reception of universals via induction from perceptual experience, whereas AI accounts for our ability to use/exercise previously acquired concepts by combining them into judgements. The initial acquiring of a concept is passive as it depends on perceptual exposure to the world, while the use of concepts in propositions is active and does not further depend on present particulars. Although attractive, this view requires the attribution of eternity and immortality to AI to be taken as somehow metaphorical, similar to a rhetorical emphasis without real commitment. How could Aristotle talk so loosely within such a serious context? In any case, I cannot see how to make sense of the idea that our judgemental activity is immortal and eternal. Furthermore, making AI into a sort of second actuality[45] – exercise of a previously acquired conceptual capacity – is incompatible with it being a *condition* of PI, rather than a consequence of it. In addition, what would it mean to say that the propositional exercise of our conceptual repertoire is in actuality through its own essence? Would that not boil down to a tautology, namely, that an exercise is an exercise? Finally, we could not maintain that AI simply makes all that PIs become (2), because propositional syntheses are not concepts, even though the latter can be constituents of the former. More generally, such attempts tend to disregard the neatly contrastive language by which AI and PI are opposed[46] and the ontological chasm such a language puts between them.

To sum up, HI accounts for (1), (2), (3), (5), (7), (9), (10) and (b) but does *not* account for (4), (6), (8) and (g).

II.3 *The "Social" Interpretation (SI)*

According to the SI – which may be taken as a *non-internalist* and *non-individualist* variation of the HI – AI is neither God nor a part/function of our soul, but it is rather *the possession of principles of science by the human*

---

45 See MODRAK (1991), p. 766, and KOSMAN (1992) who identifies AI with contemplation as consciousness.

46 τι τὸ μὲν/ἕτερον δὲ (a10-11), ὁ μὲν/ὁ δὲ (a14-15), οὗτος ὁ νοῦς (implicitly contrasted with *another* one, a17), (τὸ ποιοῦν/τοῦ πάσχοντος: one superior to the other, a19), τοῦτο μόνον (*this alone* is immortal and eternal, a23), τοῦτο μὲν/ὁ δὲ παθητικὸς (a23).

kind in general.[47] Such a possession at a species-level is deathless and eternal – as for (8)(l) – insofar as the human species is: although it is only eternal through being always and forever instantiated by individuals, it may be thought of as superior to each of its instantiations. Likewise, for (5)(f), humankind knowledge is superior to individual knowledge. As it is a *habitus* rather than a subject, it does not think at all, so it will be not the case that it thinks only intermittently and thus (6)(h)[48] can be accounted for. It is separable – modal meaning of χωριστός – from *each* of its individual instantiations, even though it must be instantiated to exist at all, so not only is it impassive and unmixed (like individual PI) but it is also in actuality by virtue of its own essence.[49] Indeed, as a *habit* it is a first actuality, and as an eternal and always present possession it is essentially in actuality, so SI therefore fits well with (4)(e). We can make sense of the idea that without AI, PI thinks nothing, as the human possession of principles may be thought of as a condition for the possession of principles by this or that human being, so (10)(n) can be satisfied under at least one of its possible readings.[50] Concerning the cryptic reference to our not remembering in (9)(m), Aristotle could mean that our mortal PIs cannot remember the principles – which are not already in our souls as Platonic innatism entails – but must acquire them from experience and from teachers. In fact, teaching is the most straightforward way in which general human possession becomes a new individual possession, and the transmission of knowledge at the level of noetic soul is analogous to the transmission of life from parents to offspring at the level of reproductive soul. Why would AI be just what it is only insofar as it is separated (7)(i)?

47 SI has been recently argued by BERTI (2011), (2016); but see also POLANSKY (2007) p. 462-468, KAHN (1992), MINGUCCI (2015), p. 179-194. Philoponus, *De Int.* 60, 37-43 is the first to suggest that AI is always enacted because the *human kind* is always thinking. POLANSKY (2007), p. 466: «Aristotle contrasts the human individual – born unknowingly – to the generality of the human kind». KAHN (1992) identifies AI with the "logos", broadly meant as to include *language, thought* and *culture*, so this is why I include him among the advocates of SI. According to MINGUCCI (2015), p. 192, AI is «intelligenza collettiva e storicamente depositata».
48 This is strongly emphasized by BERTI (2011), (2016).
49 With SI we can maintain ἐνεργεία at a17, as in the most part of manuscripts, so there is no need to correct it in ἐνέργεια.
50 If we read (10) as "without it, nothing thinks" we get a false statement: arguably, the Aristotelian God thinks itself quite independently of human possession of universals.

By reading χωρισθεὶς as having an aspectual value rather than a temporal one,[51] thus meaning "considered in itself" rather than "having been onto-logically separated", we can do justice to (7): the possession of principles/universals at a human-kind level can be grasped as what it is – an essentially eternal possession – only if we envisage it as only contingently instantiated in this or that PI. Furthermore, in SI our point (g) ceases to appear embarrassing and out of place, and it can be taken to be a central suggestion with argumentative import, to the extent that its excision turns out to be illegitimate and arbitrary. Actual knowledge is identical with the thing known, but for individual PI potential knowledge come first in time, although *if we consider the whole of human kind* (ὅλως, a21), actual knowledge comes first even temporally. Human kind is eternal and eternally possessing the principles, so that this possession (AI) is prior to potential knowledge not only *simpliciter* but also in time, provided that the subject is considered to be human kind.[52] As for (b), we can maintain that the difference between AI and PI holds "concerning the soul in general", rather than "into the individual soul" according to a strictly "local" reading of ἐν: it refers to the difference between the human soul in general and its instantiations.

We can now consider (1)(a) and (2)(b). Is the possession of first principles by human kind related to individual PIs as art is related to its matter? Is it productive of all things the individual PIs become? Art imposes a form upon an appropriate matter that acquires or "becomes" that form. However, it does not seem that for Aristotle the *possession* of universals by humankind in general is what makes individual PIs become these universals. In the *locus classicus* (*An. Post.* II 19) where the acquisition of universals and first principles is addressed, there is no mention of such a possession being at all relevant in the aetiology of individual knowledge. There is rather a story concerning perception, memory and induction, which are put forward as epistemological conditions for acquiring the *habitus* of first principles.[53] Moreover, we have seen that Aristotle suggests that intellection is a kind of suffering from the very same intelligible (ὑπὸ τοῦ νοητοῦ),[54] without hinting at any mediational role of the possession of these intelligibles at a species-level. No doubt teaching is of the greatest

---

51 CASTON (1999); BERTI (2016), p. 145.
52 This point is originally and elegantly made by BERTI (2011), (2016).
53 *An. Post.* II 19, 99b15-100b5.
54 *De An.* III 4, 429a14; *Metaph.* Λ 7, 1072a30.

importance for Aristotle, but he does not values so much this social aspect of cognition with respect to the acquiring of first principles,[55] and in any case teaching could only be a part of this story, because at certain points of human history there is genuine *discovery* of new principles, as Aristotle himself proclaims on several occasions.[56] Thus, (1) and (2) do not appear to be satisfied by SI. In addition, (3) is also problematic as it is an illustration of (1) and (2) through the image of light. It is true that AI and light are both said to be ἕξεις, and human possession of principles is a *habitus*, but the possession of principles as belonging to humankind does *not* seem to actualize individual intellects in the same way as light makes potential colours into actual colours. The same objection could well be raised for (8): a discovery of previously unknown principles *by some individual* may well be deathless, as it remains forever a human possession, but it can hardly be conceived of as *eternal* precisely because it is a discovery. The eternity of human possession of principles cannot be inferred from the eternity of humankind; on the contrary, Aristotle seems to consider what SI takes to be AI as *not* eternal. Thus, either Aristotle takes AI to be and not to be eternal, or SI is wrong with respect to (8).

To sum up, SI satisfies (4), (5), (6), (7), (9), (10) and (b) and elegantly accounts for the otherwise enigmatic presence of (g) in III 5, but (1), (2), (3) and (8) are problematic.

II.4 Beyond DI, HI and SI: The Content Interpretation (CI)

In arguing for SI, Berti[57] reminds us that Themistius and Thomas considered those who proposed the view, but only to ridicule them as deaf and not worthy of even being called by name. While Thomas represents them

---

55 It is true that in *Top.* I 2, 101a36-101b4 dialectics – a cooperative art *par excellence* – is said to be useful in regards to the first principles of science and to allow the way towards principles, but his role is preparatory: Aristotelian dialectics is not epistemologically self-sufficient for reaching grasp of first principles, much the less is it sufficient to obtain scientific knowledge from them.

56 Some well-known examples are the progressive discovery of causes/principles and the *birth* of philosophy itself from myth (*Metaph.* A). In *Soph. El.* XXXIV Aristotle says that before his inquiry there was nothing at all on the topic. More generally, Aristotle is certainly conscious of the progress of sciences, driven by the accumulation of discoveries.

57 BERTI (2011); (2016), p. 148.

as holding that AI is «the *habit* of principles»[58] – the view I have labelled SI and that Berti defends – Themistius criticizes those who believe that AI «is either the first God or is identical to the premises, and to the bodies of knowledge derived from the premises».[59] The first option attacked by Themistius refers to DI, while the second option, which I am going to defend under the label of *Content Interpretation* (CI), is quite different. The *possession* (*habitus*) of principles by humankind is one thing, while the first premises and other propositions that can be inferred through them are quite another. Themistius' second option identifies AI with certain (*possessable*) *contents*, rather than with the *possession* of them. According to CI, AI is the objective system of first principles, which *may or may not* be the object of human science, i.e., which may become a human *habitus/* possession or not.

We can thus determine whether CI satisfies (1)-(10) and (b) and (g), with a comparative reference to SI, with which CI is sometimes too quickly identified.[60] The first principles are essences and basic truths: they are objects of our PI as a cognitive excellence. PI involves a cluster of capacities, among which are judgemental syntheses, belief-formation, inferential skills and conceptual abilities in general, but its excellence consists of grasping essences and first principles, of "becoming" the formal structure of reality. Just as art imposes a given form onto a suitable matter, first

58 Thomas, *In Aristotelis librum de anima commentarium*, book III, lectio 10, c. 729.
59 Themistius, *Paraph. De an.* 102.30-33.
60 BERTI (2011), (2016) seems to me to oscillate between SI and CI. On the one hand, as for CI he holds that AI is «the patrimony of eternal *truths* that humanity has gradually *discovered* and that it will continue to discover» (2016, p. 148); on the other, as for SI, he takes AI as a habit, a *human* habit eternally belonging to humankind, so inseparable from humanity as a kind (2016, p. 147). He told me *per litteras* that his proposal is substantially not different from what I am proposing here under the label of CI: but then I cannot grasp why he insists on the eternal belonging of AI to humankind and on AI's being a human habit, unless I interpret his proposal as a declination of SI. On CI as I mean it, the belonging of AI to humankind is *not* essential, AI is *not* a human habit, its eternity is fully independent of being possessed by human intellects so of giving rise to human habits. A symptom of Berti's oscillation is his twofold reference to Frege's *Third Realm* (FREGE, 1917) and Popper's *World 3* (POPPER/ECCLES, 1977). The first is fully objective and humanity independent, so it is apt to capture CI; the second is composed of *human products* like theories, language, poetry, music and art, so it rather corresponds to SI. The second exists independently of being contained in the mind of a *single* individual, whereas the first is independent of being contained in *human minds* at all.

principles and essences inform our PI, whose negative nature is the absolute suitability for becoming *any* form whatsoever. First principles meant
as the objective essences of reality are the genuine actualizers of our intellects, and they are precisely what our intellects become when we acquire
scientific knowledge. From this viewpoint, the art/matter analogy becomes clear, so (1)(a) is satisfied; possession of principles is produced by
principles themselves, AI is *what determines* the possession, i.e., it consists
of the possessed thinkable objects, rather than being the possession itself;
the latter is just the outcome of AI acting upon our PIs. Similarly, (2)(c)
can be accommodated: when we acquire the principles, our PI becomes
the principles. The principles *as possessed* by us give rise to perfect epistemic states. These states – no matter whether they belong to individuals
or to humankind – are literally produced by their objects, the principles.
Again, the possession of principles by humankind is *not* AI, rather it is
brought about by AI. AI is exactly what our PI becomes as soon as it
grasps its object: its object! Likewise, according to (3)(d) AI makes things
potentially intelligible into actually intellected things: the principles actualize our intellects, that are a like a suitable matter/potentiality for such
an actualization. Like light with colours, the principles illuminate our
minds through becoming present in them, through making our minds
become them. Light reveals colours to us, just as AI reveals *itself* to us as it
is essentially available for knowledge by our noetic capacities: the formal
structure of reality is self-revealing. If AI is the whole unified system of
first principles, what does it mean that they are not only separable, impassive and unmixed but also *essentially* actual? Their ontological independence is absolute, and they are not existentially dependent on our possession of them. The relation between them and our acquisition of them is
radically asymmetrical as they cause our PI's knowledge of them, whereas
our PIs do not cause them to exist and be what they are. Our PIs can become *contingently* identical with them, but their very nature is not mixed
with our cognitive relation to them. They are just what they are, insofar
as they shape the very formal structure of reality, and for them being actual boils down to being *true*, *real*, and eternally self-identical. This may
well be the meaning of (4) (e). As for (5)(f), the first principles are *superi-
or* to our intellects, as the most excellent object of a cognitive capacity is
more noble than the capacity itself. Perhaps, it is not a coincidence that
elsewhere[61] the νοούμενον is said to be τιμιώτερον than the νοῦς just as

61 *Metaph.* Λ 7, 1074b29-32.

here AI is said to be τιμιώτερον than PI. In accounting for (6)(h), SI is correct in that AI does not think intermittently because it does not think at all, as it is not a subject, but not because it is a *habit*. Rather, the system of first principles is the *object* of thought, and it is always objective and true whether thought or not. AI is not characterized as a habit but as a *sort* of ἕξις, such as light. Light is a positive disposition, not an acquired state like first actualities; *contra* SI, we do not need to take ἕξις as meaning human *habitus* (in the sense of: psychological acquired capacity) in this occurrence. According to (7)(i), AI is it essentially what it is only as *separated*:[62] the system of principles is what it essentially is independently of being grasped from this or that individual intellect, *and from humankind in general*. Its separation is its absolute objectivity, and the knowable content does not need to be known by any human being in order to be itself. Only AI is deathless and eternal, and as for (8)(l), primitive truths, principles and essences do never become. CI is particularly apt in accounting for the predicate of eternity, unlike SI (cfr. *supra*). AI is such that we *cannot* remember it (9)(m): there is no room for ἀνάμνησις and Platonic innatism. Memory depends on body and sensibility, whereas the first principles can be understood only by receiving them from the world (through experience, induction and teaching). Even if you possess them, you cannot remember them[63] and you need to re-actualize them *immer wieder* to "become" them again. Without the first principles nothing thinks (10)(n): if we take νοεῖν in the strongest sense of "grasping the essences",[64] we easily get that there is no such grasp without the object to be grasped. AI is indeed the noblest content of νοεῖν. Why is the difference between AI and PI "in the soul" (b)? When I come to know a principle/essence, my PI is *identical* to this principle, though this is a *pro tempore* identity. Yet, there is a difference *in* my soul between the *objective content* (AI) my soul has become identical with and my intellect (PI) as a *capacity* to become this or other noetic contents. AI and PI are different: one is eternal and divine,

---

62 In translating, I have referred μόνον at a22 to τοῦθ'ὅπερ ἐστί rather than to χωρισθεὶς δ'ἐστὶ. But both options are fine with CI: first principles are *just* what they are insofar as they are considered as separated; first principles are what they essentially are *only* as considered independently on being grasped by us (i.e. in their absolute objectivity).

63 Unless you remember them *per accidens*: *per se* you only remember perceptual contents (*Mem.* 1, 450a23-25).

64 This is the most proper sense of νοεῖν in *De Anima*, as it is shown by BURNYEAT (2008), p. 24-25 and FRONTEROTTA (2016).

the other is mortal, but they can temporarily become identical. It must be acknowledged that (g) is not as easy to explain by CI as it is by SI. Even though a cognitive function is *by nature* posterior to its natural object, PI as a potentiality is prior *in time* to its actual identity with the Object (AI), namely, to the knowledge/possession of principles. Why then does actuality come first also temporally, if we consider it not "for the individual" but "in general"? Principles as such are already in actuality, and their actuality consists of them being *true* and *real*, and thus eternally available for understanding. *What* individuals become when they know is already there, as actual knowledge is identical to the Object known, and this Object (AI) comes before any PI. Given that for CI, AI is essentially knowable but absolutely independent of our knowledge, (g) is *poorly* satisfied by CI, because we need to take "actual knowledge" as loosely referring to "what actual knowledge is about", i.e., its objective content.

To sum up, CI appears to satisfy (1)-(10) and (b), and to poorly satisfy (g).

CI faces two major issues. First, why is AI *one*, whereas the principles are many? AI is the *unified* system of principles, the formal structure of the ordered cosmos, and it is in virtue of this that reality is intelligible at all. Even if many principles belong to AI, AI as the whole system of first principles is still a Unity rather than a disordered and juxtaposed multiplicity. Second, why qualify as νοῦς the first principles, i.e., those objective formal structures that are νοητά? After all, they are what our νοῦς *is* when it knows and understands, so they can be labelled as νοῦς in virtue of the original connaturality between cognitive principle and cognized object, which is a grounding idea of Plato that Aristotle ultimately keeps endorsing. In thinking/contemplating a geometrical theorem my PI is somehow de-individualized and *becomes* the theorem, so the theorem is nothing more than the thought of it:[65] it is not just my subjective thought, but rather the formal, objective Content my thought is now identical with. The theorem is the very principle of its own thinkability, and it is objective but ultimately connatural with thought. This is why the theorem is by nature apt to illuminate/actualize our intellects as it was light.

---

65 I agree with LEWIS (2003), p. 109-110 on that the sameness between our νοῦς and its object is *accidental*: indeed, our νοῦς becomes occasionally the same as a given intelligible (a principle or an essence), but it remains itself *in being*: in being, it remains absolutely open to any possible contents, as defined in III 4 (see *supra*, I.2).

Below is a synoptic chart of the analysis put forth so far. Of course, the advocates of one or another reading may well not be persuaded by my suggestions of what is satisfied and what is not under a particular reading. In any case, I hope to have made a plausible case for an interpretive option (CI), which perhaps deserves some attention of scholars in their future research.

De An. III 5:	Divine Int.	Human Int	"Social" Int.	*Content* Int.
1 (=a)	no	yes	No	yes
2 (=c)	no	yes	No	yes
3 (=d)	no	yes	No	yes
4 (=e)	yes	no	yes	yes
5 (=f)	yes	yes	yes	yes
6 (=h)	yes	no	yes	yes
7 (=i)	yes	yes	yes	yes
8 (=l)	yes	no	no	yes
9 (=m)	poorly	yes	yes	yes
10 (=n)	poorly	yes	yes	yes
b	poorly	yes	yes	yes
g	poorly	no	yes	poorly

References

ACCATTINO, P. (2014). Alessandro di Afrodisia interprete del *De Anima* di Aristotele. *Studia graeco-arabica*, 4, p. 275-288.

BARNES, J. (1979). Aristotle's Concept of Mind. In: Barnes, J.; Schofield, M.; Sorabji, R. (eds.). *Articles on Aristotle*, IV. London. Duckworth, p. 32-41.

BERTI, E. (2014). L'intelletto attivo: una modesta proposta, *lectio brevis* presso l'Accademia dei Lincei: http//www.accademiadeilincei.it/files/documenti/Lecti oBrevis_Berti.pdf.

_____ (2016). Aristotle's *Nous poiêtikos*: Another Modest Proposal. In: SILLITTI/ STELLA/FRONTEROTTA (2016), p.137-153.

BRENTANO, F. (1867). *Die Psychologie des Aristoteles, insbesondere seine Lehre vom ΝΟΥΣ ΠΟΙΕΤΙΚΟΣ.* Mainz. Verlag von Franz Kirchheim.

CASTON, V. (1999). Aristotle's Two Intellects: A Modest Proposal. *Phronesis*, 43, n °3, p. 199-227.

CHARLTON, W. (1991). Philoponus. *On Aristotle On the Intellect (de Anima 3.4-8)*, translated by W. Charlton. London. Duckworth.

DRISCOLL, A. (1992). The Anaxagorean Assumption in Aristotle's Account of Mind. In: Preus. A., Anton, J.P. (eds.). *Aristotle's Ontology.* Albany, N.Y. State University of New York Press, p. 273-293.

FINE, G. (1984). Separation. *Oxford Studies in Ancient Philosophy*, 2, p. 31-87.

FREDE, M. (1996). La théorie aristotélicienne de l'intellect agent. In: ROMEYER-DHERBEY/VIANO (1996), p. 377-390.

FREGE, G. (1917). *Logical Investigations.* Oxford. Blackwell.

FRONTEROTTA, F. (2007). Ou mnhmoneuen de...Aristot. De Anima Γ 5 a 23-25. *Elenchos*, 28, p. 79-104.

_____ (2016). Il significato del verbo νοεῖν in *De Anima* III 4. In: SILLITTI/STEL-LA/FRONTEROTTA (2016), p. 77-96.

GERSON, L. (2004). The Unity of Intellect in Aristotle's *De Anima. Phronesis*, 49, n°4, p. 348-373.

GREGORIC, P., PFEIFFER, CH. (2015). Grasping Aristotle's Intellect. *Documenti e studi sulla tradizione filosofica medievale*, XXVI, p.13-31.

HAMELIN, O. (1953). *La théorie de l'intellect d'après Aristote et ses commentateurs* (avec une introduction par E. Barbotin). Paris. Vrin.

HICKS, R.D. (1907). Aristotle, *De Anima*, with translation, introduction and notes. Cambridge. Cambridge University Press (reprint: Hildesheim, Georg Olms Verlag, 1990).

KAHN, CH. (1992). Aristotle on Thinking. In: NUSSMAUM/RORTY (1992), p. 359-380.

KOSMAN, A. (1992). What does the Maker Mind Make? In: NUSSBAUM/RORTY (1992), p. 343-358.

LEWIS. F.A. (1996). Self-knowledge in Aristotle. *Topoi*, 15, n° 1, p. 39-58.

_____ (2003). Is there Room for Anaxagoras in an Aristotelian Theory of Mind?. *Oxford Studies in Ancient Philosophy*, 25, p. 91-129.

MILLER, F. (2012). Aristotle on Separability of Mind. In: Shields, Ch. (ed.), *The Oxford Handbook of Aristotle*. Oxford. Oxford University Press, p. 306-342.

MINGUCCI, G. (2015). *La fisiologia del pensiero in Aristotele.* Il Mulino. Bologna.

MODRAK, D. (1986). Aristotle on Thinking. In: *Proceedings of the Boston Area Colloquium in Ancient Philosophy*, 2, n° 1. Leiden-Boston-Köln. Brill, p. 209-236.

MORAUX, P. (1978). Le *De Anima* dans la tradition greque: quelques aspects de l'interprétation du traité, de Théophraste à Thémistius. In: Lloyd, G.E.R.; Owen, G.E.L. (eds.), *Aristotle on Mind and the Senses*. Cambridge. Cambridge University Press, p. 280-324.

MORRISON, D. (1985). Χωριστός in Aristotle. *Harvard Studies in Classical Philology*, p. 89-105.

NUSSBAUM, M.; RORTY, A.O. (eds.) (1992). *Essays on Aristotle's* De Anima. Oxford. Clarendon Press.

POLANSKY, R. (2007). *Aristotle's De Anima*. Cambridge. Cambridge University Press.

POLITIS, V. (2001). Aristotle's Account of the Intellect as Pure Capacity. *Ancient Philosophy*, 21, p. 375-402.

POPPER, K.; ECCLES, J. (1977). *The Self and the Brain*. Berlin. Springer International.

RIST, J. (1966). Notes on Aristotle *De Anima* 3.5. *Classical Philology*, 61, p. 8-20.

ROMEYER-DHERBEY, G.; VIANO, C. (eds.) (1996). *Corps et Âme. Sur le* De Anima *d'Aristote*. Paris. Vrin.

ROSS, D. (1956). *Aristotelis De anima*, recognovit, brevique adnotatione critica instruxit. Oxford. Clarendon Press.

_____ (1961). Aristotle. *De Anima*, translated with an introduction and commentary. Oxford. Oxford Clarendon Press.

SHIELDS, CH. (2016). Aristotle. *De Anima*, translated with an introduction and commentary. Oxford. Clarendon Press.

SILLITTI, G.; STELLA, F.; FRONTEROTTA, F. (eds.) (2016). *Il NOÛS di Aristotele*. Sankt Augustin. Academia Verlag.

SISKO, J. (2001). Aristotle and the Modern Mind. In: Cleary, J.; Gurtler, G.M. (eds.). *Proceedings of the Boston Area Colloquium in Ancient Philosophy*, 16. Leiden, Boston, Köln. Brill, p. 177-198.

THOMAE AQUINATIS (2000). *De Unitate Intellectus Contra Averroistas*, It. tr. by A. Ghisalberti, Milano. Bompiani.

_____ (1975) *In Aristotelis librum De Anima commentarium*, It. tr. by A. Caparello, Roma. Abete.

TODD, R.B. (1996). Themistius. *On Aristotle's On the Soul*. London. Duckworth.

TRENDELENBURG, F.A. (1833). *Aristotelis De anima libri tres*, Ad interpretum graecorum auctoritatem et codicum fidem recognovit commentariis illustravit F.A. Trendelenburg, Ienae, Walz (reprint: Charleston, Nabu Press, 2010).

WEDIN, M. (1988). *Mind and Imagination in Aristotle*. New Haven. Yale University Press.

_____ (1989). Aristotle on the Mechanics of Thought. *Ancient Philosophy*, 9, 1, p. 67-86.

_____ (1993). Tracking Aristotle's νοῦς. In: Durrant, M. (eds.), *Aristotle's* De Anima *in Focus*. London. Routledge, p. 128-161.

ZUCCA, D. (2016). Di cosa parla *De Anima* Γ 5? Una modestissima proposta. *La Cultura. Rivista di filosofia e filologia*, 1/2016, p. 47-75.

Aristotle and the "Cartesians' Error"

Giulia Mingucci

I. Introduction

The title of this paper refers to the title of a famous work by Antonio Da-masio, *Descartes' Error* (DAMASIO, 1994), but with a significant variation. I will not go into the complex exegetical problems raised by the historical Descartes' views on the mind-body relationship, but I will rather deal with the influence of "Cartesian Dualism" on the contemporary debate on philosophy of mind and on the contemporary scholarship of Aristotle's psychology.[1]

We owe it to Descartes that we think of mind and matter as the two great, mutually exclusive and mutually exhaustive, divisions of the universe we inhabit (cf. KENNY, 1989, p. 1). In an attempt to reject Cartesian Dualism, philosophers and scientists of the twentieth century proposed a return to the ancient position that Descartes had opposed, i.e. Aristotle's psychological hylomorphism.[2]

---

1 Descartes' views about the relationship between self and body receive their best-known formulation in his *Meditations on First Philosophy* (1641). Often Descartes writes as if he thinks that a human person is an immaterial substance – a spirit or soul – which stands in some special relation to a certain physical body, its body ("real distinction" between mind and body). But at other times he speaks as if he thinks that a human person is some sort of combination of an immaterial soul and a physical body, which stand to one another in a rather mysterious relation of "substantial union". When philosophers today talk about "Cartesian Dualism" they usually mean the former view.

2 Bibliography on the relevance of Aristotle's psychological hylomorphism to contemporary philosophy of mind is now extensive. See, at least, Enrico Berti's pioneering studies (BERTI, 1998; 2008); the monographic volume of *Rivista di Filoso-fia Neo-Scolastica* dedicated to the topic (BERTI, 2011; GALVAN, 2011; LOWE, 2011; RUNGGALDIER, 2011); Anna Marmodoro's critical analysis of the contemporary proposals for "reconditioning" Aristotle's hylomorphism (MAR-MODORO, 2013); William Jaworski's recent publication (JAWORSKI, 2016) and his presentation of it in this volume (p. 181-196).

Psychological hylomorphism is an application to living beings of the ontological thesis according to which every substance is a compound of matter (ὕλη) and form (μορφή). On this perspective, the soul is the form of an appropriate matter, a matter that has essentially the capacity to be endowed with life: the body. The soul is the "first actuality" of the body's capacity for life: it is the actual possession of the body's capacity to perform a series of life functions. On Aristotle's view, therefore, soul and body are reciprocally interdependent aspects of the living being, so that we must consider the former as an enmattered or embodied form, and the latter as an enformed or ensouled matter.

This conception of the soul-body unity has been considered as a viable solution to the so-called "mind-body problem", which is the core of today's debate on philosophy of mind. A return to Aristotle in this area of research, however, is not simple for two fundamental reasons.

The first reason concerns the theory-laden character of the interpreters' reading of Aristotle's reflection on the relationship between soul and body, and between psychological and physical states. There is, in fact, a common tendency in the most widespread interpretations of Aristotle's hylomorphism, namely reading it by adopting conceptual categories born in modern age, and thus assuming, more or less explicitly, a certain post-Cartesian theory of mind.

The second difficulty concerns a specific area of his psychological research, namely his noetics, his conception of thought (νοῦς). Among the states of the living being that Aristotle considers hylomorphic or psychophysical, there is a singular absence: thinking is considered to be separable from the body. With regard to this claim, contemporary authors are, at best, embarrassed, noting a tension – if not even a real inconsistency – between Aristotle's hylomorphist perspective on the ψυχή-σῶμα relation and his statements in *De Anima* concerning the separability of νοῦς.

This paper addresses only the first one of the aforementioned difficulties, namely the theory-laden reading of Aristotle's psychology.[3] In particular, I intend to argue that the way Aristotle's psychological hylomorphism has been (and in most cases still is) interpreted and accepted in the twentieth century debate had been influenced by the fundamental "Cartesians' error": the distinction – if not anymore ontological at least conceptual – between the mental and the physical. I therefore begin with a brief introduction to the philosophical debate on the mind-body prob-

---

3 For the second problem, see Diego Zucca's essay in this volume (p. 139-162).

lem (see § II), and then show the influence that this debate had on the scholarship's reception of Aristotle's hylomorphism by taking, by way of example, perception (see § III).

II. The Debate on the Mind-Body Problem

In the twentieth century philosophical debate, one of the most discussed problems has been that of the nature of the mind and its place in the physical world. The question has more than one formulation: one, perhaps the best known, is expressed in terms of the relationship between mind and body. Are these entities different on the ontological level or are they the same reality considered from different points of view? Is the mind an essentially biological entity or could it be, in principle, disembodied? How can the body think? How can the mind produce physical effects? These concerns have a historical origin, i.e. the modern age, and a father, i.e. René Descartes (see, e.g., DI FRANCESCO, 2002, p. 35; KIM, 2006, p. 3; NANNINI, 2002, p. 22-24).

In the *Meditationes de prima philosophia* (1641), Descartes describes what properly characterises the human being, the soul, as something completely different from that which may be found in other sensible entities. Both Aristotle and the scholastic Aristotelians used the Latin and Greek words corresponding to soul (Lat. *anima*; Gr. ψυχή) to designate the principle of all the life functions of a natural organic body, i.e. self-nourishment, growth, and reproduction (nutritive faculty); perception, desire, and locomotion (sensory-motor faculty); thought (rational faculty). In order to distinguish his own, new, concept of the soul, in the Fifth Set of Replies Descartes provides a close criticism of this usage of the term *anima*:

> Thus, those who first gave "soul" its meaning probably didn't distinguish between two sources of energy or activity that are in us: the one by which we are nourished and grow and unthinkingly perform all the other actions that we have in common with the brutes, and the one by virtue of which we think. So they used the one word "soul" to name both [...]. Whereas I, realising that what leads to our being nourished is radically different from what leads to our thinking, have said that when the word "soul" is used to name to both of these sources it is ambiguous. If we want to take "soul" in its special sense, as mea-

ning the "first actuality" or "principal form of man", then it must be understood to apply only to the source in us of our thinking; and to avoid ambiguity I have generally used the term "mind" for this[4] (AT VII, p. 356).

This new object of inquiry, the mind, is considered by Descartes as the unitary centre of subjectivity:

> But what then am I? A thing which thinks. What is a thing which thinks? It is a thing which doubts, understands, [conceives], affirms, denies, wills, refuses, which also imagines and feels[5] (AT VII, p. 28).

Intellectual reflection ("doubting, understanding, affirming, denying"), volition ("willing, refusing"), imagination and feelings:[6] these apparently disparate characters of mental life present to Descartes a common feature, i.e. *conscientia*, i.e. the power of the rational soul to reflect of its own thoughts and experiences (see also AT VII, p. 160; VIII, p. 7).

As the sole possessor of consciousness, mind is not only a distinct *res* from the extended one (the body), but it is also something "private", which has a direct access in our own case by means of "introspection". This method, characterised by an inward examination of our thoughts and feelings, is altogether different from the scientific-experimental one adopted in physical investigations. Therefore, Cartesian Dualism favoured both an ontological distinction between mind and body, and an epistemological distinction between the sciences dealing with them, respectively psychology and physics.[7]

---

4 Sic, quia forte primi homines non distinxerunt in nobis illud principium quo nutrimur, crescimus, et reliqua omnia nobiscum brutis communia sine ulla cogitatione peragimus, ab eo quo cogitamus, utrumque unico *animae* nomine appellarunt [...]. Ego vero, animadvertens principium quo nutrimur toto genere distingui ab eo quo cogitamus, dixi *animae* nomen, cum pro utroque sumitur, esse aequivocum; atque ut specialiter sumatur pro *actu primo* sive *praecipua hominis forma*, intelligendum tantum esse de principio quo cogitamus, hocque nomine *mentis* ut plurimum appellavi ad vitandam aequivocationem. Text by ADAM/ TANNERY (1974) [AT]. English translation by HALDANE (1911).

5 Sed quid igitur sum? Res cogitans. Quid est hoc? Nempe dubitans, intelligens, affirmans, negans, volens, nolens, imaginans quoque et sentiens.

6 For a discussion of the standard and the revisionist interpretations of this passage (the former including, the latter excluding, sense perception and imagination from the category of the "mental"), see the recent study by SCOTT (2017).

7 Introspection was indeed the method of the first "scientific" school of psychology, i.e. Structuralism, led by Wilhelm Wundt in Germany since 1879 (when he

As it is understood by philosophers and scientists of mind today, Cartesian Dualism consists of two claims:

> *(SD)* Strong Dualism: The mental and the physical are separate substances *(Token Dualism)* of two fundamentally and irreducibly distinct kinds *(Type Dualism)*.
>
> *(CI)* Causal Interactionism: Mental states causally interact with physical states, both causing such states and being caused by them.

It is the conjunction of *(SD)* and *(CI)* that gave rise to the mind-body problem(s). Many of Descartes' readers found it paradoxical that two items that are radically different in nature from one another coexist in an individual and interact, giving rise to his observable behaviour.[8]

To this problem, modern philosophers advanced mainly two different solutions.[9] The first one is the rejection of *(CI)* in favour of *parallelism*, the doctrine that mental and physical states never interact causally, but merely "keep in step" with one other. The second solution is the rejection of *(SD)*: there is only one substance that exists, be it at the origin of physical and mental phenomena. This conception, known as "Ontological Monism" [**(M)**], has been a dominant position on the mind-body problem

founded the first formal laboratory for psychological research at the University of Leipzig).

8 The nature of the interaction between the mental and the physical is one of the most discussed claims in the history of the reception of Descartes' thought. Modern critics of Descartes found two types of difficulties, one conceptual and the other empirical. *Conceptual objections*: (a) causation must be local: there can be no causal interaction between something located in physical space and something that lacks physical location altogether; (b) in causation some properties of the cause must be transmitted to the effect: since mental and physical states have no properties in common, they have no properties which could be transmitted between them. *Empirical objections*: (c) according to Descartes, the nonphysical mind acts upon the body by altering the direction of motion of animal spirits; but any change of direction in the motion of the animal spirits is caused by some force acting upon them, and the nonphysical self cannot be the source of any such force. Cf. LOWE (2000), p. 21-26.

9 There is also a third solution, namely the "antimetaphysical tradition", whose leading representatives in the modern age are John Locke, David Hume and Immanuel Kant. The antimetaphysical tradition rejects the question of the nature of the soul/mind as nonsensical, and instead addresses the problem of the empirical functioning of it. The question is no longer "what is soul/mind?" but "how does it actually work?". I will not take into consideration the antimetaphysical tradition in this context, since it has not influenced the exegetical debate on Aristotle's hylomorphism.

and, as we shall see, also on the debate on the interpretations of Aristotle's psychological hylomorphism.

Historically, (**M**) has been developed in three forms, depending on the nature of the substance that is assumed to be the underlying substrate of psychophysical activities:

> (**P**) Physicalism or Materialism: All that exist is physical (or material).[10]
>
> (**I**) Immaterialism: Mental items constitute the fundamental reality of the world, and physical things are mere constructs out of thoughts and other mental experiences.
>
> (**N**) Neutralism: The mental and the physical are two (independently identifiable) aspects of a single underlying substance that is in itself neither mental nor physical, but neutral or indifferent.

In the twentieth century debate on the mind-body problem, the main role has been played by (**P**), which may have two different forms:

> (*SP*) Strong Physicalism: Mental states are physical states, both in the weaker sense that each and every individual mental state is identical with some physical state (*Token Identity*) and in the stronger sense that all mental properties and kinds are identical with physical properties and kinds (*Type Identity*).
>
> (*WP*) Weak Physicalism: All that exist is physical (*Token Identity*) but may have also nonphysical, i.e. mental, properties (*Type Dualism*).

Whereas the *Token Identity Thesis* merely asserts the impossibility of the existence of nonphysical particulars, the *Type Identity Thesis* also asserts the impossibility of nonphysical descriptions. By both holding the *Token Identity Thesis*, *(SP)* and *(WP)* maintain one of the most important principles of modern physics, the *Principle of the Causal Closure of the Physical Domain*, according to which, «if a physical event has a cause (occurring) at time *t*, it has a sufficient physical cause at *t*» (cf. KIM, 2005, p. 15; 2006, p. 195). In addition, *(SP)* holds also the *Type Identity Thesis*, which answers to the requirement of the *Principle of the Explanatory Adequacy of*

---

10 The terms materialism and physicalism are often used interchangeably, although there are differences. Whereas in modern materialism the material underlying reality is defined a priori – as a solid, impenetrable, permanent substance, interacting deterministically and only by contact – , in the physicalist ontology there exists everything that is admitted, a posteriori, by the physical science, like forces, waves, and fields.

Physics that physics provides «a true and exhaustive account of all physical phenomena» (cf. LEWIS, 1966). Since mental properties, it is claimed, are merely physical properties at a different, and less precise, level of description, mentalistic descriptions are in principle replaceable by physical descriptions. Instead *(WP)*, though maintaining a physicalist ontology, rejects the *Type Identity Thesis*; that is, it admits the possibility of nonphysical descriptions. Mental properties and psychological laws are irreducible to physical properties and physical laws: *(WP)* recognises the *Explanatory Autonomy of the Mental* against the *Principle of the Explanatory Adequacy of Physics*. Therefore, according to *(WP)*, psychology and physics can develop mutually alternative systems of classification, describing differently the same (physical) reality.

The rejection of the *Type Identity Thesis* is one feature that *(WP)* has in common with **(N)**. Unlike *(WP)*, however, **(N)** rejects the physicalist ontology, arguing that the single underlying substance is not physical, but neutral or composite. It is possible to offer two different descriptions of this single underlying substance, one in purely physical terms and the other in purely mental terms. For this reason, this theory of the mind is also known by the name of "Double Aspect Theory", because it distinguishes two aspects or properties of a substance that are identifiable independently of one another.[11]

III. Aristotle's Psychological Hylomorphism under the Cartesian Lens

The modern and contemporary solutions to the mind-body problem mentioned above – Immaterialism [**(I)**], Strong Physicalism [**(SP)**], Weak Physicalism [*(WP)*], and Neutralism [**(N)**] – can also be found in today's debate on Aristotle's psychological hylomorphism. I will consider, by way of example, the major interpretations of Aristotle's analysis of perception, αἴσθησις.

In the *De Anima*, Aristotle describes perceiving as the exercise of a faculty, the faculty of perception, which essentially involves bodily organs, the sense organs; it consists in "receiving" the sensible qualities "without the matter":

---

11 I will reserve the name "Double-Aspect Theory" only for **(N)**, although many interpreters apply it also to *(WP)* by virtue of their common support for *Type Dualism*.

> We must understand as true generally of every sense that sense is that which is receptive of the form of sensible objects without the matter, just as wax receives the impression of the signet-ring without the iron or the gold, and receives the impression of the gold or bronze, but not as gold or bronze; so in every case sense is affected by that which has colour, or flavour, or sound, but by it, not *qua* having a particular identity, but *qua* having a certain quality, and in virtue of its formula (*de An.* II 12, 424a17-24).[12]

Aristotle's theory of perception has been the subject of a debate among the scholars in which one can recognise the main exegetical positions on Aristotle's psychological theory in general.

It has been said that according to *(SP)*, mental states are identical with certain physical states. The readers of Aristotle hardly understood his doctrine of the soul, as a whole, as a reductionist theory;[13] however, there are those who have interpreted some aspects of it in this sense. The most striking example is precisely the theory of perception. For the interpretation called "Literalism" can mask a reductionist hypothesis on αἴσθησις, according to which it would be nothing but a physiological process, a process of ordinary alteration whereby the sense organ literally takes on the exact same quality that is being perceived (for example, in perceiving red, the organ of sight becomes literally red). This *(SP)* interpretation is held for example by Thomas Slakey in a 1961 paper, *Aristotle on Sense Perception*:

> I therefore submit as conclusively established a literal interpretation of Aristotle's statement that perception is a process in which the perceived object makes the sense organ "such as itself actually is". This in-

---

12 Καθόλου δὲ περὶ πάσης αἰσθήσεως δεῖ λαβεῖν ὅτι ἡ μὲν αἴσθησίς ἐστι τὸ δεκτικὸν τῶν αἰσθητῶν εἰδῶν ἄνευ τῆς ὕλης, οἷον ὁ κηρὸς τοῦ δακτυλίου ἄνευ τοῦ σιδήρου καὶ τοῦ [20] χρυσοῦ δέχεται τὸ σημεῖον, λαμβάνει δὲ τὸ χρυσοῦν ἢ τὸ χαλκοῦν σημεῖον, ἀλλ' οὐχ ᾗ χρυσὸς ἢ χαλκός· ὁμοίως δὲ καὶ ἡ αἴσθησις ἑκάστου ὑπὸ τοῦ ἔχοντος χρῶμα ἢ χυμὸν ἢ ψόφον πάσχει, ἀλλ' οὐχ ᾗ ἕκαστον ἐκείνων λέγεται, ἀλλ' ᾗ τοιονδί, καὶ κατὰ τὸν λόγον. Text by ROSS (1956). English translation by HETT (2000). In the *De Anima*, Aristotle dedicates to the analysis of perception eight chapters of the second book (II 5-12) and the first two of the third (III 1-2). I chose to quote this particular passage because it is a sort of recapitulation of his theory of αἴσθησις.

13 With the exception of MATSON (1966): he claimed that all the Greeks, including Aristotle, did not have a mind-body problem because for them the mind was identical to the body.

terpretation can be expressed in the following proposition, which I will label *A: an object which is perceived to be* x *makes the sense organ involved in its perception to be itself* x [...]. The phrase "receiving forms without matter" cannot be used to explain what perception is; it simply repeats the meaning of "perceives" in obscure philosophical language. The mistake is to think that we can explain perception not only in the sense of specifying physiological phenomena upon which it depends, but in the sense that we can somehow make more clear what perception is and how it is that an animal has the power of discerning (SLAKEY, 1961, p. 474-475, 479-481).

Others propose instead that perceiving and taking on a sensible quality are *distinct types*, though closely related. Richard Sorabji, for example, proposes a literalist interpretation of αἴσθησις in accordance with (**N**) (SORABJI, 1974; 1992; 2001). According to Sorabji, perception is a psychophysical or hylomorphic phenomenon, i.e. a σύνολον of matter (the physiological process) and form (the cognitive act). He maintains that the material aspect of this hylomorphic phenomenon is the sense organ's literal assimilation of the sensible quality:

> There is good reason to interpret the reception of form without matter physiologically. It means that e.g. the organ of sight (i.e. the jelly inside the eye [...]) takes on the colour of the object seen, without taking on any material particles from the object [...]. In that case, in talking of the organ's reception of form without matter, Aristotle is so far talking only of the physiological process (SORABJI, 1974, p. 52).

Nevertheless, «the physiological process is only the material cause of anger. There is also a formal cause» (SORABJI, 1974, p. 54). Sorabji states that the formal cause of perception is the propositional content of perception, its intentional character (cf. SORABJI, 1992). It is therefore possible to offer two descriptions of perception: from a material point of view, as a process of alteration (ἀλλοίωσις); and from a formal point of view, as a cognitive or intentional act. The scientific definition of perception must include both these aspects.

Sorabji leaves open the exact nature of the relationship between the mental and the physiological types of event in perception; his definition

is simply the sum of the two components.[14] Functionalist and superveni-
ent interpreters have tried to clarify the point. According to them, the
mental is a property of a material system; mental properties are dependent on, but irreducible to the physical properties of the material system.
Functionalism and Supervenience can be therefore classified as positions
of *(WP)*, as they combine a physicalist ontology with the *Explanatory Autonomy of the Mental.*

One quote is especially representative of this position: «We could be
made of Swiss cheese and it would not matter» (PUTNAM, 1975, p. 127).
According to functionalists like Hilary Putnam, mental states are functional states independent of the particular physical system that realises
them. The same mental state can be realised in a variety of physical systems, if they preserve the defining relations to causal inputs, behavioural
outputs and other mental states, i.e. if they are "functional isomorphic"
(Multiple Realisation Thesis). Functionalists assume the artefact model, in
which the relation of form to matter is contingent. To take the example of
perception, it is contingent whether the awareness of sensible qualities is
realised in the physiological set-up of an animal eye or in the physical set-
up of a robotic eye, since these two material systems are functionally isomorphic. «What we are really interested in», says Putnam, «as Aristotle
saw, is form and not matter» (PUTNAM, 1975, p. 136). By interpreting
the Aristotelian form as a functional state of a physical system, Putnam
was the first to make Aristotle an ancient precursor to functionalism.[15]

14 Sorabji specifies the relation between the phenomenon of perception as a whole
    and its material aspect as relation of composition (cf. SORABJI, 1972, p. 55); but
    he does not specify the relation of the formal aspect to the material aspect. On
    Aristotle's view, a notion of this kind, which is held together only by the simple
    conjunction of the two components, cannot express the essential unity of the
    form and the matter of a hylomorphic compound, and therefore cannot provide
    the scientific definition of it (cf. *An. Post.* II 10, 93b35-37; *de Part. An.* I 3,
    643b17-24; *Metaph.* Z 4, 1030b7-10; 12, 1037b24-27; H 6, 1045a12-14; *Poet.* 20,
    1457a28-31).
15 Martha Craven Nussbaum was the first Aristotelian scholar that confirmed the
    convergence between Hilary Putnam's functionalism and Aristotle's hylomor-
    phism, by adopting a functionalist perspective in her translation and commen-
    tary to *De Motu Animalium* (NUSSBAUM, 1978). Since then, many interpreters
    have read Aristotle's psychological hylomorphism as a functionalist theory: see,
    at least, WILKES (1978); SHIELDS (1990); IRWIN (1991); COHEN (1992).
    Since the publication of *Philosophy and Our Mental Life* (1975), Hilary Putnam
    has modified the meaning of his reference to Aristotle, recognising a closer rela-
    tionship between form and matter (cf. NUSSBAUM/PUTNAM, 1992).

The *Multiple Realisation Thesis* fails to see how radical the soul-body unity is in Aristotle's work. Though Aristotle's use of artefacts to exemplify the relationship between form and matter in the living compound is not rare (see, e.g., *Phys*. II 2, 194a21-27; 8, 199a8-20; 9, 199a34-200b8; *de An*. I 1, 403a29-b7; II 1, 412b11-17; *de Part. An*. I 1, 639b11-30; 640b17-29; 641a5-17; 642a6-13; *Metaph*. H 2, 1043a14-28), to him the soul-body unity has peculiar features compared to other hylomorphic compounds (see esp. *Phys*. II 1, 192b8-32). According to Aristotle, the living body contains within itself the ἀρχή of all its life functions; when it performs them, it naturally brings into realisation the selfsame capacities by which it is defined. Therefore, it cannot be composed of a matter whatsoever: it must be composed of a very specific matter organised in a determinate way in order to perform the "multi-tasking" function by which it is defined, that is, *living*. A body composed of a different matter or arranged in different structure would not be capable of living, and thus would fail its intrinsic goal, being a "body" only homonymously, as Aristotle puts it (cf. *de Part. An*. I 1, 640b34-641a6): it would have only the name, but not the definition corresponding to the name, of a living body (cf. *Cat*. 1, 1a1-6).

Supervenience seems to establish a closer relationship between the mental properties and the physical properties of a material system. In fact, according to what is established by one of the most representative interpreters supporting this position, Victor Caston,[16] the fundamental tenet of Supervenience is the *Nonsymmetric Covariation Thesis*. According to it, there cannot be a difference in mental states without a difference in physical states (cf. CASTON, 1997, p. 313-314).

By arguing that mental variations "follow from" physical variations, Supervenience gives the matter ontological and explanatory priority over the form, thus overturning Aristotle's teleological perspective. According to Aristotle, bodily structures and processes depend on the soul and its functions, and not *vice versa*. With the intent to recognise priority of the form over the matter, Caston combines the *Nonsymmetric Covariation Thesis* with the *Causal Efficacy of the Mental* (cf. CASTON, 1997, p. 338). According to this type of Supervenience, known as *Emergentism*, mental pro-

---

16 Victor Caston believes that the first supporter of Supervenience was Alexander of Aphrodisias. According to Caston, Alexander took the soul to be a power that "supervenes" on the temperament of the body (cf. Alex.Aphr. *de An*. 25.2-3) – where by "supervenes", Alexander would have meant "follows from" (cf. *de An*. 104.27-34: «the difference in soul follows from the temperament of the body's being of a certain sort»): see CASTON (1997), p. 247-350.

perties "emerge" from matter when it reaches a certain level of complexity as genuinely new, irreducible causal powers obeying their own laws (i.e. laws which are not deducible from physical laws):

> [...] Aristotle might tend towards an emergentist solution, that is, one that accepts downward causation while upholding the supervenience of the mental [...]. On this view, which properties a living thing has, including its causal powers, will be fully *determined* by its elemental constitution. Nevertheless, not all behaviour will be *caused* by its elemental powers. Some behaviour will result from contribution of new, emergent causal powers that arise, necessarily, from matter. Emergentism thus accounts for the preeminence Aristotle gives to form, without undercutting the supporting role matter plays (CASTON, 1993, p. 332, 337-338).

Emergentism, though, seems to run into over-determination, since it maintains both the *Principle of the Causal Closure of the Physical Domain* and the *Causal Efficacy of the Mental*.[17] The emergentist appears to have two choices to consider. Either *(a)* she can recognise that the causal work is made at the physical level, that is, at the level of the physical system that underlies the mental state, or *(b)* she can opt to abandon physical causal closure. In case *(a)*, the mental state would not work at all; in other words, it would be an epiphenomenal property (*Epiphenomenalism*).[18] In case *(b)*, the emergentist would reject what is held to be the "characteristic principle" of Physicalism [(**P**)] (cf. POPPER, 1977, p. 51) and, with

---

17 The argument, known as the *Causal Closure Argument*, has three premises: (1) At every time at which a physical state has a cause, it has a fully sufficient physical cause (*Principle of the Causal Closure of the Physical*); (2) Some physical states have mental states amongst their causes (*Causal Efficacy of the Mental*); (3) When a physical state has a mental state amongst its causes, it is not overdetermined by that mental state and some other physical state (*Principle of Causal Non-overdetermination*). Premise (3) rules out the possibility that the physical effect P of a certain mental state M simultaneously has independent but fully sufficient physical causes $P(1)$, $P(2)$... $P(n)$; therefore we have no option but to identify the mental state M with one or another of the physical states $P(1)$, $P(2)$...$P(n)$. Cf. LOWE (2000), p. 26-29.

18 According to the definitions provided by Victor Caston himself, both Emergentism and Epiphenomenalism hold the thesis of the supervenience of the mental on the physical, but whereas Emergentism recognises the *Causal Efficacy of the Mental*, Epiphenomenalism rejects it: according to this latter, the mental properties are causally impotent. Cf. CASTON (1997), p. 310-319.

it, (**P**) itself; in short, she would embrace a form of Strong Dualism [(**SD**)].[19]

To strip the physical-physiological aspect off of perception is Myles Burnyeat (BURNYEAT, 1992; 1995; 2001; 2002). In 1983 Burnyeat began to deliver a paper aimed at refuting Richard Sorabji's interpretation, along with the functionalist reading Burnyeat took it to support.[20] According to him, perception is a "spiritual change" that does not involve any "material change":

> All these physical-seeming descriptions – the organ's becoming like the object, its being affected, acted on, or altered by sensible qualities, its taking on sensible form without the matter – all these are referring to what Aquinas calls a "spiritual" change, a becoming aware of some sensible quality in the environment [...]. The only necessary conditions are states of receptivity to sensible form [...]. When these have been specified, the material side of the story of perception is complete (BURNYEAT, 1992, p. 21, 23).[21]

Burnyeat's reading gave rise to a dispute between the "literalists" (e.g., Richard Sorabji, John E. Sisko, Stephen Everson) and those that begun to be labelled "spiritualists" (e.g., Myles Burnyeat, Sarah Broadie, Thomas K. Johansen) following Burnyeat's borrowing of the expression "spiritual change" from Thomas Aquinas[22] (on this dispute, see esp. CASTON, 2005).

19 Most contemporary emergentists find neither option tolerable; nevertheless, the *Causal Closure Argument* is an objection they must take seriously.
20 According to Burnyeat, Sorabji's interpretation of the "reception of form without matter" as a literal physiological change of the quality in the organ offers the "material side" of perception, and in doing so, it supports the *Type Dualism* held by the functionalist interpretation. Cf. BURNYEAT (1992), p. 15.
21 This is the published version of Burnyeat's 1983 paper.
22 The idea of "spiritual change" is stated by John Philoponus, Thomas Aquinas, and Franz Brentano. Aquinas' exegesis – which has been classified also by others as a "spiritualist interpretation of hylomorphism": see, e.g., NANNINI (2002), p. 18 – has been particularly important to Burnyeat (cf. BURNYEAT, 2001, p. 130). Aquinas describes perception as a "spiritual immutation": «Immutatio vero spiritualis est secundum quod species recipitur in organo sensus aut in medio per modum intentionis, et non per modum naturalis formae. Non enim sic recipitur species sensibilis in sensu secundum illud esse quod habet in re sensibili» (*in de An*. § 418). The sensible form is in the sense organ in a way different than the one it is in the sensible object, because in the latter «it has a natural mode of

On Burnyeat's reading, perception is just a cognitive state, i.e. the awareness of colours, sounds, smells and other sensible qualities in the environment. There is no physiological process that stands to perceptual awareness as matter to form. Perception is a "pure transition of form".

Burnyeat recognises that there are some standing material conditions which are necessary for perception to take place, such as the transparency of the eye-jelly, the intermediate temperature and hardness of the organ of touch. But these conditions are for Burnyeat merely "states of receptivity to sensible form", static conditions ensuring the proper disposition of the sense organ: when these have been specified, the material side of the theory of perception is complete (cf. BURNYEAT, 1992, p. 23; 1995). Even when some material changes are involved in perceptual acts, they are nothing but mere accidental accompaniments (κατὰ συμβεβηκός), which are irrelevant for the scientific account of perception (cf. BURNYEAT, 2001).

Spiritualism can be considered as a peculiar form of Immaterialism [(I)]. Burnyeat assumes that the underlying subject of cognitive states such as perception and thought is a very particular kind of matter, a matter that is essentially «pregnant with consciousness, needing only to be awakened to red or warmth» (BURNYEAT, 1992, p. 19). Given this quasi-vitalist definition of biological matter, it would logically follow that any change it undergoes is, in a sense, "spiritual". But it is not clear, in Burnyeat's perspective, whether it is the *whole* living body or just the physical material of which the *sense organs* are made that is «*essentially* alive, *essentially* capable of awareness» (BURNYEAT, 1992, p. 26). By intentionally excluding from his spiritualist analysis vegetative life functions such as nutrition, growth and reproduction, and also passions (cf. BURNYEAT, 1995, p. 432-433; 2001, p. 129-130), Burnyeat treats their bodily side as "mere matter", capable of undergoing "mere material changes". In so doing, Burnyeat shows a dependence on Descartes' distinction between mental functions, characterised by awareness, and bodily functions, characterised by matter in motion.[23] But it is exactly this dependence on Cartesian Dualism that, according to Burnyeat himself, prevents today's Aristoteli-

being (*habet esse naturale*), but in the sense it has an intentional and spiritual mode of being (*habet esse intentionale et spirituale*)» (*in de An.* § 553).

23 Cf. esp. BURNYEAT (1995), p. 433: «If you ask why perception and its objects should be singled out for special status, I can only guess. What is special about perception is that it is a low-grade form of *knowledge*».

an scholars from understanding Aristotle (cf. BURNYEAT, 1992, p. 16, 22).

IV. Conclusive Remarks

Most contemporary philosophers would disown Cartesian Dualism; but even those who explicitly renounce it are often profoundly influenced by it. This is the case, for example, of theories of mind such as Neutralism, Functionalism, and Supervenience. They have in common the rejection of the *Type Identity Thesis*, the thesis that all mental properties and kinds are physical properties and kinds. They accept, instead, the thesis that there are realities (*physical*, according to Functionalism and Supervenience; *neutral* or *composite* according to Neutralism), which may also possess nonphysical, mental properties. Mental properties and psychological laws are not reducible to physical properties and physical laws: the mental is explanatory autonomous.

Even the more "extreme" options of Strong Physicalism and Spiritualism maintain a conceptual distinction between the mental (or "spiritual") and the physical (or material). For both the reductionists and the spiritualists, in order to support, the former, the identity of mental states with their physical equivalents, and the latter the accidentality of "material changes" with respect to "spiritual changes", must distinguish the referent of our psychological expressions (what can be said "mental" or "spiritual") by the referent of our physicalist expressions (what can be said "physical" or "material"). If they did not recognise a conceptual distinction between the mental and the physical, they could not ask the question about the nature of their relationship and therefore not even answer in terms, the reductionists, of identity, and the spiritualists, of accidentality.

Despite their reciprocal differences, the above mentioned interpretations of Aristotle's psychological hylomorphism fall precisely in that "Cartesian error" they wish to avoid: the sharp distinction between a "pure" mental component and a "pure" physical component in the life functions of the living being – that is, between a mental component and a physical component that can be identified and defined independently of each other.[24]

The heredity of Descartes' thought seems to have prevented today's Aristotelian scholarship from getting out of the dualistic frame outlined by his philosophy. In this, Descartes succeeded in obtaining his purpose: to make his readers «accustom themselves to [his] principles and recognise the truth in them before they notice that they destroy those of Aristotle» (AT III, p. 298).

References

ADAM, C.; TANNERY, P. (eds.) (1974). *Œuvres de Descartes*. Paris. Vrin.

BERTI, E. (1998). Aristotele e il "Mind-Body Problem". *Iride*, 11, n° 23, p. 43-62.

_____ (2008). *Aristotele nel Novecento*. Roma-Bari. Laterza.

_____ (2011). L'ilemorfismo da Aristotele a oggi. *Rivista di Filosofia Neo-Scolastica*, 2, p. 173-180.

BURNYEAT, M.F. (1992). Is an Aristotelian Philosophy of Mind Still Credible? (A Draft). In: NUSSBAUM/RORTY (1995), p. 15-26.

_____ (1995). How Much Happens When Aristotle Sees Red and Hears Middle C? Remarks on *De Anima* II, 7-8. In: NUSSBAUM/RORTY (1995), p. 421-434.

_____ (2001). Aquinas on "Spiritual Change" in Perception. In: Perler, D. (ed.). *Ancient and Medieval Theories of Intentionality*. Leiden, Boston. Brill, p. 129-153.

_____ (2002). *De anima* II 5. *Phronesis*, 47, n° 1, p. 28-90.

CASTON, V. (1993). Aristotle and Supervenience. *Southern Journal of Philosophy*, Supp. 31, p. 107-135.

_____ (1997). Epiphenomenalism, Ancient and Modern. *Philosophical Review*, 106, p. 309-363.

_____ (2008). Commentary on Charles. *Proceedings of the Boston Area Colloquium in Ancient Philosophy*, 24, p. 30-47.

_____ (2005). The Spirit and the Letter: Aristotle on Perception. In: Salles, R. (ed.). *Metaphysics, Soul and Ethics in Ancient Thought. Themes from the Work of Richard Sorabji*. Oxford. Oxford University Press, p. 245-320.

24 A similar criticism to the "hidden Cartesianism" in contemporary interpretations of Aristotle's psychological hylomorphism has also been moved by David Charles (CHARLES, 2008, p. 1-3). Charles stated a "third exegetical way" with respect to (conceptual or ontological) dualism and (materialist or spiritualist) monism: the "Inextricability Thesis". For an analysis and a criticism of Charles' position, see CASTON (2008); for a defence of it, see MINGUCCI (2015), p. 19-153.

_____ (2006). Aristotle's Psychology. In Gill M.L.; Pellegrin, P. (eds.). *A Companion to Ancient Philosophy*. Oxford. Blackwell, p. 316-346.

_____ (2008). Commentary on Charles. *Proceedings of the Boston Area Colloquium in Ancient Philosophy*, 24, p. 30-47.

CHARLES, D. (2008). Aristotle's Psychological Theory. *Proceedings of the Boston Area Colloquium in Ancient Philosophy*, 24, p. 1-29.

COHEN, S.M. (1992). Hylomorphism and Functionalism. In: NUSSBAUM/ RORTY (1995), p. 57-74.

DAMASIO, A. (1994). *Descartes' Error: Emotion, Reason, and the Human Brain*. New York. Putnam.

DI FRANCESCO, M. (2009). *Introduzione alla filosofia della mente*, 5th edition. Roma. Carocci.

GALVAN, S. (2011). L'ilemorfismo nella filosofia contemporanea. *Rivista di Filosofia Neo-Scolastica*, 2, p. 167-171.

HALDANE, E.S. (1911). René Descartes. *Meditations on First Philosophy*. In: *The Philosophical Works of Descartes*. Cambridge. Cambridge University Press.

HETT, W.S. (2000). Aristotle. *On the Soul, Parva Naturalia, On Breath*, 5th Edition. Cambridge (Mass.). Harvard University Press, London. Heinemann.

IRWIN, T.H. (1991). Aristotle's Philosophy of Mind. In: Everson, S. (ed.). *Psychology. Vol. 1. Companions to Ancient Thought*. Cambridge. Cambridge University Press, p. 56-83.

JAWORSKI, W. (2016). *Structure and the Metaphysics of Mind: How Hylomorphism Solves the Mind-Body Problem*. Oxford. Oxford University Press.

KENNY, A. (1989). Descartes' Myth. In: Id. *The Metaphysics of Mind*. Oxford. Clarendon Press, p. 1-16.

KIM, J. (2005). *Physicalism, Or Something Near Enough*. Princeton. Princeton University Press.

_____ (2006). *Philosophy of Mind*. Oxford. Westview.

LEWIS, D.K. (1966). An Argument for the Identity Theory. *The Journal of Philosophy*, 63, n° 1, p. 17-25.

LOWE, E.J. (2000). *An Introduction to the Philosophy of Mind*. Cambridge. Cambridge University Press.

_____ (2011). Body, Soul, and Self. *Rivista di Filosofia Neo-Scolastica*, 2, p. 201-215.

MARMODORO, A. (2013). Aristotle's Hylomorphism without Reconditioning. *Philosophical Inquiry*, 36, n° 1-2, p. 5-22.

MATSON, W.I. (1966). Why Isn't the Mind-Body Problem Ancient?. In: Feyerabend, P.K.; Maxwell, G. (eds.). *Mind, Matter, and Method: Essays in Philosophy and Science in Honor of Herbert Feigl*. Minneapolis. University of Minnesota Press, p. 92-102.

MINGUCCI, G. (2015). *La fisiologia del pensiero in Aristotele*. Bologna. Il Mulino.

NANNINI, S. (2002). *L'anima e il corpo. Un'introduzione storica alla filosofia della mente*. Roma-Bari. Laterza.

NUSSBAUM, M.C. (1978). *Aristotle's De Motu Animalium*, Text with Translation, Commentary and Interpretive Essays. Princeton. Princeton University Press.

NUSSBAUM, M.C.; PUTNAM, H. (1992). Changing Aristotle's Mind. In: NUSSBAUM/RORTY (1995), p. 27-76.

NUSSBAUM, M.C.; RORTY, A.O. (1995) (eds.). *Essays on Aristotle's De anima*, 2nd Edition. Oxford. Clarendon Press (orig. ed. 1992).

POPPER, K.; ECCLES, J. (1977). *The Self and its Brain*. New York. Springer.

PUTNAM. H. (1975). Philosophy and Our Mental Life. In: Id. *Mind, Language and Reality*. Cambridge. Cambridge University Press, p. 127-137.

ROSS, W.D. (1956). *Aristotelis De anima*. Oxford. Clarendon Press.

RUNGGALDIER, E. (2011). Concezioni ilemorfiche dell'anima. *Rivista di Filosofia Neo-Scolastica*, 2, p. 181-200.

SCOTT, D. (2017). Descartes's "Considerable List": A Small but Important Passage in His Philosophy. *International Philosophical Quarterly*, 57, n° 4, p. 381-399.

SHIELDS, CH. (1990). The First Functionalist. In: Smith, J.C. (ed.). *The Historical Foundations of Cognitive Science*. Dordrecht. Kluwer Academic Publishers, p. 19-33.

SLAKEY, T. (1961). Aristotle on Sense Perception. *Philosophical Review*, 70, n°4, p. 470-484.

SORABJI, R. (1974). Body and Soul in Aristotle. *Philosophy*, 49, p. 63-89.

_____ (1992). Intentionality and Physiological Processes: Aristotle's Theory of Sense-Perception. In: NUSSBAUM/RORTY (1995), p. 195-225.

_____ (2001). Aristotle on Sensory Processes and Intentionality: A Reply to Myles Burnyeat. In: Perler, D. (ed.). *Ancient and Medieval Theories of Intentionality*. Leiden, Boston. Brill, p. 49-61.

WILKES, K.V. (1978). *Physicalism*. London. Routledge & Kegan Paul.

Contemporary Hylomorphism and the Problems of Mind versus Body

William Jaworski

During the late 1980s Martha Nussbaum and Hilary Putnam (NUSS-BAUM/PUTNAM, 1992) circulated a coauthored paper that renewed interest in the idea that Aristotelian hylomorphism might provide resources for solving problems in the philosophy of mind. It would nevertheless take over a decade for their idea to catch on. Contributing to an area like philosophy of mind requires formulating theories in ways that make it evident how they solve problems within that area, and it was unclear to most philosophers of mind exactly what a hylomorphic psychology claimed and how it could solve mind-body problems.

The difficulty was abetted by disagreements about what exactly Aristotle's psychology was. Some claimed it was a form of substance dualism (ROBINSON, 1983), or dual-attribute theory (BARNES, 1972); others, a version of the psychophysical identity theory (SLAKEY, 1961), functionalism (WILKES, 1974; HARTMAN, 1977), neoparallelism (ROSS, 1973), or panpsychism (BURNYEAT, 1992), and yet others a view that was ultimately incoherent (GRANGER, 1996), or (perhaps more charitably) a view that waffled between incoherence and nonreductive physicalism (WILLIAMS, 1986). Philosophers of mind could thus see little value in studying Aristotle's psychology: not only it was unclear what it claimed, but whatever it claimed, they were assured by the experts that it was a theory of some already familiar sort. Why, then, look to a figure separated from us in time and, more importantly, conceptual space, who wrote in a defunct language that was difficult to decipher both in translation and in the original, who lived before the Scientific Revolution, and whose ideas on so many topics had been proven false by the enhanced methods for studying the natural world that the Revolution introduced? Why turn to Aristotle, moreover, when it was so much easier to look to contemporary exemplars of whatever kind of view he must have endorsed?

The result shouldn't be surprising. Aristotle himself noted that we understand things initially in terms of what is better known to us, and what is better known to contemporary philosophers are ways of conceptualizing things that have been inherited largely from Descartes. Little wonder if even specialists have trouble understanding a pre-Cartesian view. It was the elaboration of Aristotelian themes in metaphysics – particularly work on powers and composition – that ultimately enabled Nussbaum and Putnam's idea to be more than a mere suggestion. It enabled contemporary hylomorphists to formulate the basic principles of their theory in a way that could contribute to current debates and solve mind-body problems.

Mind-body problems are persistent problems understanding how thought, feeling, perception, and other paradigmatically mental phenomena fit into the natural world. The problem of emergence is an example; it demands an explanation for how physical interactions devoid of consciousness manage to give rise to thoughts, feelings, perceptions and other conscious states. How is it that the movements of tiny particles in my brain give rise to the rich conscious experiences I have? The answer is not obvious since the following claims all seem plausible:

(1) We have conscious experiences.
(2) We are composed of physical particles.
(3) The properties of a composite whole are determined by the properties of the particles composing it.
(4) Physical particles do not have conscious experiences.
(5) No number of non-conscious particles could combine to produce a whole with conscious experiences.

It seems obvious that we have conscious experiences as claim (1) says. Claim (2), moreover, seems well-supported empirically: we seem to be composed of the same materials as everything else in the physical universe, and our best physics suggests that those materials are microscopic particles. Many examples seem to illustrate claim (3). I have the mass I have, for instance, because I am composed of physical particles with smaller masses that collectively add up to my bigger mass. Likewise, I have the position and velocity I do because the particles composing me are located and moving the ways they are. Given that so many of the properties of a whole are determined by the properties of its constituent particles, it's not implausible to suppose that all the properties of a whole are determined by the properties of those particles. It seems, moreover, that the behavior of those particles can be described and explained exhaustively by physics, as per claim (4): we needn't invoke a psychological or even a biological vocabulary to describe and explain what they are and what they can do. There also seem to be good reasons to endorse claim (5). One particle by itself does not have the power to produce conscious experiences. If it did, then consciousness would have emerged much earlier in the universe's history than we think it did, and it would also be more widespread – even rocks, tables, oxygen atoms, and electrons could be conscious. But if one particle by itself does not have the power to produce conscious experiences, then it is difficult to see how any number of particles could combine to produce conscious experiences. For suppose that some number of particles, N, do not have the power to produce conscious experiences. If one particle does not make a difference to whether or not something is conscious, then clearly $N+1$ particles will not have the power to produce conscious experiences either. Since N can be any number one likes, it seems to follow that no number of non-conscious particles has the power to produce a whole with conscious experiences.

It is thus plausible to suppose that claims (1)-(5) are all true, yet they cannot all be true because jointly those claims are inconsistent: claim (1) implies that we have conscious experiences, yet claims (2)-(5) together imply that we do not. At least one of the claims must therefore be false, yet the lines of reasoning just described make it difficult to say which.

Mind-body problems like the foregoing have a common architecture. On the one hand, they take the physical universe to be a vast undifferentiated sea of matter and energy that can in principle be described exhaustively by our best current or future physics. On the other hand, they take seriously the idea that we have (or at least appear to have) capacities that cannot be exhaustively described using the conceptual resources of physics, for the vocabulary of physics doesn't include predicates and terms such as 'believes', 'hopes', 'feels', and 'wants'. There is, then, a problem understanding how the capacities for believing, hoping, feeling, and wanting fit into the universe that physics describes.

The assumptions that generate mind-body problems are widespread, but that doesn't make them true, and hylomorphism implies that they are false. Hylomorphism's basic idea, stated very roughly, is that some things are composed of physical materials with a specific form or structure. A human being, for instance, is not composed of physical materials configured in any way whatsoever, but physical materials configured in a very specific way. In some cases, a thing's configuration (its form or structure) is something static, like the relatively unchanging spatial arrangements of atoms in a crystal, but in the most interesting cases, the configuration comprises dynamic interactions among an individual's components. The configurations of matter and energy that make human beings and other complex living things what they are cannot be characterized apart from the dynamic interactions among their various organ systems, along with their component organs, tissues, cells, and the molecules, atoms, and fundamental physical materials ultimately composing them.

Aristotle originally introduced hylomorphism to account for change or coming-to-be. Every change, he said, involves two explanatory factors (*Phys.* I 7, 190a15ff.).[1] First, there is something that exists prior to the change and persists through it. Second, there is a characteristic or form (*eidos*) which the persisting thing previously lacked, or (depending on the case) which it previously had, and which it subsequently comes to have (or comes to lack). To say that Socrates becomes musical at *t* thus implies that Socrates exists prior to *t*, that he lacked the form of being musical, but took on that form at *t*. A persisting thing coming to have different forms at different times is therefore what change consists in.

Aristotle extended this way of understanding the coming-to-be of properties to account for the coming-to-be of substances: in each case, there is something that exists prior to a substance coming to be and that persists through its coming to be (*Phys.* I 7, 190b1ff.): a statue comes to be from some pre-existing stuff on account of that stuff changing its shape, a house comes to be on account of putting some pre-existing things together house-wise, and the same goes mutatis mutandis for natural things such as Socrates, which are substances in the strictest sense (*Phys.* I 7, 190b17ff.).

Natural things, for Aristotle, include plants and animals, their parts, and the simple bodies: earth, air, fire, and water (*Phys.* II 1, 192b8-13; *Metaph.* H 1, 1042a8-10). What qualifies these as natural is that each has within itself a source of change and stability. Unlike the case of an artifact such as a table, which comes to have its characteristic shape on account of an external agent, a human develops its distinctive array of parts and carries on its distinctive metabolic processes and other activities not on ac-

---

1 The term "factor" here translates the Greek word *archê* which designates a source, origin, or starting point. Although Aristotle sometimes refers to a linguistic entity, such as the major premise of an argument, as an *archê*, the latter need not be linguistic entities. To call *a*'s matter an *archê*, for instance, implies that *a*'s matter explains something about *a*. The same is true mutatis mutandis of *a*'s form. This does not imply that either the matter or the form is a linguistic entity.

count of an external agent but on account of itself: it is itself the source of the distinctively human characteristics it takes on.

Natural things are the ultimate engines of change on Aristotle's view; they are the things that are ultimately responsible for why anything undergoes the changes it does. Tracing the provenance of any putative change will eventually yield an explanation that has as its truthmaker a natural substance or substances acquiring or losing some form or forms.

Among the changes natural things undergo, some fall into stereotypical patterns. Biological development is the paradigm: fish grow gills and scales, not lungs and skin, whereas humans do the opposite. These occurrences cannot happen by chance, Aristotle argues, for things that happen by chance do not display the kind of regularity we find in cases like biological development (*Phys.* II 8, 198b33ff.) Developmental changes happen instead on account of the natures (*phuseis*) of things. Behavioral regularities, whether in living things or in nonliving materials, are due to the natures things have.

The changes that are due to something's nature are those which it undergoes on account of itself (*kath'hauto*), that is on account of its being an instance of its natural kind. A thing's nature comprises both its matter and its form (*Phys.* II 1, 193a10-b20): both make a difference to what something is and what it does. A human being will fall downward on account of its matter, for the latter includes a large portion of the element earth. Since it is in the nature of earth to move downward, on Aristotle's view, it is in the nature of anything composed of a sufficiently large quantity of earth to move downward as well. Likewise, it is in the nature of fire to move upward. Because of this upward-moving nature, a human is able to grow and maintain itself. If Socrates were composed of earth alone, he would collapse in a heap of earthy rubble. Fire counteracts this tendency, but the presence of fire is not the only thing needed to explain human growth and homeostasis. Left to their own devices earth and fire would separate themselves from each other completely with the result that living things like Socrates would be torn apart: the fiery materials composing them would ascend skyward while their earthy materials would accumulate on the ground in a heap (*de An.* II 4, 416a6-9). Something prevents this from happening. Something about a living whole directs, proportions, and regulates the activities of the materials composing it, and ensures that the whole itself remains a unified persisting individual. That something is form.

Form explains what unifies diverse materials into a single whole (*de An.* I 5, 411b5-13; *Metaph.* H 6, 1045a23-b6). There is no unified composite individual apart from a form. Destroying something's form results in a disunified heap (*Metaph. Z* 17, 1041b11-18). The remains of a human – what are often referred to, confusedly from an Aristotelian perspective, using singular terms such as "human body" or "corpse" – do not compose a single individual at all; they are instead materials that used to compose an individual but that no longer do. Form also explains diachronic unity or persistence: why a living whole such as Socrates can exist one and the same over time even though the materials composing him are in constant flux (*de Gen. et. Corr.* I 5, 321b25-27): Socrates persists so long as his form does (*de Gen. et Corr.* I 5, 321a13-25). Likewise, the biological processes in which Socrates engages are directed toward developing and maintaining a mature, properly-functioning member of the human kind. What unifies various stages of the developmental process, as well as various metabolic processes, is their directedness to this end.

With this outline of Aristotle's hylomorphism in place, it is possible to identify the roles that the concept of form is supposed to play within his framework. These roles supply an implicit definition of form:

> *Change:* Form is what accounts for change or generation, especially the generation of composite wholes;
> *Unity:* Form is what accounts for the unity of composite wholes;
> *Persistence:* Form is what accounts for a composite whole's persistence through time, especially in cases in which it changes its matter over time;
> *Kind Membership:* Form is what accounts for kind membership, especially membership in natural kinds;
> *Behavioral Regularity:* Form is what accounts for behavioral regularities, especially the self-maintaining and developmental processes in which living things engage.[2]

In Aristotle's philosophy, then, form is what plays the foregoing theoretical roles. Aristotle's is not the only hylomorphic theory however, and not all hylomorphic theories have form playing the roles that Aristotle's does.

---

2 Aristotle also intends form to play epistemological roles: *Perceptual and Cognitive Knowledge:* Form is what accounts for the ability to know things themselves in perception and understanding. But these roles do not bear directly on our present inquiry.

For example, contemporary hylomorphic theories that place few restrictions on the kinds of predicates or functions that express hylomorphic forms have difficulty accommodating Behavioral Regularity. These include the hylomorphic theories of Kit Fine (FINE, 1999, 2008) and Mark Johnston (JOHNSTON, 2006). Their theories are committed to something like the following principle:

> *Abundant Matter Principle:* For any objects, a_1, a_2,..., a_n, there is a form F and an object s such that F is s's form, and the as are s's matter.

Given a principle of this sort, nothing prevents us from constructing hylomorphic composites in any way we please, for given any n-tuple of objects, we can construct a function that corresponds to a hylomorphic form.

Consider three objects: a particular hydrogen atom h, my left foot, and the Empire State Building. Each of these objects occupies various positions at various times. These positions, let us suppose, are specified in a description D. On Fine's theory, we can define a hylomorphic composite c (what he calls a "variable embodiment") which is composed of h, my left foot, and the Empire State Building exactly if those three objects occupy the positions at times specified in D. This result is likely to strike many hylomorphists as bizarre. We cannot bring new things into existence simply by stipulation, they will say – simply by formulating a definition. One reason for thinking this is that intuitively c does not have any causal powers beyond those of h, my left foot, and the Empire State Building; it doesn't do anything other than what h, my left foot, and the Empire State Building by themselves do. To use Aristotle's term, c has no nature of its own. Any powers or activities we might attribute to it are really just the powers and activities of h, my left foot, and the Empire State Building. The latter objects operate, moreover, completely independent of their status as parts of c. The latter thus adds nothing to the causal inventory of the world. Because theories like Fine's admit composite entities like c, it is difficult to see how forms could play the role of Behavioral Regularity. On these views, hylomorphic forms have no essential connection to the causal powers that things have.

Problems in philosophy of mind, however, often concern causal powers. The problem of emergence, for instance, concerns how physical changes can cause mental states, and the well-rehearsed problem of downward causation concerns how mental states can cause physical changes (KIM, 2006). Because theories like Fine's divest forms of distinctive causal roles, they hold little promise for solving mind-body problems. I'll thus put them to one side and focus on a hylomorphic theory that can accommodate Behavioral Regularity.

I've described that theory in detail elsewhere (JAWORSKI, 2016, 2017). It understands forms in terms of a metaphysics of powers: forms, it says, make a difference to what things can do – the powers they have. In particular, forms confer powers on composite individuals that are not had by the components of those individuals taken by themselves. Socrates, for instance, has powers that earth and fire by themselves lack – the power, for instance, to maintain himself one and the same over time despite changes in the materials composing him. That power is one that Socrates is essentially and continuously manifesting: he is essentially and continuously engaged in regulating, proportioning, and directing the way his composing materials operate. This ongoing configuring activity is how he manages to unify those materials into a single whole, both synchronically and diachronically. It also confers on him further powers, such as the powers to walk, talk, sing, dance, run, jump, and engage in the various other activities he does.

Socrates engages in these activities by imposing an order on the ways his parts manifest their powers. Walking, talking, playing an instrument, and so on are not random sequences of physiological changes; each is instead an activity composed of a sequence of physiological changes with a certain order or coordination. That coordination is another species of structuring – the manifestation of a further power Socrates has for coordinating or structuring the way his parts (and in some cases external objects) operate. When he walks, talks, or plays, he structures walking- talking- or playing-wise the way his parts and external objects manifest their powers. In some cases, this structuring is conscious and intentional as in producing the precise limb movements in a dance, but in many cases the structuring is neither conscious nor intentional as in digesting food or increasing blood flow to the legs in response to something fearful. In whatever way it occurs, whether consciously and intentionally or not, the result of this structuring is a unified activity that is composed of the simpler activities of his parts (and in some cases external objects).

The structured activities in which Socrates engages include thinking, feeling, and perceiving. When he experiences an emotion, he is engaging in an activity in which various parts of his nervous system and various objects in the environment manifest their powers in a coordinated way that unifies them into a single event. Just as physical materials compose an individual exactly if they are structured the right way, likewise various events compose an activity of thinking, feeling, or perceiving exactly if they are structured the right way.

Based on what's been said, it is possible to get a rough sense for how hylomorphists approach mind-body problems. Those problems, they say, are byproducts of a worldview that rejects hylomorphic structure. Structure carves out distinctive individuals from the otherwise undifferentiated sea of matter and energy described by our best physics, and it confers on those individuals distinctive powers. If hylomorphic structure exists, the physical universe is punctuated with pockets of organized change and stability – composite physical objects (paradigmatically living things) whose structures confer on them powers that distinguish what they can do from what unstructured materials can do. Those powers include the powers to think, feel, and perceive. A worldview that rejects hylomorphic structure, by contrast, lacks a basic principle that distinguishes the parts of the physical universe that can think, feel, and perceive from those that can't, and without a basic principle that carves out zones with distinctive powers, the existence of those powers in the natural world can start to look inexplicable and mysterious. If there is nothing built into the basic fabric of the universe that explains why Zone A has powers that Zone B lacks – if nothing explains why you, say, have the power to think, feel, and perceive, while the materials surrounding you do not, then the options for understanding the existence of those powers in the natural world become constrained: either they must be identified with the powers of physical materials taken by themselves or in combination (as panpsychists and many physicalists claim), or their existence must be taken as an inexplicable matter of fact (as many emergentists and epiphenomenalists claim), or else their existence in the natural world must be denied altogether (as substance dualists and eliminative physicalists claim). If there is hylomorphic structure, however, the options are no longer constrained in this way. The existence of thinking, feeling, and perceiving in the natural world is no more mysterious than the existence of walking or talking: all are manifestations of distinctive powers that beings like us have, and those powers exist in the natural world because structure does.

But are there hylomorphic structures? Are there such things as Aristotle's forms? Hylomorphism has long been sidelined in serious philosophical discussions due a widespread perception that it is unscientific – that the Scientific Revolution proved that the notion of form was empty, that it had no real-world application. In fact, this attitude represents a misconception about what the Scientific Revolution accomplished – something that is especially evident when we turn to biology.

Marjorie Grene noticed the similarity between Aristotelian form (*eidos*) and the notion of organization at home in modern biology:

> *Eidos* [...] functions in a number of striking respects in the same way as the concept of organization... in modern biology [...]. The *eidos* of an entity or process is its organizing principle, the way it works to organize some substrate [...]. [F]orm in nature [...] exists in, and only in, that which it informs [...] *as* the organizing principle [...] in an appropriate matter [...]. *Eidos* in the sense of organizing principle is [...] a definitive concept for biological method [...] [though] its modern counterpart is couched in different terms (GRENE, 1972, p. 409-410).

To illustrate Grene's point about the notion of organization in modern biology, consider an example from a popular college-level biology textbook:

> Life is highly organized into a hierarchy of structural levels, with each level building on the levels below it... Biological order exists at all levels [...]. [A]toms [...] are ordered into complex biological molecules [...]. [Those] molecules [...] are arranged into minute structures called organelles, which are in turn the components of cells. Cells are [in turn] subunits of organisms [...]. The organism [...] is not a random collection of individual cells, but a multicellular cooperative [...]. Identifying biological organization at its many levels is fundamental to the study of life [...]. With each step upward in the hierarchy of biological order, novel properties emerge that were not present at the simpler levels of organization [...]. A molecule such as a protein has attributes not exhibited by any of its component atoms, and a cell is certainly much more than a bag of molecules. If the intricate organization of the human brain is disrupted by a head injury, that organ will cease to function properly [...]. And an organism is a living whole greater than the sum of its parts [...]. [W]e cannot fully explain a higher level of order by breaking it down into its parts (CAMPBELL, 1996, p. 2-4).

This passage suggests that organization (or order, structure, or arrangement) is a real feature of things, one that plays an important role in them being the kinds of things they are, and in explaining the kinds of things they can do. It suggests, in other words, that structure or organization is a real ontological and explanatory principle – one that cannot be reduced to mere spatial arrangements or causal relations among something's parts.[3] The materials composing Socrates can change their spatial and causal relations, and yet Socrates persists all the same. Form is instead what is responsible for ensuring that the spatial and causal relations among those materials remain within the parameters necessary for Socrates to continue to exist.

Appeals to a notion of organization or structure along these lines appear throughout biology and biological subdisciplines such as neuroscience.[4] These empirical appeals provide the basis for an argument in favor of hylomorphism. It depends on two premises: first, a broadly Quinean premise about ontological commitment: we are committed to all the entities postulated by our best descriptions and explanations of reality; second, our best descriptions and explanations of reality derive from empirical sources such as the natural and social sciences. Suppose we take the natural-language sentences in which our best empirical descriptions and explanations are formulated and reformulate them in a quantifier-variable idiom the way QUINE (1948) suggests. In that case, we would be committed to the existence of all the entities needed to make those descriptions and explanations true. Consequently, if our best empirical descriptions and explanations posit various kinds of organization or structure, then we have good prima facie reason to think those structures exist. But appeals to organization or structure are ubiquitous in the biological sciences. The theoretical roles those notions are expected to play, moreover, are the theoretical roles that hylomorphic form is supposed to play. We thus have good prima facie reason to think that there are hylomorphic forms. Far from being unscientific, then, hylomorphism seems to be

---

3 The term 'principle' here translates the Greek word *archê* which designates a source, origin, or starting point. See footnote 1.
4 Philosophers and scientists who invoke a similar notion of organization or structure (typically without appreciating the ontological implications of that invocation) include ARMSTRONG (1968), p. 11; BECHTEL (2007), p. 174, 185-186; CAMAZINE, et al. (2001), p. 12-13; DEWEY (1958), p. 253-258; HALDANE (1947), p. 54-56; HEIL (2003), p. 245; KITCHER (1984), p. 369, 373; MAYR (1982), p. 2, 52; MILLER (1978), p. 140-141; RUSE (2001), p. 79; SIMPSON (1964), p. 113, and SOMMERHOFF (1969), p. 147-148. The principle of ontological naturalism discussed below puts pressure on philosophers and scientists like these to endorse a notion of structure like the hylomorphic one.

an implication of our best empirical descriptions and explanations of living things.

With the foregoing ideas in place, let us return to the mind-body problem with which we began: the problem of emergence. It requests an explanation of how physical factors produce thoughts, feelings, perceptions, and other paradigmatically mental phenomena. Within a hylomorphic framework, this request for an explanation is illegitimate. It is legitimate to request an explanation of how it is possible that p only if it is possible that p, and according to hylomorphists, it is not possible for physiological occurrences to produce thoughts, feelings, and perceptions.

According to hylomorphists, a thought, feeling, or perception is an activity composed of physical occurrences with a structure, and structured entities in general are not generated or produced by the things that compose them. Socrates' act of talking is not produced by states of his muscles and nerves; it is instead an activity that occurs when he coordinates or structures the states of his muscles and nerves talking-wise. Likewise, Socrates' brain states do not generate or produce his thoughts, feelings, and perceptions; each is instead an activity that occurs when he structures the way parts of his nervous system operate – when he coordinates their operations thinking-, feeling-, or perceiving-wise. On the hylomorphic view, structured things in general are not causal byproducts of the things they structure. Consequently, requesting an explanation of how unstructured occurrences generate structured phenomena misunderstands the hylomorphic notion of structure. It assumes, contrary to hylomorphism, that structure is not a basic principle but is instead something that is derived from unstructured things. Demanding that hylomorphists explain how brains produce consciousness thus implicitly begs the question against their view, for it assumes the existence of a kind of occurrence that hylomorphists deny exists, namely the generation of structured phenomena by unstructured things. On hylomorphists' own terms, it is not legitimate to request an explanation of this any more than it is legitimate to request that a meteorologist explain how the will of Zeus produces rain. Opponents of hylomorphism are free to reject the view wholesale, but within the hylomorphic framework itself, requesting such an explanation is illegitimate. Moreover, the very fact that the problem of emergence arises for opponents but not for hylomorphists weighs in favor of taking hylomorphic structure as a primitive.

Opponents might argue that hylomorphists face their own problem of emergence. What, after all, explains the emergence of structure itself on the hylomorphic view? What physical conditions are responsible for bringing it into existence? Hylomorphists respond once again that on their view structure is basic – every bit as basic as things that get structured. Asking why either structure or materials exist on the hylomorphic view comes close to asking why the universe as a whole exists, or why there is something instead of nothing. It is possible to reject the hylomorphic worldview and with it the claim that structure is basic. But to request that hylomorphists explain how structure emerges is to request something that hylomorphism implies cannot be done.

Hylomorphists do not deny that we can ask how particular structures came to be in place. It is legitimate to ask how my distinctively human structure came initially to inform various biotic materials. The answer has to do presumably with my parents' reproductive activity. Likewise, it is a legitimate empirical endeavor to attempt to discover how the first living things emerged; that is, how the first living structures came to inform various prebiotic materials. What is not legitimate to ask, according to hylomorphists, is what is responsible for continually generating the structures that I and other living things have. My structure is not something continually generated by some external source or by the materials that compose me; it is instead a self-maintaining configuring activity in which I continuously and essentially engage. There is no sense, then, in which hylomorphists' refusal to answer a request to explain the emergence of structure can count as a strike against their view, at least not without begging the question and assuming from the outset that the hylomorphic view is false.

What of the five jointly inconsistent claims discussed earlier – the ones that appear to make the existence of emergent phenomena problematic? It should be evident that hylomorphists reject claim (3): they deny that the properties of a composite whole are determined by the properties of the particles composing it. There may be some properties of this sort – mass might be an example. But hylomorphists deny that all properties are like this: some properties of a composite whole are determined by its structure. This was evident in the example discussed earlier: because Socrates is composed of a sufficiently large quantity of earth, he has a tendency to move downward, and because he is also composed of fire, parts of him have a tendency to move in the contrary direction, yet the earth and fire composing him do not separate themselves from each other completely as they would if left to their own devices. Socrates persists – a unified whole – on account of something else: his ongoing structuring activity, which directs, proportions, and regulates the activities of the materials composing him. This is not a power of the materials themselves, but of Socrates, the structure whole.

For simplicity this example was borrowed from Aristotle and formulated in terms of his physics. But it would be easy enough to reformulate the example of Socrates in terms of the physical materials postulated by contemporary biology; it would simply make the description unwieldy for our present purposes, and I trust that the philosophical point remains the same: according to hylomorphism, not all the properties of a composite entity are determined by its composing materials, some are due to its structure – an idea that Aristotle expresses by saying that a thing's nature comprises both its matter and its form (*Phys.* II 1-2, 193a10-194b15; *Metaph.* Z 11, 1036b22-32).

What I've described is an empirically-based hylomorphic theory formulated in a way that makes it evident how it implies a solution to a live problem in the philosophy of mind. Elsewhere, moreover, I've described in detail how this same theory implies a solution not just to the problem of emergence, but to the problem of mental causation and the problem of other minds (JAWORSKI 2016). It establishes that Nussbaum and Putnam had a real insight into the nature of mind-body problems and the philosophical potential of Aristotle's hylomorphic psychology.

At the beginning of the 21st Century, we are better positioned to retrieve the insights of Aristotelian philosophy than at any time since the Scientific Revolution. Contemporary metaphysical accounts of composition and powers that challenge deep-seated Cartesian and Humean assumptions about the natural world provide a basis for retrieving the insights of hylomorphic psychology in particular, and for marrying those insights to the descriptions and explanations supplied by our best scientific accounts of living phenomena.

References

ARMSTRONG, D.M. (1968). *A Materialist Theory of the Mind*. London. Routledge & Kegan Paul.

BARNES, J. (1972). Aristotle's Concept of Mind. *Proceedings of the Aristotelian Society*, 72, p. 101-114.

BECHTEL, W. (2007). Reducing Psychology while Maintaining its Autonomy via Mechanistic Explanations. In: Schouten, M.; Looren de Jong, H. (eds.) *The Matter of the Mind*. Oxford. Blackwell Publishing, p. 172-198.

BURNYEAT, M.F. (1992). Is an Aristotelian Theory of Mind Still Credible? (a Draft). In: NUSSBAUM/RORTY (1992), p. 15-26.

CAMAZINE, S. et al. (2001). *Self-Organization in Biological Systems*. Princeton. Princeton University Press.

CAMPBELL, N.A. (1996). *Biology*, 4th Edition. Menlo Park, CA. The Benjamin/ Cummings Publishing Company, Inc.

DEWEY, J. (1958). *Experience and Nature*. New York, NY. Dover Publications.

FINE, K. (1999). Things and Their Parts. *Midwest Studies in Philosophy*, 23, p. 61-74.

_____ (2008). Form and Coincidence. *Proceedings of the Aristotelian Society*, Supplementary Volume 82, p. 101-118.

GRANGER, H. (1996). *Aristotle's Idea of the Soul*. Dordrecht. Kluwer Academic.

GRENE, M. (1972). Aristotle and Modern Biology. *Journal of the History of Ideas*, 33, p. 395-424.

HALDANE, J.B.S. (1947). *What Is Life?*. New York. Boni and Gaer.

HARTMAN, E. (1977). *Substance, Body, and Soul: Aristotelian Investigations*. Princeton. Princeton University Press.

HEIL, J. (2003). *From an Ontological Point of View*. Oxford. Clarendon Press.

JAWORSKI, W. (2016). *Structure and the Metaphysics of Mind: How Hylomorphism Solves the Mind-Body Problem*. Oxford. Oxford University Press.

_____ (2017). Psychology without a Mental-Physical Dichotomy. In: Simpson, W.; Koons, R.; Teh, N. (eds.). *Neo-Aristotelian Perspectives on Modern Science*. Abingdon on Thames. Routledge, p. 261-292.

JOHNSTON, M. (2006). Hylomorphism. *Journal of Philosophy*, 103, p. 652-698.

KIM, J. (2006). Emergence: Core Ideas and Issues. *Synthese*, 151, p. 547-559.

KITCHER, P. (1984). 1953 and All That: A Tale of Two Sciences. *Philosophical Review* 93, p. 335-373.

MAYR, E. (1982). *The Growth of Biological Thought: Diversity, Evolution, and Inheritance*. Cambridge, MA. The Belknap Press of Harvard University.

MILLER, J. (1978). *The Body in Question*. New York, NY. Random House.

NUSSBAUM, M.; RORTY, A. (1992). *Essays on Aristotle's De Anima*. New York. Oxford University Press.

NUSSBAUM, M.; PUTNAM, H. (1992). Changing Aristotle's Mind. In: NUSSBAUM/RORTY (1992), p. 27-56.

QUINE, W.V. (1948). On What There Is. *Review of Metaphysics*, 2, p. 21-38.

ROBINSON, H. (1983). Aristotelian Dualism. *Oxford Studies in Ancient Philosophy*, 1, p. 1-25.

ROSS, G.R.T. (1973). *De Sensu and De Memoria*. New York. Arno Press.

RUSE, M. (2001). *Can a Darwinian Be a Christian? The Relationship between Science and Religion*. Cambridge (Mass.). Cambridge University Press.

SIMPSON, G.G. (1964). *This View of Life: The World of an Evolutionist*. New York. Harcourt, Brace and World.

SLAKEY, T.J. (1961). Aristotle on Sense Perception. *Philosophical Review*, 70, p. 470-484.

SOMMERHOFF, G. (1969). The Abstract Characteristics of Living Systems. In: Emery, F.E. (ed.). *Systems Thinking: Selected Readings*. Harmondsworth. Penguin, p. 147-202.

WILKES, K.V. (1978). *Physicalism*. Atlantic Highlands. Humanities Press.

WILLIAMS, B. (1986). Hylomorphism. *Oxford Studies in Philosophy*, 4, p. 189-199.

Bio of the Editors

Diego Zucca works as a researcher in the History of Ancient Philosophy at the Department of History, Human Sciences and Education of the University of Sassari (Italy). His research interests are mainly concerned with Aristotle (especially psychology, epistemology, philosophy of nature and ethics) and with philosophy of mind (especially philosophy of perception).

Roberto Medda is a post-doc research fellow at the Department of Pedagogy, Psychology and Philosophy of the University of Cagliari (Italy). His work concentrates on the history of ancient philosophy, especially on Aristotle's epistemology, psychology and ethics.

Index of Authors (with the exceptions of 'Socrates', 'Plato' and 'Aristotle')

ANCIENT:

Aeschilus, 102n.
Alexander of Aphrodisias, 15n., 17, 89, 90, 93, 93n., 139, 139n., 140n., 142n., 154, 169n.
Anaxagoras, 9, 11,155
Antisthenes, 73
Apollonius Dyscolus, 8n.
Atticus, 93
Cicero, 15n., 132
Clement of Alexandria, 15-17
Chrysippus, 7, 8, 11n., 64
Diogenes Laertius, 9n., 64n.
Empedocles, 63, 64, 74, 90, 119
Galen, 15n.
Gorgias, 66, 66n., 73
Heraclitus, 73, 103, 104, 104n., 105n., 112
Herodotus, 102n., 112
Homer, 21n., 86, 88, 102
Lysias, 21
Melissus, 66n., 73
Parmenides, 63, 64, 73, 74
Philoponus, 89-91, 100, 144n., 147n., 155, 171n.
Plotinus, 75, 76, 78, 79, 93, 94
Porphyry, 93
Protagoras, XII, 55-57, 60, 61, 64, 65, 67, 68, 73, 74
Pythagoras, 73
Seneca, 7n., 15n.
Sextus Empiricus, 7-9, 16, 66n.
Simplicius, 14, 14n., 15, 15n., 17, 89n., 100, 139n.
Sophonia, 100
Stobaeus, 7, 8, 11n.
Tertullian, 64, 64n.
Themistius, 89n., 100, 144n., 145n., 149, 150, 150n., 155, 156
Theophrastus, 96n., 139n., 144n., 156
Thomas Aquinas, 144n., 145n., 149, 150n., 156, 171, 171n., 174
Xenophanes, 66n., 73
Xenophon, 96n.
Zeno of Citium, 7n.

MODERN:

Ackrill J.L., 107n., 112
Adam Ch., 162n., 174
Annas J., 16, 51n., 54
Anscombe G.E.M., 116n., 131
Armstrong A.H., 76
Armstrong D.M., 187n., 191
Arthur J., 116n., 131
Aubenque P., 119n., 131
Balme D.M., 112
Barnes J., XIX, 5-9, 13, 14n., 16, 17, 112, 113, 145n., 154, 177, 191
Battegazzore A.M., 73
Bechtel W., 187n., 191
Bekker I., 98
Berti E., 6n., 17, 147-150, 154, 159n., 174
Besser-Jones L., 132
Betegh G., 64n., 73
Bobzien S., 7, 8, 8n., 15n., 17
Bodeüs R., 92, 94
Bonelli M., VIII, IX, 3, 3n., 15-17
Bonitz H., 100, 100n., 102n., 112
Bostock D., 7n., 17
Boudouris K., 73
Brancacci A., XI, XII, 55, 55n., 67n., 73
Brentano F., 139n., 144n., 155, 171n.
Broadie S., 42, 42n., 54, 171
Bruns I., 139n., 140n., 142n.
Brunschwig J., 54
Burnet J., 104n., 112
Burnyeat M.F., XVIII, 62, 62n., 73, 97n., 112, 122, 122n., 131, 138n., 139n., 143n., 145n., 152n., 171-174, 176, 177, 180, 191
Bywater I., 118n., 136n.
Camazine S., 187n., 191
Campbell N.A., 186, 191
Caparello A., 156
Carr D., 116n., 131
Casertano G., 73
Cassin B., 66n., 73
Caston V., XVIII, 125n., 131, 139-143, 145n., 148n., 155, 169, 169-171, 174, 174n.
Catapano G., 78, 94
Cattanei E., V, 37n., 39, 122, 131, 132
Chappell T.D.J., 131
Charles D., 124n., 131, 174, 174n., 175
Charlton W., 155
Cleary J.J., 156
Code A., 107n., 112
Cohen S.M., 107n., 112, 168n., 175
Consigny S., 66n., 73
Cooper J.M., 3, 10, 11, 17, 47n., 54, 111n., 112, 117n., 131
Corcilius K., 92, 94, 115n., 124n., 125n., 131
Corradi M., 67n., 73

Damasio A., XVIII, 159, 175
Descartes R., VII, XVII, XIX, 54, 159, 159n., 161-163, 172, 174-176, 178
Dewey J., 187n., 191
Di Francesco M., 161, 175
Diels H., 112
Dillon J., 54
Dixsaut M., 54, 63, 63n., 65, 65n., 72n., 73
Drefcinski S., 120n., 131
Driscoll J., 137n., 155
Durrant M., 157
Eccles J., 150n., 156, 176
Erler M., 54
Eustacchi F., 37n., 39
Everson S., 171, 175
Feigl H., 175
Feola G., XIV, XV, 95, 108n., 112
Fermani A., 37, 39, 74, 94, 131
Feyerabend P.K., 175
Fine G., XIX, 54, 136n., 155
Fine K., 183, 191
Fleet B., 14, 14n., 17
Fossheim H.J., 129n., 131
Fowler H.N., 56n., 73, 77, 81, 85, 88
Frede D., 54, 79n., 82n., 94, 127n., 131
Frede M., 7n., 8n., 11n., 15n., 17, 44n., 54, 139n., 140n., 155
Frege G., 150n., 155
Fronterotta F., 11n., 17, 138n., 141n., 152n., 154-156
Furth M., 110n., 112
Gabbe M., 98n., 112
Gadamer H.-G., 93n., 94
Galvan S., 159n., 175
Gerson L., 79n., 94, 144n., 155
Ghisalberti A., 156
Giannantoni G., 94
Gill M.L., 175
Gotthelf A., 112
Graeser A., 68n., 73
Granger H., 177, 191
Gregoric P., 115n., 124n., 125n., 131, 137n., 155
Grene M., 186, 191
Gurtler G.M., 156
Haldane E.S., 162n., 175
Haldane J.B.S., 187n., 191
Hankinson R.J., 4n., 17, 115n., 132
Hartman E., 177, 191
Havrda M., 16, 17
Hegel G.W.F., 64
Heil J., 187n., 191
Hett W.S., 92, 94, 166n., 175
Hicks R.D., 89n., 92, 94, 95n., 98n., 100, 101, 103, 105, 109n., 112, 142n., 155
Hude C., 112
Hume D., 163n.
Hursthouse R.J., 116n., 121, 132

Hutchinson D.S., 3, 10, 11, 17, 47n., 54
Irwin T.H., 118n., 123n., 132, 168n., 175
Jaworski W., XVIII-XX, 159n., 175, 177, 184, 190, 191
Johansen Th., 46n., 48, 48n., 54, 171
Johnston M., XIX, 183, 191
Jones H.S., 100n., 112
Kahn Ch., 147n., 155
Kant I., 59, 64, 163n.
Kennedy G.A., 124n., 132
Kenny A., 159, 175
Kerferd G.B., 66n., 73
Kim J., 161, 164, 175, 183, 191
Kitcher P., 187n., 191
Koons R., 191
Kornmeier U., 42n., 54
Kosman A., 141n., 146n., 155
Kranz W., 112
Kristjánsson K., 116n., 131
Kuhar M., 124n., 131
Lane M., 79n., 94
Laurenti R., 92, 94
Leunissen M., 123n., 132
Lewis D.K., 165, 175
Lewis F.A., 137n., 153n., 155
Liddell H., 100n., 112
Lloyd G.E.R., 54, 73, 156
Locke J., 163n.
Looren de Jong H., 191
López Férez J.A., 74
Louis P., 101n., 112
Lowe E.J., 159n., 163n., 170n., 175
Luraghi S., 61n., 74
Mahonney T., 79n., 94
Manuli P., 124n., 132
Marmodoro A., 159n., 175
Matson W.I., 166n., 175
Maxwell G., 175
Mayr E., 187n., 191
Medda R., VI, XV, XVI, 53n., 115, 130n., 132, 193
Meloni G., V, 53n.
Merritt M., XV, 121, 121n., 132
Migliori M., V, IX, 19, 19n., 20n. 23n., 25, 25n., 28n., 31n., 32n., 37n., 39, 74, 94, 131
Miller J., 136n., 137n., 155, 187n., 191
Mingucci G., XVII, XVIII, 124n., 132, 147n., 155, 159, 174n., 175
Modrak D., 146n., 155
Moravcsik, 107n., 112
Moraux P., 139n., 156
Morrison D., 136n., 156
Moss J., 115, 115n., 116n., 124n., 125n., 132
Mourelatos A.P.D., 66n., 74
Movia G., 91, 91n., 92, 94
Nannini S., 161, 171n., 176
Napolitano Valditara L.M., 74, 94

Narcy M., 61, 61n., 73, 74
Natali C., 4n., 5n., 8n, 17, 118n., 122n., 132
Natorp P., 62, 62n., 66, 74
Nussbaum M.C., XVIII, XIX, 97n., 107n., 112, 113, 131, 155, 156, 168n., 174-178, 190, 191, 192
O'Brien D., 54
O'Brien F., 51n., 52n., 54
Obbink D., 73
Oppedisano C., 108n., 113
Owen G.E.L., 73, 156
Palpacelli L., 37n., 39
Patzig G., 7n., 17
Peck A.L., 113
Pellegrin P., 175
Perler D., 174, 176
Pfeiffer Ch., 137n., 155
Polansky R., 98n., 100, 100n., 109n., 113, 147n., 156
Politis V., 137n., 156
Popper K., 150n., 156, 170, 176
Putnam H., XIX, 97n., 107n., 113, 168, 168n., 176-178, 190, 192
Quarantotto D., 13n., 17
Quine W.V., 187, 192
Rackham H., 118n.
Rademaker A., 67n., 74
Reale G., 28n., 39, 63, 63n., 74
Reeve, 118n.
Reis B., 54, 131
Rist J., 144n., 156
Robinson H., 177, 192
Robinson R., 63, 63n., 74
Robinson T.M., 63n., 74
Romeyer-Dherbey G., 73, 155, 156
Rorty A.O., 106n., 112, 113, 131, 155, 156, 174-176, 191
Ross G.R.T., XIX, 177, 192
Ross W.D., 13n., 17, 89, 89n., 91, 92, 94, 95n., 98n., 100, 100n., 103, 103n., 105n., 109n., 112, 113, 133n., 136n., 139n., 142-145, 156, 166n., 176
Rowe Ch., X, XI, 41, 43n., 44n., 48n., 50n., 51n., 54
Rue R., 79n., 94
Runggaldier E., 159n., 176
Ruse M., 187n., 192
Salles R., 131, 174
Sanna M., 132
Sassi M.M., 64n., 74
Schofield M., 112, 113, 154
Schouten M., 191
Scott D., 162n., 176
Scott R., 100n., 112
Scotti Muth N., 17
Sedley D., 48n., 49n., 50n., 54, 63, 63n., 74
Shields Ch., 155, 156, 168n., 176
Sider D., 73
Sillitti G., 139n., 154, 155, 156
Simpson G.G., 187n., 192
Simpson W., 191

Singer P.N., 64n., 74
Sisko J.E., 137n., 144n., 156, 171
Slakey T.J., XVIII, XIX, 166, 167, 176, 177, 192
Slote M., 132
Smith J.C., 176
Sommerhoff G., 187n., 192
Sorabji R., XVIII, 107n., 112, 113, 131, 154, 167, 168n., 171, 171n., 174, 176
Stella F., 154-156
Stork P., 73, 74
Tannery P., 162n., 174
Teh N., 191
Todd R.B., 156
Torstrik A., 133n. 139n.
Trabattoni F., XII, XIII, 5n., 17, 63, 63n., 74, 75, 80n., 82n., 87n., 94
Trendelenburg F.A., 133n., 144n., 156
Tulli M., 54
Vakirtzis A., 130n., 132
van Ophuijsen J.M., 73, 74
van Raalte M., 74, 74
Vegetti M., 124n., 132
Viano C., 17, 155, 156
Vlastos G., 4n., 17
Wedin M., 141n., 145n., 156
White N., 117n., 132
Whiting J., 107n., 113
Wilkes K.V., XIX, 168n., 176, 177, 192
Williams B., 177, 192
Wisse J., 124n., 132
Wittgenstein L., 22, 39
Wundt W., 162n.
Zagzebski L., XV, 116, 116n., 120, 120n., 123n., 132
Zeyl D., 47n.
Zingano M., 17
Zucca D., V, VI, XVI, XX, 53n., 125n., 127n., 132, 133, 157, 160n., 193